ANNABEL KARMEL
FIRST MEALS

ANNABEL KARMEL
FIRST MEALS

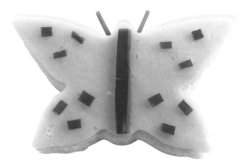

THE COMPLETE COOKBOOK AND NUTRITION GUIDE

DK

LONDON, NEW YORK, MUNICH,
MELBOURNE, DELHI

Revised edition

Senior editor Salima Hirani
U.S. Senior editor Jennifer Williams
Art editor Nicola Rodway
Project editors Jane Laing, Angela Baynham
Designer Christine Lacey
DTP designer Karen Constanti
Production controller Kevin Ward
Managing editor Anna Davidson
Managing art editor Glenda Fisher
Art director Carole Ash
Food photography Dave King
Model photography Vanessa Davies
Photographic art director Toni Kay
Americanizer Christine Heilman
Category publisher Corinne Roberts

Original edition

Project editor Lorna Damms
Editor Lorraine Turner
Art editors Carmel O'Neill & Emy Manby
Senior art editor Carole Oliver
DTP designer Bridget Roseberry
Production controller Martin Croshaw
Deputy art director Carole Ash
Managing editors Corinne Roberts & Mary Ling
Consultant editor (child development) Caroline Greene
Food photography Ian O'Leary
Home economist Janice Murfitt

Note on the nutritional breakdowns of recipes
All information is approximate and based on figures from food
composition tables, not on direct analysis of prepared dishes.
Thus analyses should be used as a guide, not as guaranteed figures.
Because some ingredients are not specified by weight, an estimated
weight has been used. No analyses have been provided for
recipe variations. Analyses are per portion.
Since many vitamins are destroyed when exposed to air or light,
the guidelines on sources apply to dishes served immediately after
preparation. Where recipes are frozen immediately, they will, in
general, still provide a useful amount of the nutrients indicated.

First American Edition, 1999
07 08 10 9 8 7 6 5 4
Revised edition published in 2004

Published in the United States by
DK Publishing, Inc., 375 Hudson Street
New York, New York 10014

Copyright © 1999, 2004 Dorling Kindersley Limited
Text copyright © Annabel Karmel, 1999, 2004

A Cataloging-in-Publication record for this book is available from the
Library of Congress
ISBN-13: 978-0-7566-0365-6

Reproduced in Italy by GRB
Printed and bound in China by Hung Hing

Discover more at
www.dk.com

Contents

Weaning your baby

This chapter explains all you need to know to wean your baby successfully, showing how to prepare his first meals and feed him for the first time, when to introduce more advanced purées, and which foods provide a gentle introduction to exciting new tastes and textures. Now is the best time to establish sensible eating patterns and an enjoyment of good food. There are 47 healthy and tasty recipes that are simple to make and will start your baby off in the right direction.

9 to 12 months

Your older baby's dexterity is developing rapidly, as is his sense of independence. With these comes his desire to start feeding himself. This chapter shows you how to encourage self-feeding with finger foods and includes 17 delicious recipes.

12 to 18 months

By now your baby's dietary needs are changing, along with his attitude toward food and mealtimes. This chapter discusses how to encourage your lively baby to join in family meals and includes 19 tantalizing recipes to keep him interested.

18 months to 2 years

It's hard to get toddlers to sit down to eat, so you'll need plenty of good ideas for healthy, energy-boosting snacks to fuel your child's energetic explorations of the world. Most toddlers go through a phase of picky eating, so you'll also need some sensible strategies to keep him well fed. This chapter contains 43 recipes that are ideal for growing toddlers.

2 to 3 years

This chapter contains constructive tips on planning easy and nutritious meals for young children with busy lives, along with 22 creative recipes designed to appeal to two-year-olds.

3 to 7 years

Encourage your preschool child to follow a healthy, varied diet and enjoy family meals from around the world—there are 47 delicious recipes the entire family can enjoy in this chapter. There are also 21 recipes and further suggestions for healthy and tasty lunch boxes and snacks.

My children Scarlett (top), Lara (middle), and Nicholas (bottom) grew up on my recipes, and now they enjoy eating a wide variety of healthy foods. Many of their favorite recipes are in this book.

Introduction

When it comes to the health and happiness of their children, I think that all parents will agree that only the very best will do. I lost my first child, Natasha, at the heartbreakingly early age of 13 weeks, after she contracted a viral infection. Though this illness was not diet-related, Natasha's loss made me even more determined to give my second child, Nicholas, the best possible start in life. It was Nicholas who gave me my first experience of coping with a picky eater. Indeed, my interest in the whole subject of child nutrition was born out of my own frustrations with feeding a child who for a time would eat only a limited range of foods. Thus the strategies and solutions for common feeding problems that are presented in this book are based not only on current nutritional guidelines, but on experience and a conviction that food is one of the best forms of preventive medicine.

At the time when diet is most crucial to health, we should not be reliant upon processed foods from jars and boxes. After all, there is no great mystique to making baby food, and there is nothing better for your child than home-cooked food made from fresh ingredients. Home cooking is an economical option and, as the recipes in this book show, it need not be time-consuming. There are many excellent purées that do not involve cooking and other recipes suitable for batch-cooking that allow a whole month's food supply to be prepared in just a couple of hours and then frozen. These homemade meals get babies accustomed to the natural variations in the taste of freshly cooked food, and this helps them adapt to family meals and grow up to be less-picky eaters. So while parents are giving their baby the best nutritional start in life, they are also helping to guard against future feeding difficulties.

Unfortunately, for many children, convenience and junk foods are a regular part of their diet: fewer and fewer families are sitting down to meals together. Instead, children are often raised on a depressingly familiar repertoire of processed, packaged foods and "TV dinners"— pizza, chicken nuggets, french fries, and canned pasta. It can seem that "real" food is only for adults, and that children have a special diet consisting of some of the poorest-quality, most unhealthy food available. Yet parents are the ones in charge of what their children eat, and it is up to parents to give their children the opportunity to follow a varied, healthy diet.

My three children, Nicholas, Lara, and Scarlett, have been my constant inspiration over the years, but I am also grateful to all the babies and young children who have contributed to my research into nutrition and development, albeit unknowingly, and tested my new recipes. Children are exacting critics, and while they are rarely interested in whether their food is healthy, they do care if it tastes good. Accordingly, the recipes in this book are designed to combine "child appeal" with sound nutritional principles.

Many parents have been kind enough to say how helpful they found the first edition of this book. In this totally revised and extended edition, I have changed many existing recipes to make them even tastier than before, and I have added more than 85 delicious new recipes. There are now two completely new sections in the book, providing recipes to tempt the picky eater and ideas for healthy snacks, picnics, and lunch boxes. There are more recipes to appeal to the whole family and more vegetarian dishes throughout. In addition, all the nutritional information has been completely updated in accordance with the latest research into child nutrition.

When you prepare food for your children using fresh ingredients, you know you are giving them the very best start in life. I hope that many of my recipes will become firm family favorites for years to come.

Annabel Karmel

Early nutrition

"For his first six months, all your baby's nutritional needs are fulfilled by breast milk or formula."

A balanced diet is one that perfectly suits your growing child's needs. Breast milk or formula is the essential source of nourishment throughout the first year of your baby's life, but from the time you begin weaning him, you should try to establish a diet that provides the five essential nutrient groups: carbohydrates, protein, fat, vitamins, and minerals. Remember that your child's needs are different from your own. Children under five need significantly more fat and concentrated sources of calories and nutrients than adults in order to fuel their rapid growth during the early years.

Your baby's milk

During his first six months, your baby is dependent on breast milk or formula for all his nutritional needs. Although you may have begun weaning him at four or five months, his solid intake is so small that these "real" foods are little more than taste experiences, and it is vital not to reduce milk feedings.

Whole cow's milk can be used in cooking or with cereal from six months but should not be given as your baby's main drink before age one, mainly because it is low in iron and vitamin C. Once he reaches his first birthday, cow's milk can become his usual drink, but until then he needs the vitamins and iron found in breast milk or formula. Do not give him fat-free milk before his fifth birthday because it provides too little energy. However, low-fat milk can be given from the age of two if your child is eating well.

Benefits of breastfeeding

The American Academy of Pediatrics (AAP) advocates exclusive breastfeeding for approximately the first six months after birth. However, if you are uncomfortable about breastfeeding, or unable to breastfeed, you can still give your baby a good start with infant formula. Between four and six months, babies should be fed 20–27 fl oz (600–800ml) of breast milk or formula per day. It is important to ensure that up to the age of eight months your baby drinks milk at least four times a day.

There are proven health benefits to breastfeeding for both child and mother in the short and long term.
• Breastfeeding helps strengthen your baby's immune system. Breastfed babies have a lower risk of respiratory or ear infections and gastroenteritis.
• Breastfeeding for six months has been shown to delay the onset, and reduce the severity, of allergies in children from families with a history of asthma, hay fever, eczema, and food allergies.

• Breast milk is easily digested and lessens the risk of constipation.
• Breastfed children may be at lower risk of becoming obese.
• Breast milk provides a balance of essential fatty acids, which are important for brain development.
• Breastfeeding can help mothers lose excess weight gained during pregnancy.
• The risk of premenopausal breast cancer in mothers is reduced the longer they breastfeed.

Water

Babies are vulnerable to dehydration, and it is essential to maintain their fluid intake. If your baby is breastfed, your milk will supply the necessary fluids (he may need extra feedings on hot days). The same should be true for bottle-fed babies, but they may need sips of cooled boiled water on hot days.

Once your baby is on a mainly solid diet, you will need to boost his fluid intake. Cooled boiled tap water is accessible and the best thirst-quencher.

Young babies will need only a few sips of water, but it is wise to encourage your child to drink water from an early age: most herbal and fruit drinks marketed for babies contain sugar, which can harm developing teeth and give your baby a taste for sweet drinks.

Do not offer mineral water or use it to make up feedings: it is not bacteriologically safe unless boiled and may contain a higher level of sodium than is recommended for babies.

Carbohydrates

Carbohydrates are the body's main source of energy. The body breaks them down to release glucose, thereby providing itself with energy. There are two main types: slow-burning carbohydrates and fast-burning carbohydrates. Complex carbohydrates, such as root vegetables and whole-wheat bread, release glucose slowly to provide long-lasting energy. Simple carbohydrates, such as bananas and white rice, release glucose quickly to provide a quick burst of energy. Although very useful at times, fast-burning carbohydrates cause a rapid rise in blood-sugar levels, which can cause the body to overcompensate. This results in a subsequent sudden

dip in blood sugar levels and a low level of energy. Both types of carbohydrates contain vitamins, minerals, and fiber that are useful to the body, and between them should make up 40–50 percent of your child's diet, depending on age.

Refined carbohydrates have usually been stripped of their natural fiber during processing and have decreased levels of their valuable nutrients. Cakes, cookies, and sugary cereals (unless fortified) all fall into this category. Such foods are turned into glucose very rapidly, producing a short-lived energy "high" followed by an energy "low." Limit consumption of these types of foods, since they supply few nutrients but lots of "empty" calories.

What milk when
• From birth to one year, feed your baby breast milk or infant formula (cow's milk modified to resemble human breast milk).
• From six months to one year, you can feed your baby follow-up formula if you feel he is getting insufficient nutrients from a combination of regular formula and solids. He should be drinking 17–27 fl oz (500–800ml) of breast milk or formula each day.
• From six months, you can introduce whole cow's milk in cooking only.
• From one year, give your baby whole cow's milk as a drink. One- to seven-year-olds should drink at least 14 fl oz (400ml) of milk a day, or consume the equivalent in dairy products.

Sources of slow-burning carbohydrates
• whole-grain breakfast cereals
• whole-wheat flour and bread
• oats • apples • carrots
• sweet corn • pasta • lentils

Sources of fast-burning carbohydrates
• tropical fruit, such as melons, pineapples, kiwi fruit, bananas • corn flakes • white bread • white rice • sugar
• sweetened breakfast cereals
• most manufactured cookies, cakes, and pastry

Protein

Protein is essential for growth and repair of body tissues. It provides the building blocks of all cells in the body and makes up a large portion of children's muscles, internal organs, skin, and hair. If we have inadequate protein, our resistance to disease and infection is lowered. Protein is made up of amino acids, some of which the body can manufacture and some of which must be obtained from food. Animal proteins, including milk, contain all the amino acids the body needs. Soy is the only plant-based food that contains all of them. Other foods must be combined to provide complete proteins: for example, grains with legumes. These foods do not need to be combined at one meal, but can be eaten during the course of a day.

Children grow rapidly and need more protein in relation to their size than adults. However, protein-rich foods should not be the major part of a baby's meal—a high-protein diet can put strain on immature kidneys.

Because protein is not stored by the body, children need two portions of protein-rich foods each day. They should ideally eat meat three or four times a week and fish two or three times, of which one portion should be an oily fish, such as salmon, tuna, or sardines. Protein foods such as cheese or eggs are good for breakfast. Try to include some vegetable proteins, such as beans and lentils, since they contain important minerals and phytochemicals, and are a good source of fiber.

Fat

Fats provide the most concentrated source of energy, and babies need proportionately more fat in their diet than adults do. They need energy-dense foods such as cheese, meat, and eggs to fuel their rapid growth and development. Up to the age of one, children should derive 40–50 percent of their energy from fat (breast milk contains more than 50 percent fat). After that they should derive around 35 percent of their total energy from fat. However, all fats are not equal, and it is important to distinguish between different fats when checking the amount of fat in your child's diet.

• **Saturated fat** is derived mainly from animal sources and is solid at room temperature. Butter, lard, and the fat in meat and dairy products are mainly saturated. Saturated fats can increase blood cholesterol levels, and high intakes are linked to heart disease in adults. Limit these fats in your child's diet: choose lean meats, use vegetable oils instead of butter for frying, and broil,

grill, steam, or stir-fry food whenever possible. Milk and cheese contain saturated fats but are also a good source of calcium, protein, and vitamins.

• **Monounsaturated fats** tend to be liquid at room temperature. Olive oil, canola oil, and the fat found in most nuts and avocados are mainly monounsaturated. This type of fat can help lower cholesterol levels and so can some offer protection against heart disease, as studies of the traditional Mediterranean diet, which is high in olive oil, have shown. Olive oil and canola oil are also the safest for cooking at high temperatures.

• **Polyunsaturated fats**—oils with a high percentage of polyunsaturates, such as corn, safflower, and sunflower oils, also lower cholesterol levels, but it's good to get a balance between different unsaturated fats for good health, so don't just use these types.

• **Trans fats** are unsaturated fatty acids that have been hardened in

the manufacture of commercial foods. They can be found in some margarines, low-fat spreads, cookies, and cakes. They no longer have the properties of unsaturated fat and are nutritionally similar to saturated fats. Many experts believe that trans fats are even more harmful than saturated fats and should be avoided whenever possible.
• **Essential fatty acids (EFAs)** are essential for brain and visual development. There are two types of EFAs: omega-3 and omega-6. Both should be included in the diet because, unlike other fats, they cannot be made in the body. Currently we eat around 10 times more omega-6 fats than omega-3 fats. DHA, found in oily fish, is an omega-3 fatty acid that makes up a significant proportion of human brain tissue. It is important for regulating attention and controlling behavior. Some research suggests that a diet rich in EFAs may improve the performance of children with dyspraxia, dyslexia, and attention deficit disorder.

Remember
If you leave the skin on roast chicken but cut the visible fat off roast beef, the chicken will contain more fat than the beef.

Vitamins

Vitamins are essential for maintaining health. They are either water-soluble (B complex and C) or fat-soluble (A, D, E, and K). Water-soluble vitamins can be destroyed by heat and, as their name indicates, dissolve in water, so do not overcook foods rich in these vitamins. Fat-soluble vitamins are stored in the body and may be harmful in large doses. Children aged six months to two years may be deficient in vitamins A and D. A baby may need supplements if he is breastfed after six months or taking less than 17 fl oz (500ml) of formula per day.
• **Vitamin A**, including beta-carotene and retinol, is essential for growth, fighting infection, healthy skin, good vision, and strong bones.
• **B complex vitamins**, including folate, are essential for growth, energy, the development of a healthy nervous system, and to aid digestion.
• **Vitamin C** is required for growth, tissue repair, healthy skin, and to aid iron absorption.
• **Vitamin D** is manufactured by skin exposed to sunlight and is needed to absorb calcium and phosphorus for healthy bones and teeth.

• **Vitamin E** is needed for the maintenance of the body's cell structure: it helps the body to create and maintain red blood cells.

Sources of vitamin A
• carrots • red peppers
• sweet corn • sweet potatoes
• tomatoes • melons
• apricots • mangoes • liver
• butter and margarine

Sources of B-complex vitamins
• meat, especially liver • tofu
• sardines • eggs • nuts
• dark green vegetables
• dairy products • whole-grain cereals • avocados • bananas

Sources of vitamin C
• citrus fruits • strawberries
• kiwi fruit • dark green leafy vegetables • potatoes
• peppers

Sources of vitamin D
• salmon • tuna • sardines
• milk • cheese • eggs

Sources of vitamin E
• vegetable oils • wheat germ
• avocados • nuts

"A carefully balanced vegetarian diet can be perfectly adequate for babies and small children, as long as meals do not contain too much fiber."

Calcium

Calcium is important for the formation and health of bones and teeth. 14 fl oz (400ml) of milk a day provides an adequate amount for children between the ages of one and five years.

Zinc

Zinc is essential for normal growth and for the efficient functioning of the immune system. A varied diet should provide all the body's daily zinc requirements.

Iron

Iron is needed for both physical and mental development. Babies are born with a store of iron that lasts for about six months. After this time it is important to make sure they get the iron they need from the solid food they eat, because iron deficiency, which can lead to anemia if unchecked, leaves children feeling run-down and tired and can make them more susceptible to infection. Premature babies are especially vulnerable to iron depletion—their store of iron may last for only six weeks. If your baby was born prematurely, you may be advised by your doctor to give him an iron supplement until he is one year old.

A baby's iron requirements are particularly high between the ages of six months and two years. This is a critical time for brain development and a lack of iron in the diet can lead to impaired mental development and lack of concentration. Follow-up formula, which contains more iron than standard infant formula, can be given to babies between six months and two years of age. Follow-up formula is not necessary for most babies but can provide a useful nutritional safety net if your baby is a very picky eater.

Identifying iron deficiency

Iron deficiency is the most common childhood nutritional deficiency—25 percent of children do not have enough iron in their bodies. Iron deficiency can be difficult to spot because the symptoms are not as easily identifiable as those of an infectious illness. If you notice pallor, listlessness, and fatigue in your child, he is probably deficient in iron. You can rectify the problem quickly by providing adequate dietary sources of iron—talk to your healthcare provider.

Dietary sources of iron

Iron from animal sources, such as red meat, particularly liver, or oily fish (salmon, sardines, mackerel, or pilchards, for example), is easily absorbed by the body. Plant food sources, such as legumes and green, leafy vegetables, and iron added by manufacturers to foods such as breakfast cereals, is absorbed less easily. However, if foods or drinks containing vitamin C are eaten at the same meal as a plant-based source of iron, then the iron is absorbed better. Offer kiwi fruit, citrus fruit, or berries, or some diluted pure fruit juice with the meal. Alternatively, serve a few chunks of vitamin C–rich sweet red pepper or cauliflower florets with an iron-rich spinach or lentil dish. In both cases, the vitamin C will improve iron absorption in your child's body.

Protein-rich foods also aid iron absorption. By serving fish, lean red meat, or chicken with dark green, leafy vegetables or lentils, you will improve the absorption of the vegetable sources of iron by about three times.

Vegetarian diet

Parents who follow a vegetarian diet sometimes worry that it may not be suitable for their children. In fact, only a bulky, high-fiber vegetarian diet is unsuitable for growing young children, because it is too low in calories and essential fats, and hinders the absorption of iron. However, a vegetarian diet can be perfectly adequate for babies and small children as long as the meals are carefully balanced and do not contain too much fiber.

Boosting protein
Animal proteins, including those found in egg and dairy products, are high-quality and contain essential amino acids. Vegetable proteins, such as those found in beans, legumes, and seeds, provide a lower-quality protein. Soy is the only plant-based food that contains all the amino acids.

If your child is following a vegetarian diet, ensure that he receives enough high-quality protein by serving cereal or vegetable proteins, such as pasta, bread, rice, or lentils, with small quantities of dairy foods or eggs. Alternatively, you could include two vegetable-protein food groups. There are three groups: legumes, such as beans, lentils, and chickpeas; grains, such as wheat, rice, oats, bread, and pasta; and nuts and seeds.

A good way to improve the protein in a baby's diet is to make up some cheese sauce and freeze it. Then, when you give your baby some vegetable purée, simply add cheese sauce.

Here are some examples of good vegetarian dishes for babies and young children:
- lentil and vegetable purée with cheese
- peanut-butter sandwiches
- baked potato with cheese and milk
- pasta with cheese sauce
- baked beans on toast
- rice and lentils.

Improving iron absorption
Children brought up on a vegetarian diet can sometimes be deficient in iron, since red meat provides the best and most easily absorbed source of iron. Plant food sources of iron are more difficult to absorb. So it's especially important to remember that vitamin C–rich foods given with your child's meal (see under Iron) greatly increase the absorption of iron from plant sources.

Vegan option
If you want your child to follow a vegan diet (that is, without meat, dairy products or eggs), you will need to plan his diet carefully, in consultation with your healthcare provider.

Sources of calcium
- milk • cheese • yogurt
- leafy vegetables • tofu • nuts
- sardines • sesame paste

Sources of zinc
- shellfish • red meat
- peanuts • sunflower seeds
- fortified breakfast cereals

Sources of iron
- liver and red meats • egg yolks • oily fish, fresh or canned
- legumes, such as lentils and baked beans • fortified breakfast cereals • bread
- green leafy vegetables
- dried fruits, such as apricots

Vegetarian sources of iron
- fortified breakfast cereals
- egg yolks • whole-wheat bread • beans and lentils
- dark green leafy vegetables
- dried fruit, such as apricots

Healthy eating

"95–99 percent of all food products advertised during children's television are high in fat, sugar, and/or salt."

The most common nutritional disorder in the Western world is obesity. Obese children as young as five are displaying early warning signs of heart disease. Type 2 diabetes—once called adult-onset diabetes—is now appearing in teenagers. There are other dietary concerns. Too much salt is linked to high blood pressure, which can lead to heart disease and strokes, and most children eat two to three times the daily recommended salt intake. Most children fall far short of the five daily portions of fruit or vegetables recommended to boost the immune system and reduce the adult incidence of cancer.

Reducing obesity

In the US, almost one-fourth of children ages 2 to 17 are classified as obese. Thanks to the popularity of computer games, television, and videos, children are only too happy to stay in their rooms moving nothing more than a few fingers on a keyboard. A couch-potato generation of junk-food addicts is storing up serious health problems for the future—ultimately, one-third of these sedentary youngsters will die from a diet-related disease. Children do not make food choices in a vacuum; they are influenced by the products they see on television, what their favorite sports stars or pop groups are seen eating or drinking, and peer pressure. Advertising that relies on "pester power"—kids' ability to wear down their parents by constantly asking for a certain product—is ultimately dangerous, since food marketed directly to children is some of the most

unhealthy food available. Whether it's packs of chicken nuggets or the children's menu in a restaurant, children's food is generally over-processed and high in saturated fat; it is often high in sugar and salt, too. Most children have intakes of saturated fat that exceed the maximum level for adults.

A balanced diet
Children who are overweight should not be put on a restricted diet. Unlike adults, children are still growing, and it is important that they eat a broad variety of healthy foods that provide plenty of calcium, protein, iron, and other essential nutrients.

By adopting a long-term approach to healthy eating, it should be possible for your child to maintain a steady weight instead of losing weight and, as he grows taller, he will "grow into" the extra weight and become proportionately slimmer.

Encourage exercise
Overweight children are often embarrassed by their bodies and dislike taking part in school sports. They are usually the last to be picked for team sports.

Set a good example yourself—children of active parents are much more likely to be active themselves. Limit television and computer games and find a sport or physical activity your child enjoys.

Provide play equipment such as a jungle gym or a trampoline. Encourage family activities, such as trips to the pool, bicycle rides, inline skating, ball games, or racket sports. It's a good idea to introduce a regular time for such a family exercise, even if it's just walking in the park, to help make regular exercise a habit. Consider enrolling your child in gymnastics, swimming, or dance classes.

Watch the salt

Over half of all children eat twice as much salt as they should. It is estimated that by reducing salt intake by just 3g a day for adults, 14 percent fewer people would suffer strokes and there would be 10 percent fewer heart attacks. Bones would benefit, too, since excess salt causes a loss of calcium, which could lead to bone thinning, a higher risk of fractures, and osteoporosis.

The liking for salt and salty foods is a learned taste preference. During the first year, babies are not given any salt in their diet, and they don't miss it. However, after this, more and more salt creeps into your child's food. There is hidden salt in foods such as bread and breakfast cereals. In fact, corn flakes contain as much salt as seawater. Approximately three-quarters of the salt children consume comes from processed foods. To reduce your child's salt intake, you must limit the amount of processed foods, snacks, and fast food, such as pizza, chicken nuggets, canned pasta, and potato chips, that your child consumes. As far as possible, ensure that your child eats freshly cooked food that does not contain added salt.

Most foods are labeled with grams of sodium per 100g. One gram of sodium is equivalent to 2.5g of salt, so anything with more than 0.5g sodium per 100g is too high in salt. Try to buy foods with less than 0.2g of sodium per 100g.

Salt issues
• Recommended salt intake per day is 2g for 1- to 3- year-olds, 3g for 4- to 6-year-olds, and 5g (or 1 teaspoon) for 7- to 10-year-olds.

• Potassium's relationship with salt is like a seesaw: if your potassium intake is high, your body's level of sodium (the key element in salt) will be healthier. Dried fruits, nuts, bananas, onions, potatoes, and legumes are all good sources of potassium.

Eating more fruit and vegetables

Researchers estimate that a diet filled with fruit and vegetables instead of unhealthy fats and refined foods, combined with increased exercise, could reduce the incidence of cancer by at least 30 percent. Health experts recommend that we eat at least five portions of fruit and vegetables each day.

Fruit and vegetables are packed with powerful natural compounds called phytochemicals. Many of the bright colors in fruit and vegetables come from phytochemicals, and they can help to protect the body from heart disease and cancer, boost immunity, and fight harmful bacteria and viruses.

Fruit and vegetables also contain antioxidants, which protect the body by neutralizing free radicals that can damage cells and lead to poor health.

In general, the more colorful the food, the more nutritious it is. For example, spinach rates more highly than lettuce, and sweet potato is better for you than an ordinary potato. Lycopene gives fruits such as tomatoes and watermelons their red color. It is a very powerful antioxidant that can protect against heart disease and some forms of cancer. Different-colored fruits and vegetables contain different nutrients, so aim for a mix of colors.

Rainbow fruit & vegetables
Try to include different-colored fruit and vegetables to provide a wide variety of nutrients.

Orange/yellow: carrots
• mangoes • papayas
• sweet potatoes

Red: tomatoes • red peppers
• strawberries • raspberries

Green: broccoli • spinach
• peas • kiwi fruit

Purple/blue: blueberries
• grapes • blackberries
• purple figs

White: cauliflower • onions
• garlic • potatoes • pears

Food allergies

An allergic reaction occurs when the immune system perceives a harmless substance as a threat and overreacts, triggering unpleasant, occasionally dangerous, side effects. Because young babies' immune systems are not fully developed, they are more likely to become sensitized to common allergens, such as eggs and gluten, which is why the introduction of these foods should be delayed. Children who do experience a food allergy may outgrow it by the age of three, but occasionally an allergy will persist and the only option is avoidance.

Common allergies

The foods most likely to trigger an allergic reaction in babies include:
- cow's milk and dairy products
- nuts and seeds • eggs
- wheat-based products • fish and shellfish • soy. Sesame seeds, berries, citrus fruits, and kiwi fruits can sometimes cause a reaction in susceptible babies.

Cow's milk (protein) allergy
An allergic reaction to one of the proteins found in cow's milk, cow's-milk-based infant formulas, and dairy products can give rise to diverse symptoms, namely diarrhea, vomiting, abdominal pains, eczema, and lactose intolerance (see opposite). Babies who experience this allergic reaction can be given a soy-based or hypoallergenic formula milk, on the advice of a doctor, if breast milk is not an option. Older children need a dairy-free diet (consult your healthcare provider).

Nut allergy
Although allergy to tree nuts is relatively rare, the peanut can be a trigger for one of the most severe allergic reactions, anaphylactic shock (in which the throat swells and breathing becomes difficult). In families with a history of any kind of allergy, including hay fever, asthma, eczema, or food allergy, it is advisable to avoid products containing peanuts or unrefined peanut oil until the child is three years old. If there is no history of allergy, peanuts of a suitable consistency (for example, creamy peanut butter) can be introduced from six months. Whole nuts should not be given to children under five because of the risk of choking.

A growing number of people are experiencing an allergy to sesame seeds. Although much less common than peanut allergy (1 in 2,000), the symptoms can be just as severe.

Symptoms of food allergy
Allergic reactions usually manifest as:
- swelling of the lips or tongue with a runny nose

- persistent diarrhea
- vomiting
- wheezing or difficulty breathing
- abdominal pain
- in extreme cases, anaphylactic shock—a sudden and life-threatening reaction with wheezing, hives, swelling of the throat, and shock (peanuts are the most common cause of this serious reaction).

Diagnosing a food allergy
The most accurate way to diagnose a food allergy is to eliminate all the suspected foods from your child's diet, wait for the symptoms to cease, and, after a period of several weeks, start to reintroduce these foods one by one until the symptoms reappear. The last food to be reintroduced is usually the one producing the allergic reaction. This process should be carried out under medical supervision only.

Do not remove key foods from your child's diet. If you suspect she is allergic to a common food, such as milk or wheat, seek expert advice (from your healthcare provider) to confirm the diagnosis and help plan a balanced diet before taking any action yourself.

What is food intolerance?

A person is said to have an intolerance to a food or food substance if eating that food leads to an adverse reaction not involving the immune system. The body is temporarily incapable of digesting certain foods. This is generally short-lived, unlike a true food allergy.

Lactose intolerance
Children who suffer permanent lactose intolerance lack a substance called lactase, an enzyme needed in order to digest the lactose (milk sugar) in milk. These babies cannot drink breast milk or cow's milk formula and need a special low-lactose infant formula (available only with a prescription). Lactose intolerance may cause diarrhea and gas after drinking milk or eating other dairy products.

Temporary lactose intolerance—usually caused by gastroenteritis from bacteria or viruses damaging the gut, where lactase is produced—is more common. Once the gut repairs the damage (which may take from a few days to a few weeks), the enzyme is produced once more and the intolerance disappears. While the condition lasts, it can be managed with a soy-based formula or a low-lactose infant formula.

Gluten intolerance
Wheat, barley, rye, and possibly oats and their products contain gluten, a type of protein. Intolerance to gluten causes celiac disease, a genetically linked, lifelong condition that can appear at any age. Foods containing gluten should not be introduced into a baby's diet until he is six months old. If there is a family history of gluten intolerance, advice is to introduce gluten after six months, as normal, so it can be clearly diagnosed.

In most cases, the condition disappears once the gut has had time to recover from the gastroenteritic illness. Symptoms of gluten intolerance include frequent, bulky, pale, foul-smelling stools, loss of appetite, failure to thrive, distended stomach, sticklike limbs, irritability and lethargy, and saggy, flat buttocks.

The later introduction (after six months) of solid foods including gluten delays the appearance of the intolerance until the infant is stronger. If celiac disease is diagnosed, careful dietary and medical management will be required. Gluten-free cereals, such as rice, millet, and corn, can be introduced once weaning starts.

Full-size processor with mini bowl attachment

Food mill

Collapsible steamer   *Stacking steamer*

Kitchen basics

There are many kitchen tools and shortcuts you can learn to help make the entire process of food preparation for your baby or young child quick, simple, and stress-free. There are certain pieces of equipment, pantry essentials, and cooking techniques that are invaluable, and you'll need to know how to freeze baby food safely if you want to avoid cooking every day. A little knowledge of food hygiene will also help you keep your baby healthy.

Equipment

You will probably find that you already have most of the equipment needed to make home-cooked meals for your child, but there are certain additional items that will facilitate food preparation and prove useful for general family cooking. Equipment need not be expensive or complicated, but you should look for items that will make preparing solids easy for you and that will later help your baby learn how to feed himself.

Sterilizing equipment

Warm milk is the perfect breeding ground for bacteria, so bottles must be scrupulously washed and sterilized. Sterilize all bottles, nipples, and feeding cup spouts up to one year, and sterilize feeding spoons for the first six months. You can simply boil feeding equipment in a pot of water for ten minutes, or use a dishwasher, especially if it has a hot cycle.

Processors & blenders

Electric food processors, blenders, or hand blenders make it easy to purée large quantities of food quickly. Some foods, such as cooked apples, will purée to a smooth consistency; other, coarser foods, such as peas or dried apricots, should be strained through a metal sieve after puréeing to remove the fibrous, indigestible material.

- **Mini processors** are useful for making baby foods in small portions.
- **Full-size processors** facilitate cooking food in large batches, but a mini bowl attachment will work better if you are mainly preparing small quantities.
- **Food mills** purée foods while holding back any indigestible husks or skins. This is ideal in the early stages when serving nutritious foods such as dried apricots and peas, whose skins are indigestible for young babies.
- **Handheld blenders** are easy to clean and ideal for puréeing small quantities in the container provided with the blender.
- **A metal-mesh sieve** can be used to eliminate any fibrous material from purées for babies.

Steamers

Steaming vegetables preserves maximum nutrients, so it's worth buying a steamer. There are two types.
- **A multilayered steamer** allows you to stack several foods in the same pan so that you can cook them simultaneously. You can boil one ingredient in the bottom and steam others in the layers above.
- **A collapsible steamer** rests in any pan with a lid. It fits various sizes of pans and is a versatile alternative to a stacked steamer.

Freezer containers

Tiny portions of purée can be spooned into ice-cube trays, then frozen (see page 22). You can buy small freezer-proof tubs with snap-on lids that hold larger portions. These are particularly useful because they can be transferred straight from freezer to microwave.

• **Several ice-cube trays** will allow you to freeze meal-size portions of a variety of purées. Flexible rubber trays can be twisted to release the cubes easily.

• **Freezer tubs** with snap-on lids are useful—use them as extra feeding bowls. They are also easy to transport.

Baby chairs

A good bouncy chair that supports the back is ideal for babies who cannot yet sit unaided. A baby car seat can double as a feeding chair. Once he can sit up, your baby can progress to a high chair with safety straps. A clip-on chair with safety straps is a light, transportable, space-saving alternative.

• **Bouncy chairs** are lightweight and recline slightly. Wipe-clean or washable finishes are useful.

• **High chairs** should be wide-based and sturdy, with a wipe-clean tray.

• **Clip-on chairs** may be clamped to a sturdy table that can take the weight. Do not clamp them over a tablecloth.

Feeding kit

There are many varieties of feeding bowls and spoons available. All that is needed to start is a small weaning bowl and a shallow plastic spoon, preferably made of soft, flexible plastic that will not hurt tender gums. Later on, bowls with suction cups or thermal linings, feeding cups, and children's cutlery become useful.

• **Weaning bowls** should be made of heatproof plastic. Choose one with a hand-grip.

• **Heat-sensitive bowls** and spoons quickly change color to indicate that the food is too hot.

• **Suction cups** on bowls allow them to be secured to high-chair trays.

• **Weaning spoons** should have a small, shallow bowl with no hard edges.

• **Feeding cups** enable babies to learn to drink fluids independently. Most babies graduate from bottles to cups with a spout and snap-tight lid and then to an open cup. A nonspill "tippy" cup is ideal.

Bibs

Feeding can be a messy business for young babies, parents, and even the surrounding walls. Protect your baby's clothes from the worst of the mess with a bib, and place a large, square plastic splash mat, or an old plastic tablecloth, under feeding chairs.

• **Soft cotton bibs** should have a plastic backing and a Velcro fastener.

• **Bibs with sleeves** and ties at the back give the best allover protection when your baby starts to feed himself.

• **Soft plastic bibs** with a shallow trough are suitable for older babies. Their wipe-clean surface makes them a very practical alternative to cotton bibs.

Weaning bowl

Heat-sensitive bowl

Bowl with suction cups

Weaning spoon

Graduated feeding cup   *Feeding cup*

Stocking the pantry

A well-stocked pantry is invaluable in any kitchen. If you don't have time to go shopping, you can use ingredients already on hand to make a quick and nutritious meal for your children, or indeed for the whole family. While the lists of foods on this page are by no means exhaustive, they represent a useful and highly versatile selection of standby foods. Check the ingredients lists on canned foods because some common commercial additives, such as the food colorings annatto and FD & C Yellow No. 5 (tartrazine), can provoke an allergic reaction in sensitive young children.

PANTRY ESSENTIALS

Dried staple foods

Bread and other grain products, such as pasta and rice, are invaluable sources of carbohydrates that can form the basis for quick, healthy meals. Although dried beans and lentils generally require some advance preparation, they are both nutritious and economical. Keep flour and cornstarch in the cupboard, too.

Bread products Stock whole-wheat and white bread, bread sticks, English muffins, and taco shells.

Beans & legumes Include red kidney beans, red and green lentils, and haricot beans.

Dried fruit Include apricots, mangoes, peaches, prunes, apple rings, raisins, and pineapple.

Rice Stock baby rice cereal for purées, white and brown long-grain rice, and risotto rice.

Pasta Include soup pasta, farfalle, rotini, spaghetti, lasagna, cannelloni, and Chinese egg noodles.

Couscous & other wheat products Include semolina and bulgur wheat.

Breakfast cereals

Choose low-sugar cereals made with rice, oats, or wheat. A whole-grain variety is preferable, but for children avoid bran-based products with added fiber.

Commercial cereals Stock corn flakes, puffed rice, and shredded wheat. Check the sugar content.

Muesli Make with a mixture of rolled oats, mixed grains, toasted wheat germ, and chopped dried fruit.

Eggs & dairy products

Eggs Choose organic, free-range, or omega-3-enriched eggs and store in the refrigerator. They make a nutritious meal in minutes.

Dairy products Choose full-fat, pasteurized products for children under five years old.

Cheeses Stock soft cream cheese for dips and spreads, mild or medium cheddar, Edam, or Gruyère, cottage cheese, and fresh Parmesan.

Milk Choose full-fat and pasteurized, whether cow's or goat's milk.

Yogurt Choose full-fat natural plain yogurt and low-sugar fruit or vanilla yogurt (preferably a live, organic variety).

Butter Choose unsalted or lightly salted butter or a soft margarine for spreading on bread and for shallow frying and baking.

Sauces, oils, & seasonings

A plentiful supply of bottled sauces and oils, herbs, and spices will give plenty of culinary scope.

Sauces & flavorings Include soy sauce, oyster sauce, tomato purée, Worcestershire sauce, pesto, and low-sodium vegetable and chicken stock.

Oils & vinegars Include olive oil, sunflower oil, vegetable oil, sesame oil, and balsamic and wine vinegars for cooking and salad dressings.

Herbs Include mixed dried herbs, bay leaves, oregano, thyme, bouquet garni, fresh basil, fresh and dried parsley.

Spices Include powdered cinnamon, mixed spice, and ginger for baking, and nutmeg (buy the whole spice), fresh ginger root, and mild paprika.

Frozen foods

Many vegetables and fruits, such as peas and sweet corn, are frozen within two to three hours of being picked, ensuring that they retain valuable nutrients. In fact, fresh vegetables that are stored for several days often contain fewer nutrients than frozen vegetables.

Frozen chicken portions and fish fillets are good standbys. If buying breaded fish, choose larger portion sizes, since there will be less breading in proportion to the fish.

Freeze bread and butter for emergencies, and stock ice cream for quick desserts.

Canned foods

Some canned processed foods are high in sugar and salt, and all contain additives, so always read the labels carefully before you decide what to buy. However, many canned products are valuable nutritionally. Make sure you keep the following standbys in stock: tuna, sardines, baked beans, kidney beans, tomatoes, and sweet corn.

Preparing baby food

The ingredients of most commercial baby foods have been heated to very high temperatures and then cooled, giving them a long shelf life (usually two years) but destroying the flavor and some of the nutrients. By making baby food yourself, you can be sure of using only the best-quality ingredients to create fresh-tasting, nutrient-packed purées without thickeners or additives. You can also introduce a wide range of foods to your baby and make up your own combinations to suit his taste. The cooking methods shown here are useful for making the smooth purées suitable for the early stages of weaning (see pages 36–39 for recipes).

Choosing produce carefully

Babies are far more susceptible than adults to pesticide residues and other harmful artificial chemicals found in conventional food.

• **Organic agriculture** uses minimal antibiotics, no artificial fertilizers or pesticides, and no genetically modified organisms. However, although environmentally friendly, organic produce is more expensive to buy. In addition, since it contains no chemical preservatives, you will need to buy fresh fruit and vegetables several times a week.

• **The use of pesticides** is controlled by law, so a nonorganic diet is not necessarily unhealthy. Most residues in fresh produce are in the skin, so peel fruit and remove and discard the outer leaves of cabbage and lettuce.

Different cooking techniques

You don't need any special expertise to prepare baby foods, but there are ways to streamline the process so that even busy parents can produce meals that perfectly suit their babies' needs. Many first foods, such as mashed bananas and avocados, make excellent baby purées and do not require any cooking at all. For other meals, you can either set aside unseasoned portions of food, such as vegetables, that are being cooked for the rest of the family, or cook batches of puréed foods just for your baby and freeze them.

• **Steaming** helps to preserve the taste and nutrient content of fresh produce and preserves more antioxidants than either boiling or microwaving. Water-soluble vitamins B and C can be destroyed by overcooking: broccoli loses 60 percent of its vitamin C if boiled, 20 percent if steamed.

• **Boiling** can destroy nutrients, so ingredients should be cooked just until tender in the minimum amount of water. Be careful not to overcook.

• **Microwaving** destroys antioxidants contained in fresh produce, according to new research, so is best avoided.

• **Baking** is a nutrient-retaining, labor-saving cooking method. Potatoes, sweet potatoes, and squash can be washed, pricked with a fork, and baked until tender. The flesh can then be scooped out and mashed.

Blending purées

Blending uncooked soft fruits or steamed harder fruits or vegetables in a food processor is the quickest and easiest way of making smooth purées.

Cook small pieces of vegetable or fruit until tender. Drain, retaining

"Making baby food at home is more economical than routinely buying commercial brands and means that you can establish a varied and healthy diet from the start."

a tablespoon or two of the cooking liquid, then pour into the bowl of the food processor.

Run the food processor until a smooth, even-textured purée is produced. If necessary, add a little of the cooking water to thin the mixture, and then pulse briefly.

The final texture of the purée should be completely smooth. It can be thinned with breast milk, formula, or cooled boiled water for young babies.

To blend fibrous ingredients, such as peas and dried apricots, use a food mill. Fit the fine blade, then place the ingredients in the food mill and set it over a bowl. Turn the handle to rotate the blade. Continue grinding until most of the ingredients are pushed through the screen, then discard the fibrous pulp that is left behind.

The finished purée has a smooth, uniform texture.

Freezing & reheating

"Preparing large quantities of purées and freezing them in batches makes it easy and practical to feed your baby homemade food."

Batch-cooking and freezing purées is by far the most time-economical way to make food for your baby. Only a few first purées—banana, avocado, melon, and eggplant, for example— do not freeze well.

Food should be stored in a freezer that freezes food to 0°F (−18°C) or below in 24 hours. Food that has thawed should never be refrozen, although defrosted raw food, such as frozen peas, may be cooked and then frozen again for later use.

Freezing purées
Allow freshly cooked purée to cool to room temperature, then spoon it into clean ice-cube trays. Wrap in a freezer bag and transfer the trays to the freezer. When frozen, remove the trays from the freezer and push out the cubes of frozen purée onto a plate. Transfer the cubes to a fresh freezer bag, seal tightly, then label and date the contents. Return to the freezer and store for up to six weeks.

When you wish to use the frozen purée, take the required number of cubes from the freezer and heat in a pan or microwave until piping hot. Stir and allow to cool before serving.

Reheating rules

It is safe to thaw purées in a microwave or saucepan, as long as the food is throughly heated until piping hot. If using a microwave, be particularly vigilant—microwaves can heat food unevenly, producing "hot spots" but leaving other parts of the food cold. Let the purée cool after heating, and test the temperature before offering it to your baby. A baby's mouth is more sensitive to heat than an adult's, so food should be given at room temperature or lukewarm. If you are worried about estimating the temperature, use a heat-sensitive weaning spoon, which changes color according to the temperature of the food.

Food hygiene

Babies and young children are especially vulnerable to the effects of food poisoning, so it is essential that their food is prepared and stored correctly. In the first few months of a baby's life, extra care must be taken (see page 18), but once your baby is mobile and exploring objects with his mouth, there is little point in sterilizing anything except bottles and nipples. Attention to food safety rules, however, remains crucial.

Food safety

• **Keep raw meat, fish, and eggs away from other foods**. Wash hands well after contact with any of these foods. Keep two chopping boards—one for meat and fish and another for fruit and vegetables.
• **Only reheat food once**, and ensure that it is reheated to a high temperature to kill off bacteria.

• **Do not keep your baby's half-eaten food for a later meal** because the saliva introduced from your baby's spoon will breed bacteria. If you are feeding from a jar that contains more than one portion, transfer a serving portion into a weaning bowl and feed from the bowl.
• **Always date frozen food** so that it is never offered if it is past its best.
• **Do not leave food unrefrigerated** because bacteria multiply rapidly at room temperature. Cool food quickly if it is to be refrigerated or frozen. You can accelerate cooling by placing a bowl of cooked baby food in ice water.
• **Use up baby food** that is stored in the refrigerator within 24 hours.
• **Cover all food and drink** securely to protect it from contamination by germ-carrying insects, and keep pets away from food and work surfaces.

Kitchen hygiene
Adhering to a few simple rules will minimize the likelihood of food contamination.

• Always wash your hands before preparing food, and make sure your child's hands are washed before eating.
• Wipe daily, using an anti-bacterial agent, any surfaces that come in contact with your baby's food.
• Wash chopping boards and kitchen knives immediately after use, and leave equipment to air-dry.
• Use only perfectly clean dish towels to dry your baby's feeding equipment.

TIP When batch-cooking, cool food as quickly as possible and then freeze it right away. Don't leave it in the refrigerator for several days before freezing.

Weaning your baby

Starting solids

The first year of life is a period of rapid growth and development, with most babies at least doubling their birthweight by the time they reach six months. Don't be in a hurry to wean your baby onto solids. Solids should not be introduced until at least 17 weeks after your baby's due date. Her digestive and immune systems are not sufficiently developed before this time and there is a greater risk of triggering an allergy. Until six months or so, breast milk or formula provides all the nutrients your baby needs, but after six months, her digestive system will be ready for solids, and so will her appetite!

When does my baby need solids?

At around 26 weeks your baby will reach a stage where she needs solid foods as well as milk in her diet. For example, the iron inherited from her mother will have been used up. This is when the World Health Organization recommends that you introduce your baby to solids. Her first taste of solid food will be a significant milestone and mark the beginning of a gradual shift to a solid diet.

While sucking is a natural reflex, so is gagging on unaccustomed solids. And if weaning is delayed beyond six months, some babies have difficulty learning to swallow and chew food.

"Begin with one tablespoon of single-ingredient fruit or vegetable purée that has the consistency of runny yogurt."

All babies need to learn the skill of pushing food to the back of the mouth with their tongues and swallowing.

Recognizing that she's ready
Your baby may show signs that indicate she's ready for solids.

• She may seem dissatisfied by her milk feedings and become unsettled.
• She may start waking in the night, demanding a feeding when previously she was sleeping through.
• She might start showing an interest in the things you eat.

Ideal first foods
(see pages 34–35)
• baby rice cereal • sweet apple
• pears • papayas • bananas
• avocados • broccoli • carrots
• potatoes • sweet potatoes
• butternut squash or pumpkin

Foods for weaning

Baby rice cereal, mixed with expressed breast milk or formula, is a good starter food, but you can also introduce single-ingredient purées during the first four weeks of weaning. Simple purées enable you to assess how each new food suits your child, and get her accustomed to a wide range of single fruits and vegetables before they are mixed together. Avoid any foods that might cause early allergies (see page 16).

Root vegetables tend to be the most popular with young babies because of their naturally sweet flavor and smooth texture once puréed. Dessert apples and pears are ideal first fruits, but taste them yourself before cooking because they must be ripe and naturally sweet. Remember that baby rice cereal is an excellent mixer, too—it can make strongly flavored foods more palatable to some babies. Alternatively, foods such as mashed bananas, papayas, or avocados make nutritionally excellent no-cook purées.

Why homemade is best
If you make baby food yourself, you can be sure of using only the best ingredients, without the need for thickeners or additives. It is also more economical and easier to establish a varied diet with food combinations designed to suit your baby. Homemade food has a fresher taste than store-bought baby foods, which may contain preservatives and tend to be uniform and bland.

Remember
• Always wash your hands thoroughly before preparing or offering food, and wash your baby's hands before every meal.

• For thinning purées to the desired consistency of runny yogurt, use cooled boiled tap water, a little cooking water, or your baby's usual milk.

• Do not use bottled mineral water in food—it is not sterile and also tends to have a high sodium content.

• All your baby's feeding equipment should be washed in water that is hotter than 176°F/80°C (you will need to wear rubber gloves) and dried with a perfectly clean, dry towel. Alternatively, wash them in a dishwasher.

Getting started

Preparing tiny amounts of purée is time-consuming, so batch-cook and freeze portions in ice-cube trays, perhaps once a week (see page 22). At first your baby will manage only a "solid" consistency similar to runny yogurt, so the thickness of your purées will change over the weeks.

Alternatively, your baby's food can be prepared alongside the rest of the family's: if you are cooking vegetables for your dinner, for example, simply cook without adding any seasoning, set aside a small portion for your baby, and purée it in a blender when she is ready for her meal.

Special equipment
You will find suggestions for food preparation equipment on page 18. Your baby can take her first taste of solids from the tip of your finger, but once she is more accustomed to solids, you can use a small plastic weaning spoon and bowl.

Some weaning spoons are made of soft plastic that is kinder to tender gums. The spoon should be shallow so your baby can easily suck the food from it. The bowl may have a handle that allows you to hold it up to your baby. Cover her clothes with a bib and have wipes or a damp cloth on hand.

Introducing your baby to solids

"Don't worry if your baby refuses solids at first—many babies take a little while to get used to the idea. Simply try again the next day."

Pick a time of day for your baby's meal when you are not rushed or likely to be distracted. If possible, choose the same time every day (perhaps lunchtime) so that you can begin to establish a routine. You may want to give your baby half her usual milk feeding before her solids so that she is not extremely hungry.

Judging quantities

All babies' appetites and needs are different, but you will probably find that your baby initially takes one to two teaspoons of purée, so allow one tablespoon or one ice-cube portion. As she develops, offer a little more and continue feeding until her interest starts to wane. When she has had enough of the solid food, finish off with the second half of her milk feeding.

Taking it slowly

Even though your baby may relish her solid food from the start, it will still take time for her to master the art of swallowing it. Let her enjoy her mealtimes by being relaxed yourself and taking things at your baby's pace. Avoid times when she is overtired or restless. Talk to her encouragingly and make sure she is comfortable, whether she is in a bouncy chair, or sitting on your lap. Show her that the experience is enjoyable by smiling and making eye contact—and be prepared to get smeared with baby food, too.

Foods to avoid

It is best to avoid giving your baby the following foods to minimize the risk of infection and allergic reaction and to set up a healthy eating pattern.

• **Salt** Babies under a year should not have any salt added to their food, since this can strain immature kidneys and cause dehydration. A preference for salt can become established at an early age, and eating too much salt may lead to high blood pressure later in life. You should also avoid smoked foods.

• **Sugar** Unless food is really tart, don't add sugar to it. Added sugar is habit-forming and increases the risk of tooth decay.

• **Raw or lightly cooked eggs** Due to the risk of salmonella infection, eggs should be cooked until the yolk and white are both solid.

• **Unpasteurized cheese** To avoid the risk of listeria infection, avoid cheeses such as Brie and Camembert.

• **Foods containing gluten** Do not introduce wheat, oats, barley, or rye before six months (see page 17).

• **Nuts** Chopped and whole nuts are not recommended before the age of five due to the risk of choking. There is also a risk of allergic reaction to nuts (see page 16).

FIRST TASTES

Wash your hands thoroughly, then dip the tip of your finger into the food to test its temperature—it should be room temperature or lukewarm. If it is cool enough, let your baby suck the food

from your finger to introduce her to the taste. The feel of your finger is probably familiar to her and lessens the strangeness of tasting "solids." You can then switch to a spoon.

▶ To begin with, offer a small amount of purée from the tip of your scrupulously clean finger and let her suck the food off it.

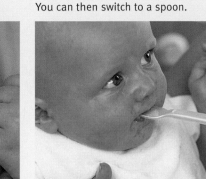

▶ Coat the tip of a soft, shallow weaning spoon with purée. Place the spoon between her lips and let her suck the food off. If she spits the purée out, scrape it up and offer it again.

• **Honey** Honey can contain a type of bacteria that, if eaten by a baby under the age of one, can produce toxins in the baby's intestine. This can result in a potentially life-threatening illness called infant botulism.

• **Shellfish** A major cause of food poisoning, shellfish can also cause an allergic reaction in young children.
• **High-fiber foods** Excessive amounts of high-fiber foods may interfere with the absorption of important minerals.

If your baby rejects food

Your baby may be one of the many who refuse solids on the first try. Be patient; it doesn't mean that she will never eat them. Wait and try again the next day. Initially, you are offering solids purely to introduce your baby to different foods. Do not cut down on the amount of milk you give, since at this point, solids are not replacing any part of her milk diet. If your baby seems to dislike a certain purée, try mixing it with a familiar or bland taste, such as breast milk, baby rice cereal, or puréed potatoes, for a gentler introduction. If this does not work, simply stop offering that food and try it again at a

later date. Weaning is unlikely to take an uninterrupted course; there may be days when your baby refuses solids, perhaps if she is feeling sick or is in an unfamiliar environment, and wants only her comforting milk. Don't be anxious about this: a short break from solids will not harm your baby. Try reintroducing solid food after a few days, or prepare a runnier purée that is easier for your baby to swallow. At this early stage, as long as your baby is getting her nutrition from milk, and as long as she continues to gain weight over a period of several days, she is probably getting enough food.

Remember
• Babies are born with a tongue-thrust reflex—if you introduce solids too early, your baby will poke out both the food and his tongue almost immediately. This reflex clears any foreign bodies, including food, out of his mouth and protects him from choking. Some time between four and six months, this reflex disappears.

• Test the temperature of all food. If using defrosted food, reheat until piping hot and leave to cool. Stir well and make sure the temperature is lukewarm before offering it to your baby.

• Do not reheat food more than once. Use a small quantity and leave the rest refrigerated.

• Use only breast milk, formula, or cooled boiled tap water to make purées or to dilute them if they seem too thick.

• Do not save your baby's half-eaten food, since bacteria-carrying saliva from the spoon will have been introduced.

• Do not overload the spoon with purée—this will make your baby splutter.

• When freezing food, try to fill containers right to the top without too much of an air pocket above and seal well to maintain the quality of baby purées.

• Although current guidelines recommend that you do not give your baby any solid food before six months, if you do start earlier, avoid any eggs, citrus fruit or juices, and shellfish until he is at least six months old.

Exploring tastes

"Gradually introduce your baby to coarser textures and new flavors: mash, grate, and finely chop food instead of puréeing, and combine sweet with savory ingredients."

The period between six and nine months is a time of rapid development, and your baby will spend many more hours awake than previously. It is a good idea to introduce plenty of new flavors in addition to the ones she already knows. Since everything is new for her, she will be receptive to these changes. This is the stage when solids should become a fixed part of your baby's daily diet.

Moving on from purées

Learning to chew

Every baby develops at her own pace, but your baby's first tooth (a front incisor) will probably come in at six or seven months; the remaining incisors usually follow in the next five months. As teeth begin to emerge, you can introduce coarser textures. Your baby will mostly use her gums to chew, so mashed and finely chopped food will provide ample chewing practice. It is not a good idea to offer smooth purées for too long because your baby may become lazy about chewing and have difficulty developing the tongue movements needed to deal with real solids. If she refuses lumpy food, make the transition easier by introducing a little mashed or grated food into her usual purées, or perhaps make a favorite meal in a thicker or coarser form. Introduce wider combinations of ingredients and don't be afraid to mix sweet with savory: fruit combined with vegetables, fish, or meat often appeals to babies.

Milk & dairy products

From the age of six months to one year, babies should have between 17 and 27 fl oz (500 and 800ml) of milk each day, mostly in the form of breast milk or formula. While you can use cow's milk in cooking and with breakfast cereals, breast milk or formula should remain your baby's main drink, since these contain nutrients that cow's milk lacks, such as iron and vitamin C.

If your baby is breastfed or if she is taking less than 17 fl oz (500ml) a day of a fortified infant milk, she also needs supplementary vitamins A, C, and D up until at least one year of age.

A portion of the milk intake can come from dairy products, including cheese and yogurt or milk used to prepare cooked foods, such as a cheese sauce. If your baby is not hungry at mealtimes, you may find that cutting down on the amount of milk she drinks helps.

With the introduction of solids, your baby may become more thirsty than she was on her milk-only diet. If you think this is the case, offer her some water or very diluted fruit juice in a cup at mealtimes once she is six months or older.

New foods for your baby

- **Bread and cereals**, including whole-wheat bread and whole-grain low-sugar breakfast cereals (such as shredded wheat or oatmeal) can now be given. Remember not to introduce gluten before six months. Avoid large amounts of high-fiber foods, such as high-fiber bread or bran flakes—this may fill up your baby without giving her the nutrients she needs for healthy growth and development.
- **Dairy products**, such as pasteurized whole-milk yogurt, cottage cheese, cream cheese, and mild hard cheeses including cheddar and Edam, are excellent nutrient-rich foods. Low-fat foods, such as reduced-fat spreads, are not suitable because they are too low in calories for a growing baby.
- **Eggs**, if hard-boiled, and dishes made with well-cooked eggs, such as french toast, omelets, frittatas, or scrambled eggs, are quick to cook and nutritious. Do not serve raw or lightly cooked eggs to babies under one year old (there is some risk of salmonella poisoning). The white and yolk should both be cooked until solid.
- **Fish fillets**, such as sole or cod, may be made into a purée with root vegetables or green vegetables such as zucchini or broccoli, or perhaps blended into a homemade cheese sauce. Oily fish, such as sardines, salmon, and tuna, are good sources of essential fatty acids, which are important for brain development. Carefully check all fish for bones before serving.

- **Red meat**, such as lean ground beef or lamb, can be combined with sautéed onion, potatoes, and mushrooms, then finely chopped in a blender. Organic liver, which is easily digested, provides the best source of iron. Slow-cooked lamb, pork, or beef casseroles make good purées.
- **Chicken** is generally popular with babies because of its mild taste. Serve it chopped or puréed, casseroled or poached. It combines well with root vegetables, such as potatoes and carrots, and with fruits such as dessert apples, grapes, mangoes, or papayas.
- **Vegetables**, including onions, leeks, cabbage, kale, green beans, spinach and other leafy green vegetables, red peppers, tomatoes, sweetcorn, peas, and mushrooms, greatly expand the dietary repertoire. Frozen vegetables often have as many nutrients as fresh ones.
- **Fruits**, particularly mangoes, grapes (peeled, deseeded, and halved), citrus fruits, and berries, can be served. Remove pith from citrus fruits and sieve out berry seeds. Use berries in small quantities, since they can be hard to digest. (Some babies are also allergic to strawberries.) Do not serve kiwi fruit to babies under nine months, and watch carefully for an allergic reaction.
- **Beans and legumes** are ideal for boosting meat purées, and are especially valuable for vegetarian babies. Lentils and dried legumes (such as split peas or butter beans) are a good source of protein and iron. Tofu (soybean curd) is a good meat alternative.

New tastes & textures
- whole-grain, low-sugar breakfast cereals • rice cakes
- whole-milk yogurt • hard-boiled eggs • oily fish, such as salmon • organic liver
- chicken puréed with carrots • green vegetables
- tofu • mangoes • lentils

Remember
- If you begin weaning before six months, do not introduce gluten to your baby's diet before she is six months old.
- Do not serve raw or lightly cooked eggs to babies under one year old.
- Strawberries can sometimes cause an allergic reaction. Watch your baby carefully, especially if she suffers from conditions such as eczema or asthma.

Family meals with your baby

Once your baby can support her head and upper body, you can introduce her to a high chair. As long as her back is supported, she will feel comfortable, and she will enjoy being higher up and able to see what is going on around her. Put her in a safety harness so that she can't fall out, and pull the chair away from the wall and put a splash mat on the floor to make cleaning up easier. Let her get used to being in the chair, wearing a bib, and having a tray in front of her by giving her the chance to play there with her favorite toys. When you feed her, give her her own plastic spoon to hold. If she drinks milk from a bottle, let her have that in the high chair at first. She will soon be ready to enjoy eating there.

First refusals

If she finds it strange to be fed in this new way, she may even reject the food, turning her head away each time. Don't be discouraged by her initial refusal. Gently encourage her to feed herself, even though it is a messy business. Her hand–eye coordination will be improving all the time, and she'll soon start dipping her spoon in and out of the food and aiming it at her mouth.

Joining in

Even though your baby has only just begun to eat solids and has many more meals than older members of the family, draw her high chair up to the table so that she can join you at meals as often as possible. She will learn that meals are sociable and fun, as well as satisfying for her stomach. Try to plan and vary her menus along the lines of the family mealtimes. For example, give her baby rice cereal for breakfast, a savory dish followed by pieces of fruit or cheese for lunch, and perhaps a selection of finger foods along with her milk drink for dinner.

"Your baby will quickly learn that mealtimes not only satisfy his hunger, but are sociable and fun, too."

Drinks other than milk

Water is the best alternative drink to milk to give your baby if she is thirsty. For babies under six months, take water from the kitchen faucet and boil it, then allow to cool before giving to your baby. Bottled mineral water can contain high concentrations of mineral salts, which are unsuitable for young babies. Breastfed babies don't usually need water until they start eating solid foods, when they will need extra fluid to quench their thirst.

Fruit juices, such as pure orange or cranberry juice, are useful sources of vitamin C, which helps our bodies to absorb iron from the food we eat. However, fruit and herbal baby drinks can sometimes contain large amounts of sugar, which can lead to tooth decay. A label stating "no added sugar" does not mean that the drink is sugar-free. It may contain a different type of sugar, such as fructose or glucose. Even natural fruit sugars can rot teeth. Consequently, it is best to give your baby very diluted fruit juice only occasionally with her meal. Make sure that she drinks it from a cup instead of a bottle.

Drinks with added sugar or artificial sweeteners are completely unsuitable for babies or toddlers.

Drinking from a cup

Although your baby will still be getting most of her liquid from her usual milk feedings and some from the purées she eats, she will enjoy having a cup of water that she can handle for herself. This will give her the freedom to choose when she wants to drink and how much.

As soon as your baby is ready to hold one, introduce a two-handled training cup. These have lids and come in a variety of designs. Your baby may prefer to have one that allows her to use the familiar sucking mechanism.

Cups with soft, flexible spouts can eventually be replaced by cups with shorter, firmer spouts, and later by open cups.

Drinks & tooth care

Comfort sucking on sweetened drinks is the main cause of tooth decay in babies and toddlers. Nursing-bottle caries, also known as baby-bottle tooth decay, occurs when a baby or young child is frequently given sugary drinks in a bottle. Drinking from a bottle is worse for teeth than drinking from a cup because the drink is in contact with the teeth for longer. The bacteria present on teeth use the sugar to produce acid, which attacks the tooth enamel, leading to tooth decay.

It is even worse to give a baby a bottle to suck at night because there is less saliva in her mouth than usual at this time, so the sugar clings to the teeth all night. If your baby insists on a bottle at bedtime, then fill it with either water or milk—not fruit juice. Try to wean your baby off a bottle and onto a cup by the time she is one year old, with the possible exception of a bottle of milk or water at bedtime.

Remember

• Never leave your baby alone when she is eating. If she is in a high chair, always use a safety harness.

• Never force your baby to eat a food she does not want or to finish a meal. Let your baby's appetite be your guide.

• Allow your baby to practice feeding herself. This will be messy, so position her away from the walls and put a splash mat or an old plastic tablecloth under her chair to make cleaning easier.

• Eat with your baby whenever possible. Try to make eating a sociable experience from the beginning.

• Don't give children tea or coffee because they hinder iron absorption. High-fiber cereals have the same effect.

Preventing tooth decay

• Use a cup as soon as your baby is able to handle one.

• Put only milk or water in your baby's bottle.

• Avoid putting your baby to bed with a bottle.

• It is much better to give water between meals, saving diluted fruit juice for mealtimes only.

• Do not add sugar to weaning foods except when it is absolutely necessary.

• Dilute all juices for your baby (at this age, one part juice to at least five parts cooled boiled water), since even natural fruit sugars can cause tooth decay.

First tastes

Very first foods must be easy to digest and made of ingredients that will gently introduce your baby to new flavors and textures. Although your baby may like fairly strong flavors, such as sweet potato, parsnip, or carrot, many babies prefer to begin with blander tastes, such as milky baby rice cereal or a potato purée. At first, purées should be runny and absolutely smooth, similar to runny yogurt in consistency, and made up of only one or two ingredients.

1 Baby rice cereal
Baby rice cereal is fine-textured and easily digested. Its milky taste makes for an easy transition to solids. Mix with cooled boiled water, breast milk, or formula.

2 Potato purée
The mild taste of potatoes makes them a good weaning food. Boil, mash, and purée in a food mill or press through a sieve. (See First vegetable purée, page 37.)

3 Carrot purée
The sweet taste of carrots appeals to babies. Steam or boil, and blend with a little cooking water. (See First vegetable purée, page 37.)

4 Broccoli & potato purée
Broccoli is a good source of vitamins. Combine with sieved boiled potatoes or puréed sweet potatoes for a creamy purée. (See page 39.)

5 Baby rice cereal & dried apricot purée
Dried apricots are rich in iron and beta-carotene. Purée with baby rice cereal for a gentle introduction to the fruit. (See Dried apricot purée, page 38.)

6 Apple purée
Sweet eating apples make a smooth apple sauce. Try combining with some puréed pear for a tasty combination. (See First fruit purée, page 36.)

7 Banana purée
A fully ripe banana makes an instant purée when well mashed. Make it less sticky by adding a little breast milk or formula. (See First fruit purée, page 36.)

8 Pear purée
Ripe pear steamed until soft or cooked in a heavy saucepan makes an ideal first food. Try combining with a little baby rice cereal for a creamier finish. (See First fruit purée, page 36.)

9 Papaya purée
A fully ripe papaya needs no cooking. A rich source of antioxidants, it has a naturally sweet flavor. (See First fruit purée, page 36.)

10 Parsnip & carrot purée
Parsnips have a sweet taste that babies enjoy. Cook in the same way as carrots. They combine well with apple, too.

11 Butternut squash or pumpkin purée
Both these vegetables are good sources of vitamin A. Steam or boil until tender, then purée. (See page 39.)

12 Sweet potato purée
Sweet potatoes are an excellent source of vitamin A and babies like their naturally sweet taste. Steam or boil until tender.

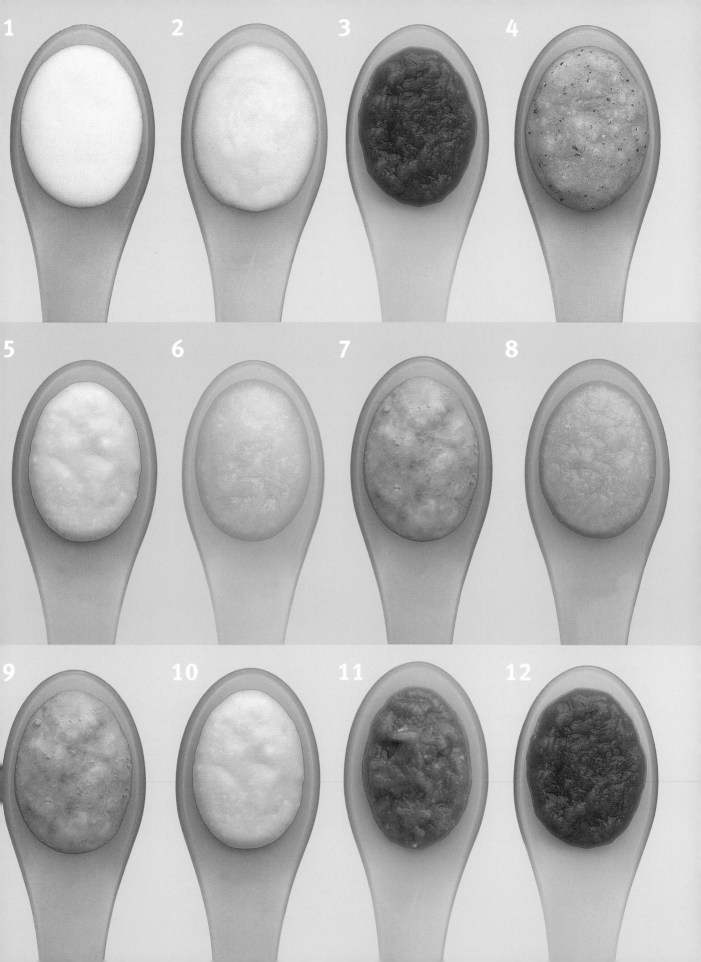

First fruit purée

⟳ Preparation: 5 minutes; cooking: 8 minutes for apples, 3–4 minutes for pears

✓ Makes 6 portions　❄ Suitable for freezing

Fruit purées make ideal first meals. Choose only sweet fruit that is completely ripe for your baby. Once he is accustomed to eating an apple or a pear purée on its own, try combining the two fruits to give him a taste of a mixed flavor. This purée will be a little thinner than vegetable purées.

▶ Chop your chosen fruit into small, even-sized pieces. Put these pieces in a heavy-bottomed saucepan with the water or apple juice (if the pears are ripe, you may not need water or juice). Cover and cook over low heat until the fruit is tender. Or steam the fruit over water for the same amounts of time (see above).

▶ Blend the fruit to a smooth purée with a hand blender. Add a little apple juice, boiled water, or water from the bottom of the steamer to the purée.

▶ Spoon a little purée into your baby's bowl and serve lukewarm. Pour the remainder into an ice-cube tray and freeze (see page 22).

Variation

▶ Mash a raw banana or half a papaya and purée with a little breast milk or formula. If necessary, the banana can be heated in a microwave for a few seconds to make it easier to mash. These variations are not suitable for freezing.

2 medium **sweet eating apples** or **ripe pears,** peeled and cored

3 tbsp **boiled water** or **pure apple juice**

TIPS All fruits for very first purées, except for bananas, papayas, and avocados, must be cooked. A month after beginning to wean your baby, you can use raw pears, peaches, mangoes, plums, and melons, if they are ripe and juicy.

You can thicken pear puree by stirring in a little baby rice cereal.

Apple and pear are good combined together.

First vegetable purée

⟳ Preparation: 5 minutes; cooking: 15–20 minutes   ⊘ Makes 8 portions
❉ Suitable for freezing

Your baby's first foods should be mild in taste, easy to digest, completely smooth, and unlikely to provoke an allergic reaction. Begin with single-ingredient purées in the first week or two, then progress to combinations of root vegetables (see pages 26–29).

▶ Chop the vegetables into small pieces. Put in a steamer or colander set over boiling water and cook for 15–20 minutes, or until tender. Alternatively, place in a pan, pour over just enough boiling water to cover, and simmer, covered, for 15 minutes or until soft.
▶ Blend the vegetable to a purée using some of the liquid from the bottom of the steamer or the pan (see page 22).

▶ Spoon a little purée into your baby's bowl and serve lukewarm. Pour the remainder into an ice-cube tray and freeze (see page 22).

Variation
▶ Substitute other root vegetables, such as parsnip or rutabaga. Chop, cook, and blend as described above.

1 ½ cups **carrots, potatoes, sweet potatoes, butternut squash,** or **pumpkin,** peeled

TIP The amount of liquid needed when blending depends on whether your baby finds swallowing difficult. A general rule is to make an absolutely smooth, very runny purée, akin to runny yogurt.

TIP Do not purée potatoes or sweet potatoes in a food processor—the mixture will become starchy and gluey. Use a food mill or sieve.

Creamy vegetable purée

⟳ Preparation: 5 minutes; cooking: 2 minutes   ⊘ Makes 6 portions
❉ Suitable for freezing

Strong-tasting root vegetable purées, such as parsnip or carrot, may be made milder with the addition of baby rice cereal. Baby cereal also combines well with steamed and puréed broccoli and cauliflower.

▶ Mix together the baby rice cereal and milk according to the instructions on the box, and stir into the vegetable purée until thoroughly combined.

▶ Spoon a little purée into your baby's bowl and serve lukewarm. Pour the remainder into an ice-cube tray and freeze (see page 22).

1 tbsp sugar-free, vitamin- and iron-enriched **baby rice cereal**

3 tbsp **breast milk** or **formula**

4 tbsp **first vegetable purée** (see above)

Fruity baby rice cereal

⟳ Preparation: 5 minutes; cooking: 2 minutes   ⊘ Makes 6 portions
❉ Suitable for freezing

Baby rice cereal is a valuable first food: it is easily digested and has a milky taste that helps to ease your baby's transition from a purely milk diet to solids. It may be served plain or combined with a purée.

▶ Mix together the cereal and milk according to the instructions, and stir it into the fruit purée to give it a slightly creamy texture.

▶ Spoon a little purée into your baby's bowl and serve lukewarm. Pour the remainder into an ice-cube tray and freeze (see page 22).

1 tbsp sugar-free, vitamin- and iron-enriched **baby rice cereal**

3 tbsp **breast milk** or **formula**

4 tbsp **first fruit purée** (see opposite)

TIP Pear, peach, or plum purée mixed with baby rice cereal is often popular with babies.

"Start with single, bland purées, then gradually introduce stronger flavors and combinations of foods."

Simple fruit & vegetable purées

Once first tastes have been accepted, you can introduce a wider variety of fruits and vegetables to your baby. Some babies may find certain foods, such as dried apricots, mangoes, or cauliflower, indigestible. If this is the case, try mixing them with other foods such as bananas or root vegetables, or leave them out of your child's diet until he is a little older.

Melon purée

Take a small wedge of melon, remove the seeds, and cut the flesh away from the skin, discarding the green flesh near the skin. Blend to a purée of the desired consistency. Combines well with mashed bananas or avocadoes. Makes 1 serving.

Peach or nectarine purée

Score a cross on the base of a small, ripe peach or nectarine, then submerge in boiling water for 1 minute. Skin and chop the peach flesh, then purée in a blender. (Ripe, sweet peaches and nectarines can be used raw.) Makes 2 servings.

Dried apricot purée

Simmer a handful of dried apricots in a little water for about 5 minutes, or until tender. Blend to a purée of the desired consistency with as much cooking liquid as is needed to make a smooth pulp. Work the pulp through a food mill or purée in a blender and then push through a sieve. This purée is also good mixed with baby rice cereal or puréed apples or pears. Makes 4 servings.

Avocado purée

Choose a soft, ripe fruit and prepare when your baby is ready to eat (to avoid discoloration). Halve and pit one avocado, and mash the flesh from one half with a fork or purée to the desired consistency with about 2 tbsp of breast milk or formula. Makes 1 serving.

Cauliflower or broccoli purée

Place 2½ cups of small cauliflower or broccoli florets in a steamer and cook until tender, about 10 minutes. Drain and blend to a purée. Mix with potato purée (see First vegetable purée, page 37) or baby rice cereal. Makes 6 servings.

Zucchini purée

Place 2 cups trimmed and sliced zucchini in a steamer and cook until tender, about 12 minutes. Alternatively, put in a pan with water to cover, bring to a boil, and simmer for 6 minutes. Blend to a purée. Makes 8 servings.

Butternut squash or pumpkin purée

Peel and deseed a 1-lb squash or slice of pumpkin, then cut into small pieces. Cook as described for First vegetable purée on page 37, then blend to a purée, adding a little cooking water if necessary. Alternatively, cut the squash in half or cut a wedge of pumpkin, scoop out the seeds, and brush with melted butter. Cover with foil and bake in an oven preheated to 350°F for 1½ hours, or until tender. Makes 8 servings.

Sweet potato purée

Scrub 2½ cups sweet potatoes, pat dry, and prick with a fork. Bake in an oven preheated to 400°F for 45 minutes to 1 hour. Scoop out the flesh and mash with 1–2 tbsp of breast milk or formula. Alternatively, peel and cube the sweet potatoes and cook as for First vegetable purée on page 37. This purée blends well with apple, peach, or broccoli purées. Makes 8 servings.

Nutrition matters

- **Cantaloupe** is the most nutritious of all the melon varieties—it is rich in vitamin C and also provides beta-carotene and potassium.
- **Peaches** provide vitamin C.
- **Nectarines** provide vitamin C and potassium.
- **Dried apricots** provide beta-carotene, iron, and potassium, and are very useful when fresh fruit is scarce.
- **Avocadoes** provide potassium and vitamins B6 and E. They have a buttery flavor and texture that are usually popular with babies.
- **Cauliflower** provides folate, potassium, and vitamin C.
- **Broccoli** provides beta-carotene, folate, potassium, and vitamin C.
- **Zucchini** provides beta-carotene, potassium, vitamin C, and magnesium, but most of the nutrients are in the skin, so do not peel.
- **Butternut squash** provides beta-carotene, potassium, and vitamins C and E.
- **Pumpkins** provide beta-carotene and vitamin C.
- **Sweet potatoes** are an excellent source of beta-carotene, potassium, and vitamins C and E.

New tastes & textures

Once your baby has adjusted to simple purées, you can begin to introduce a broader range of flavors and textures. Keep textures smooth until your baby can cope well with chewing and swallowing. Then gradually introduce purées with thicker or lumpier textures, beginning with familiar flavors. Try adding just a little grated or mashed food to a smooth purée, or make your baby's favorite purée in a lumpier form. You can also combine more ingredients to make interesting flavors. Don't be afraid to mix sweet with savory: fruit with puréed chicken or fish, for example, is a favorite with many babies.

1 Tomato & cauliflower gratin
This blended gratin makes a good introduction to cauliflower. Cheddar cheese and deseeded tomatoes boost the flavor. (See page 49 for recipe.)

3 Fish with carrots & orange
This purée made with fresh white fish has a delicious combination of flavors and is bursting with useful nutrients. (See page 51 for recipe.)

5 First chicken casserole
Combining tender chicken breast with sweet root vegetables gives it a flavor and smooth texture that appeals to babies. (See page 53 for recipe.)

2 Spinach, potato, parsnip, & leek purée
It's a good idea to combine stronger-tasting vegetables such as spinach with root vegetables or cheese sauce. (See page 48 for recipe.)

4 Peach, apple, & strawberry purée
Make this purée when peaches are in season and soft fruit is perfectly ripe and sweet. Mix with baby rice cereal for a milder taste. (See page 45 for recipe.)

6 Banana with mango or papaya
Sweet ripe mangoes or papayas blended with ripe bananas make a fruity, nutritious no-cook meal. (See page 42 for recipe.)

Remember

• Foods such as mashed bananas or papayas make perfect fresh baby food in no time at all.

• Raw fruits are best, since none of the nutrients are lost in cooking. Make sure the fruit is ripe and sweet—it's a good idea to taste it yourself.

Nutrition matters

• **Bananas** provide potassium and vitamin B6.

• **Papayas** provide beta-carotene, magnesium, and vitamin C.

• **Mangoes** provide beta-carotene and vitamins C and E.

• **Blueberries** provide vitamin C.

• **Apples** provide vitamin C.

• **Plums** provides potassium.

• **Apricots (fresh)** provide beta-carotene and vitamin C.

• **Pears** provide vitamin C.

• **Strawberries** provide folate and vitamin C.

• **Cottage cheese** provides calcium, protein, and vitamins B2 and B12.

• **Yogurt** provides calcium, protein, and vitamins B2 and B12.

• **Chicken** provides iron (especially dark meat), protein, potassium, B vitamins, and zinc.

TIP It's best to prepare these purées just before your baby is ready to eat.

Instant no-cook purées

There are many fast, no-cook purées that are both delicious and nutritious for your baby. Here are some good fruit combinations to try. Each recipe on these two pages makes one portion. For the Apple purée plus three fruits recipe, you can mix and match fresh fruit with some unsweetened apple purée, either homemade (perhaps defrost a couple of ice-tray cubes) or bought. If you don't have apple purée in the freezer, you could use pear or apple-and-pear purée.

Mango & banana purée

Purée or mash the flesh of a quarter of a small, ripe mango together with half a small, ripe banana, peeled and sliced. Serve immediately.

Avocado & banana or papaya purée

Mash a quarter of a small avocado together with half a small, ripe banana and 1–2 tbsp of breast milk or formula.

You can substitute the flesh of half a papaya for the banana in this recipe—the milk is then optional.

Banana & blueberry purée

Cut a medium-size, ripe banana into pieces and simply blend together with ¼ cup blueberries. Serve immediately.

Apple purée plus three fruits

Combine one ripe peach, skinned and cut into pieces, one small, ripe banana, peeled and sliced, ¼ cup blueberries, and 2 tbsp of apple purée, and purée in a blender. For older babies, simply mash the fruit and mix with the apple purée.

Plum or apricot & pear purée

Peel and pit a ripe apricot or plum. Slice the fruit and purée or mash the flesh with the chopped soft flesh of a ripe pear. This purée is suitable for freezing.

Cantaloupe & strawberry purée

Blend together half a ripe cantaloupe, peeled and cut into chunks, with two strawberries, hulled and cut in half. Stir in 2 tsp of baby rice cereal.

Papaya & cottage cheese or yogurt purée

Cut a small, ripe papaya in half, remove the black seeds, and purée or mash the flesh of one half with 1 tbsp of sieved cottage cheese or Greek yogurt.

Papaya & chicken purée

Peel and halve a small, ripe papaya, remove the black seeds, and purée or mash the flesh of one half with ¼ cup of cooked, boneless, skinless chicken. This purée is suitable for freezing.

"Once your baby is happily eating her first purées, you can start to experiment with different combinations. Fruits blend well together and are always popular."

2 ripe **pears**, peeled, cored, and chopped

2 pitted **prunes**, chopped

1 tbsp **baby rice cereal**

Juicy pear & prune purée

⟳ Preparation: 5 minutes; cooking: 5 minutes   ✎ Makes 2 portions

✐ Provides fiber, potassium, and vitamin C   ❄ Suitable for freezing

This tasty combination of fresh and dried fruits is a useful source of fiber.

▶ Simmer the fruit in a saucepan with a little water for 5 minutes. Purée to the desired consistency, using as much cooking water as needed. Sieve to get rid of the tough prune skins.

▶ Stir in the cereal while warm.

---

1 **sweet eating apple**, peeled, cored, and chopped

1 ripe **pear**, peeled, cored, and chopped

⅓ cup **strawberries**, hulled and cut into quarters

⅓ cup **blueberries**

2 tbsp **baby rice cereal**

Apple, pear, blueberry & strawberry purée

⟳ Preparation: 3 minutes; cooking: 5 minutes   ✎ Makes 2 portions

✐ Provides fiber, potassium, and vitamin C   ❄ Suitable for freezing

▶ Put the fruit into a heavy-bottomed saucepan, cover, and cook over a low heat for about 5 minutes. Purée in a blender and stir in the baby rice cereal.

Variation

Instead of baby rice cereal, you could mix with bananas.

Apricot, pear, peach & apple compote

⏱ Preparation: 5 minutes; cooking: 10 minutes
🔪 Makes 4 portions
🍴 Provides beta-carotene, fiber, and vitamin C
❄ Suitable for freezing

3 ready-to-eat **dried apricots** or **fresh apricots,** chopped

1 **sweet eating apple**, peeled, cored, and chopped

1 large, ripe **pear**, peeled, cored, and chopped

1 large ripe **peach** or **plum**, peeled, pitted, and chopped

▶ Place all the chopped fruit in a saucepan and simmer with a little water until soft, about 8–10 minutes.
▶ Blend the mixture to a purée of the desired consistency.

Variation

For a creamier finish to this compote, mix 2 tbsp of baby rice cereal with 4 tbsp of breast milk or formula and blend with the fruit purée.

Peach, apple & strawberry purée

⏱ Preparation: 5 minutes; cooking: 9–12 minutes
🔪 Makes 4 portions
🍴 Provides fiber and vitamin C
❄ Suitable for freezing

1 **sweet eating apple**, peeled, cored, and chopped

1 large ripe **peach**, peeled, pitted, and chopped

3 large **strawberries**, hulled

NOTE *Strawberries occasionally provoke an allergic reaction in sensitive babies.*

This is a delicious fruit purée to make in the summer. It can be combined with some baby rice cereal mixed with a little milk or water.

▶ Steam the apple for about 6 minutes or until tender. Add the peaches and strawberries to the steamer, and continue to cook for about 3 minutes. Blend the fruits to a smooth purée.

Peach & banana purée

⏱ Preparation: 5 minutes; cooking: 3 minutes
🔪 Makes 1 portion
🍴 Provides potassium and vitamins B6 and C

1 small ripe **peach**, peeled, pitted, and chopped

1/2 small **banana**, peeled and sliced

1 tbsp freshly squeezed **orange juice**

Instead of peach, you could use a nectarine or two sweet, juicy plums to make this purée.

▶ Put all the ingredients into a small saucepan, cover, and cook over a low heat for 2–3 minutes, or until the fruit is slightly mushy. Blend to a purée. Allow to cool before serving.

Apple & pear with raisins & cinnamon

⏱ Preparation: 5 minutes; cooking: 8 minutes
🔪 Makes 4 portions
🍴 Provides fiber, potassium, and vitamin C
❄ Suitable for freezing

1 **sweet eating apple**, peeled, cored, and chopped

1 ripe **pear**, peeled, cored, and chopped

1 tbsp **raisins**

1 tbsp pure **apple juice**

a generous pinch of **cinnamon**

▶ Put all the ingredients into a saucepan, bring to a simmer, then cover and cook for 5 minutes. Blend to a purée and allow to cool a little.

½ small ripe **mango**, peeled and chopped

3–4 tbsp mild, full-fat **natural yogurt**

Yogurt & mango purée

🕑 Preparation: 5 minutes ⌀ Makes 2 portions 🥄 Provides beta-carotene, calcium, fiber, potassium, protein, and vitamins B2, B12, C, and E

Always choose whole-milk yogurt for babies—Greek or live natural yogurts are good. Fresh peach or dried apricot purée both also work well mixed with yogurt.

▶ Purée the mango using a handheld blender and mix together with the yogurt.

1 small ripe **banana**, peeled

2 pitted **dried prunes**, chopped

2 tbsp mild, full-fat **natural yogurt**

Banana, prune & yogurt purée

🕑 Preparation: 2 minutes ⌀ Makes 1 portion 🥄 Provides calcium, fiber, potassium, protein, and vitamins B2, B6, B12, and C

▶ Simply chop the banana and prunes into pieces.

▶ Purée together using a hand-held blender and stir in the yogurt.

⅓ cup **dried apricots**, roughly chopped

⅓ cup **boiling water**

1 small ripe **banana**, peeled and sliced

1 tbsp **custard powder**

Apricot & banana custard

🕑 Preparation: 5 minutes; cooking: 5 minutes ⌀ Makes 2 portions 🥄 Provides beta-carotene, iron, potassium, and vitamins B6 and C

Check the label of the dried apricots to make sure they have not been treated with sulfur dioxide to preserve the bright orange color, since this substance can trigger an asthma attack in susceptible babies.

▶ Put the apricots into a small saucepan and cover with 3½ tbsp boiling water. Simmer for 2–3 minutes. Blend the apricots and cooking liquid together with the banana.
▶ Put the custard powder in a small

saucepan and mix in a little of the boiling water to make a paste. Add the rest of the boiling water and stir briskly over a medium heat until smooth and creamy.
▶ Mix the custard together with the apricot and banana purée.

4 cups **butternut squash** or **pumpkin**, peeled, deseeded, and chopped

1 **sweet eating apple**, peeled, cored, and chopped

Butternut squash & apple purée

🕑 Preparation: 5 minutes; cooking: 17 minutes ⌀ Makes 4 portions 🥄 Provides beta-carotene, fiber, folate, and vitamin C ❄ Suitable for freezing

Mixing vegetables with fruit is a good way to encourage babies to eat vegetables.

▶ Put the butternut squash in a steamer and cook for about 7 minutes. Add the apple to the steamer and continue to cook for 10 minutes, or until the squash is tender. Blend to a smooth purée.

Variation
▶ Omit the apple and blend the cooked squash or pumpkin with a large, juicy, skinned raw peach.

Homemade vegetable stock

⟳ Preparation: 10 minutes; cooking: 1 hour 10 minutes   ⌀ Makes 2 pints
⚗ Provides beta-carotene, folate, and potassium   ❄ Suitable for freezing

1 **onion**, peeled

1 **garlic clove**, peeled and roughly chopped

2 large **carrots**, peeled

1 large **leek**, washed

1 stalk **celery**

1 tbsp **olive oil**

4 cups **water**

1 sprig **parsley**

1 sprig **thyme** (optional)

1 **bay leaf**

4 **peppercorns**

It's easy to make a homemade vegetable stock that will keep in the refrigerator for up to a week. Use this to form the basis of your purées instead of relying on salt-filled, store-bought stock cubes.

▶ Roughly chop all the vegetables. Heat the olive oil in a large, heavy-bottomed pan and add the vegetables and garlic. Sweat the vegetables in the oil without coloring for 5 minutes—cover with a lid if you wish.
▶ Add the cold water and bring to a boil. Add the herbs, bay leaf, and peppercorns. Reduce the heat, cover, and simmer for 1 hour.
▶ Leave to cool for a couple of hours, then strain through a sieve. Squeeze remaining juices out of the vegetables by pushing them down in the sieve with a potato masher.

Cheesy leek, sweet potato & cauliflower purée

⟳ Preparation: 5 minutes; cooking: 15 minutes   ⌀ Makes 5 portions
⚗ Provides beta-carotene, calcium, folate, potassium, protein, and vitamins A, B2, B12, and C
❄ Suitable for freezing

1 tbsp **butter**

$1/4$ cup **leeks**, washed and sliced

1 **sweet potato**, peeled and cut into chunks

1 cup **boiling water**

$3/4$ cup **cauliflower** florets

3 tbsp grated **cheddar cheese**

As well as fruit and vegetables, it's good to add foods such as cheese to your baby's meals. Babies grow very rapidly in their first year, and cheese provides a concentrated source of calories, which is important for growth.

▶ Heat the butter in a pan and add the leek. Sauté for about 3 minutes until softened. Add the sweet potato and boiling water and cook for 5 minutes.
▶ Add the cauliflower and continue to cook for 5 minutes.
▶ Strain the vegetables, reserving the cooking liquid. Blend the vegetables together with about $1/3$ cup of the reserved cooking liquid and the grated cheddar cheese.

Trio of root vegetables

⟳ Preparation: 5 minutes; cooking: 21 minutes   ⌀ Makes 6 portions
⚗ Provides beta-carotene, fiber, folate, and potassium   ❄ Suitable for freezing

$1^1/2$ cups **carrots**, peeled and chopped

$1^1/4$ cups **potatoes**, peeled and chopped

$3/4$ cup **parsnips** or **rutabaga**, peeled and chopped

Babies tend to love root vegetables because of their naturally sweet flavor.

▶ Put the vegetables into a saucepan and just cover with boiling water. Cook over medium heat for about 20 minutes, or until tender. Alternatively, steam them until tender.
▶ Blend the vegetables to a smooth purée with about $1/2$ cup of the cooking liquid, or use boiled water from the bottom of the steamer.

2 tbsp **butter**

1 **leek,** white part only, washed and sliced

1$\frac{1}{4}$ cups **potatoes,** peeled and chopped

1 cup unsalted **vegetable stock** (see page 47) or **chicken stock** (see page 52) or **water**

$\frac{1}{2}$ cup **frozen peas**

Potato, leek & pea purée

⏱ Preparation: 5 minutes; cooking: 24 minutes   🥄 Makes 4 portions
🔪 Provides fiber, folate, and vitamins A and C   ❄ Suitable for freezing

Use only fresh, unsalted stock, bought or homemade, for this recipe. To make this purée into a delicious soup for the family, add extra stock and seasoning.

▶ Warm the butter in a pan, add the leeks, and sauté until just golden, 5–6 minutes. Add the potatoes and cover with stock. Bring to a boil, then reduce the heat, cover, and simmer for 10 minutes.

▶ Add the frozen peas and continue to cook for about 6 minutes, or until the vegetables are tender. Blend to a purée using a food mill or sieve.

---

2 tbsp **butter**

1$\frac{1}{2}$ cups **leeks,** white part only, washed and finely sliced

1$\frac{1}{2}$ cups **potatoes,** peeled and chopped

$\frac{3}{4}$ cup **parsnips,** peeled and chopped

1 cup **boiling water** or unsalted **vegetable stock** (see page 47)

3 cups **fresh spinach,** washed and tough stalks removed, or $\frac{1}{3}$ cup **frozen spinach**

$\frac{1}{3}$ cup grated **cheddar cheese**

Spinach, potato, parsnip & leek purée

⏱ Preparation: 10 minutes; cooking: 30 minutes   🥄 Makes 6 portions   🔪 Provides beta-carotene, fiber, folate, potassium, protein, and vitamins A and C   ❄ Suitable for freezing

▶ Melt the butter in a saucepan, add the leeks, and sauté for 2–3 minutes. Add the potatoes and parsnips, sauté for 1 minute, and cover with boiling water or stock. Cover and simmer for 12 minutes.
▶ Add the fresh spinach leaves, if using, and continue to cook for 3–4 minutes. If using frozen spinach, cook it separately,

according to the instructions on the package, drain, and then mix with the potatoes, leeks, and parsnips. Drain the vegetables, reserving the cooking liquid.
▶ Blend the vegetables together with about 3 tbsp of the cooking liquid and the grated cheddar. Add more liquid if necessary to thin the purée.

Lentil & vegetable purée

⟳ Preparation: 10 minutes; cooking: 40 minutes   ◌ Makes 8 portions
✎ Provides beta-carotene, fiber, folate, protein, and vitamin C   ❄ Suitable for freezing

Lentils are a good source of protein. However, some babies find lentils indigestible, so they are best not given before eight months.

2 tbsp **butter**

1½ cups **leeks,** washed and finely sliced

¼ cup **celery,** chopped

1 cup **carrots,** peeled and chopped

⅓ cup **red lentils**

2 cups **sweet potatoes,** peeled and chopped

1 **bay leaf**

2 cups unsalted **vegetable stock** (see page 47) or **chicken stock** (see page 52) or **water**

▶ Melt the butter in a saucepan, add the leeks, and sauté for 2–3 minutes. Stir in the celery, carrots, and lentils, and cook for 2 minutes more.
▶ Add the sweet potatoes and bay leaf, and cover with stock or water. Bring to a boil, then reduce the heat, cover, and simmer for about 30 minutes, or until the vegetables and lentils are tender. Remove the bay leaf.
▶ Blend to a purée for younger babies. Older babies can eat it as it is.

Sweet potato, carrot & broccoli purée

⟳ Preparation: 5 minutes; cooking: 18 minutes   ◌ Makes 6 portions
✎ Provides beta-carotene, fiber, folate, and vitamin C   ❄ Suitable for freezing

It can be helpful to combine popular vegetables with varieties that children tend to like a little less. In this recipe, I have used carrots and sweet potatoes, which babies usually love to eat, to tone down the strong flavor of broccoli.

2⅓ cups **sweet potatoes,** peeled and chopped

1 large **carrot,** peeled and sliced

1⅓ cups **broccoli,** cut into florets

▶ Put the sweet potatoes and carrots in a steamer and cook for 10 minutes. Add the broccoli and continue to cook for about 7 minutes, or until all the vegetables are tender.
▶ Blend the vegetables with 6–7 tbsp of water from the bottom of the steamer to make a purée.

Tomato & cauliflower gratin

⟳ Preparation: 5 minutes; cooking: 20 minutes   ◌ Makes 4 portions
✎ Provides beta-carotene, folate, protein, and vitamins A, B12, and C   ❄ Suitable for freezing

1½ cups **cauliflower,** cut into florets

2 tbsp **butter**

1⅓ cups **tomatoes,** skinned, deseeded, and roughly chopped

¼ cup grated **cheddar cheese**

▶ Put the cauliflower florets in a steamer and cook until soft, about 12 minutes.
▶ Meanwhile, warm the butter in a pan, add the tomatoes, and sauté until mushy. Remove from the heat and add the cheese, stirring until melted. Mix the cauliflower with the tomatoes and cheese sauce, then blend to the desired consistency.

Variation

▶ Steam the cauliflower until soft, then blend it with 3 tbsp of cheese sauce (see page 77), omitting the seasoning from the sauce.

Lentil purée with carrots & sweet peppers

⏱ Preparation: 10 minutes; cooking: 34 minutes   🥄 Makes 3 portions   ⚡ Provides beta-carotene, calcium, fiber, potassium, protein, and vitamins B12 and C   ❄ Suitable for freezing

1 small **onion**, peeled and chopped

1 medium **carrot**, peeled and chopped

3 tbsp **red pepper**, cored, deseeded and chopped

1 tbsp **vegetable oil**

2 tbsp **red lentils**

1 cup **boiling water** or unsalted **vegetable stock** (see page 47)

1/3 cup grated **cheddar cheese**

▶ Sauté the onion, carrots, and red peppers in the vegetable oil for about 3–4 minutes. Rinse the lentils, add them to the pan, and cover with the boiling water or vegetable stock.

▶ Cover and simmer for 25–30 minutes or until the lentils are mushy. Top off with a little more water if necessary, but there should be only a little liquid left in the pan at the end.

▶ Stir in the cheddar cheese and purée using a handheld blender.

Fillet of cod with a trio of vegetables

⏱ Preparation: 10 minutes; cooking: 25 minutes   🥄 Makes 4 portions   ⚡ Provides beta-carotene, protein, B vitamins including folate, and vitamin C   ❄ Suitable for freezing

3/4 cup **potatoes**, peeled and chopped

1 cup **carrots**, peeled and sliced

1/4 lb **cod fillet**, skinned

3 **peppercorns**

1 **bay leaf**

sprig of **parsley**

1/3 cup **milk**

1 tbsp **butter**

1 **tomato**, skinned, deseeded, and chopped

Because the proportion of fish to vegetables is quite small, this dish has a fairly mild taste, so it makes a gentle introduction to fish for your baby.

▶ Put the vegetables in a saucepan and cover with water. Bring to a boil, then reduce the heat, cover, and cook for 20 minutes or until tender.

▶ Meanwhile, put the fish in a pan with the peppercorns, bay leaf, and parsley. Add the milk, then poach the fish for about 5 minutes, or until it flakes easily. Strain the milk from the fish and reserve. Discard the flavorings.

▶ Melt the butter in a pan, add the tomato, and sauté until mushy. Flake the fish with a fork, checking carefully for bones. Drain the vegetables, then add to the fish with the tomato and 1/4 cup of the reserved milk. Blend to a purée.

Fish with cheese sauce & broccoli

⏱ Preparation: 5 minutes; cooking: 15 minutes   🥄 Makes 4 portions   ⚡ Provides beta-carotene, calcium, potassium, protein, B vitamins including folate, and vitamin A   ❄ Suitable for freezing

1/4 lb **flounder** or **sole fillet**, skinned

3 **peppercorns**

1 **bay leaf**

sprig of **parsley**

2/3 cup **milk**

1 1/2 cups **broccoli**, cut into florets

2 tbsp **butter**

1 tbsp **flour**

1/3 cup grated **cheddar** or **Edam cheese**

TIP Use spinach or zucchini instead of broccoli if you prefer.

▶ Put the fish in a pan with the peppercorns, herbs, and milk. Bring to a boil, then simmer, covered, for about 3 minutes or until the fish flakes easily. Strain the milk and reserve. Discard the flavorings. Flake the fish with a fork, checking carefully for bones.

▶ Meanwhile, steam the broccoli for about 5 minutes or until tender.

▶ Melt the butter in a saucepan, stir in the flour, and cook over a gentle heat for 1 minute. Gradually add the reserved milk, bring to a boil, and cook, stirring until thickened. Remove the sauce from the heat and add the cheese, stirring until melted. Purée the fish with the broccoli and cheese sauce.

Fish with carrots & orange juice

Preparation: 5 minutes; cooking: 20 minutes Microwave on high or conventional oven at 350°F Makes 6 portions Provides beta-carotene, calcium, protein, and B vitamins including folate Suitable for freezing

This purée is rich in vitamins and calcium, and bursting with flavor. Sole is an excellent fish to choose for young babies because it has a very soft texture.

▶ Put the carrots and potatoes in a pan, cover with water, and boil until soft. Alternatively, place them in a steamer and cook until tender.

▶ Meanwhile, place the fish in a gratin dish, add the orange juice, sprinkle with cheese, and dot with butter. Cover, leaving an air vent, and microwave on high for 3 minutes, or until the fish flakes easily. Alternatively, cover with foil and cook in a preheated oven for about 20 minutes.

▶ Flake the fish with a fork, checking carefully for bones. Add the vegetables to the fish and its juices, then blend to a purée of the desired consistency.

$^3/_4$ cup **carrots**, peeled and sliced

$^3/_4$ cup **potatoes**, peeled and chopped

$^1/_2$ lb **sole, cod,** or **flounder fillets**

juice of 1 **orange**

$^1/_2$ cup grated **mild cheddar cheese**

pat of **butter**

1 large **chicken** with **giblets**, cut into 8 pieces and trimmed of excess fat, or 1–2 **cooked roast chicken carcasses** cut into pieces (freeze bones when you roast a chicken and save them for making stock)

12 cups **water**

2 large **onions**, peeled and roughly chopped

3 large **carrots**, peeled and roughly sliced

2 **parsnips**, peeled and roughly chopped

2 **leeks**, washed and sliced

1 **celery stalk**

2 sprigs of **parsley**

1 sprig of **thyme** (optional)

2 or 3 **chicken stock cubes** (for babies over one year old only)

NOTE Do not use stock cubes in food for babies under one year because these products contain large amounts of salt.

Grandma's chicken soup & stock

⟳ Preparation: 10 minutes plus 4 hours refrigeration; cooking: 2 hours

◔ Makes 4 pints   ✎ Provides beta-carotene, folate, and potassium

❄ Suitable for freezing

I use fresh chicken stock as the base for many of my recipes. It isn't difficult to prepare and will keep in the refrigerator for two days. It also makes a delicious soup for older family members if you add some seasoning and chicken stock cubes and possibly some cooked pasta, such as vermicelli or tiny pasta shapes. Chicken soup is well-known for its soothing properties, so it's good to give to your children when they're sick.

▶ Put the raw or cooked chicken carcass pieces into a very large pan and cover with the water. Slowly bring to a boil and skim off any scum that comes to the surface.

▶ Add all the remaining ingredients, including the stock cubes if cooking for older children. Cover and simmer for about 3 hours, checking occasionally and adding more water as necessary.

▶ Remove the pan from the heat and allow to cool. Chill for at least 4 hours or overnight in the refrigerator, and skim off the layer of fat from the surface.

▶ Strain the stock through a sieve into a clean bowl and use to make baby purées. If desired, make a purée by blending a little of the stock with some of the cooked vegetables and pieces of chicken.

3 tbsp **onion,** peeled and chopped

1 tbsp **olive oil**

¼ lb **chicken breast fillets**, cut into chunks

1 **sweet potato**, peeled and chopped

1 cup unsalted **chicken stock** (see above)

6 **seedless grapes**, peeled

Chicken with sweet potatoes & grapes

⟳ Preparation: 5 minutes; cooking: 16 minutes   ◔ Makes 6 portions

✎ Provides beta-carotene, potassium, protein, and B vitamins   ❄ Suitable for freezing

Sweet potatoes tend to be very popular because of their naturally sweet taste and smooth texture, so combining chicken with sweet potatoes makes a good introduction to chicken for your baby. Chicken also blends well with many fruits—for example, chicken with grapes or apple makes a good combination.

▶ Sauté the onion in the olive oil until softened but not colored. Add the chicken and sauté for 3–4 minutes until browned. Add the sweet potato and pour the stock over the top.

▶ Cover and simmer for about 12 minutes or until the chicken is cooked through. Add the grapes and purée in a blender until it is the desired consistency.

First chicken casserole

⟳ Preparation: 10 minutes; cooking: 22 minutes   🔪 Makes 6 portions   🥄 Provides beta-carotene, B vitamins including folate, potassium, and protein   ❄ Suitable for freezing

Babies tend to like the mild taste of chicken. Here, I've combined it with vegetables that have a naturally sweet taste. Root vegetables are also good because they help to give a smooth texture.

▶ Warm the oil in a pan, add the carrots and leeks, and sauté until softened, about 6 minutes. Add the chicken and sauté, turning occasionally, until browned.

▶ Add the potatoes and parsnips and just cover with boiling water. Cover and simmer for about 15 minutes, or until everything is tender and cooked through. Blend to a purée, or leave as it is for older babies.

1 tbsp **vegetable oil**

³/₄ cup **carrots**, peeled and chopped

²/₃ cup **leeks**, white part only, washed and sliced

¹/₄ lb **chicken breast fillets**, cut into chunks

1¹/₂ cups **potatoes**, peeled and chopped

¹/₂ cup **parsnips**, peeled and chopped

Tasty ground beef with sweet potatoes & tomatoes

⟳ Preparation: 10 minutes; cooking: 40 minutes   🔪 Makes 8 portions   🥄 Provides iron, protein, vitamin A, B vitamins including folate, and zinc   ❄ Suitable for freezing

This makes a good introduction to ground beef because it has a soft texture and a natural sweetness provided by the sweet potatoes.

▶ Heat the oil in a frying pan, add the onion, and sauté for a few minutes until softened. Add the ground beef and chicken livers, if using, and sauté, stirring occasionally, until the meat is browned all over.

▶ Add the sweet potatoes and tomatoes and stock, holding back a little if a thicker consistency is preferred, and bring to a boil. Reduce the heat, cover, and cook for 30 minutes. Blend to a purée of the desired consistency.

¹/₂ tbsp **vegetable oil**

3 tbsp **onion**, peeled and finely chopped

¹/₄ lb **lean ground beef**

¹/₄ lb **organic chicken livers** (optional)

1³/₄ cups **sweet potatoes**, peeled and chopped

2 **tomatoes**, skinned, deseeded, and chopped

1 cup unsalted **chicken stock** (see opposite) or **beef stock**

Braised beef with carrots, parsnips & potatoes

⟳ Preparation: 10 minutes; cooking: 1³/₄–2¹/₄ hours   🌡 350°F
🔪 Makes 10 portions   🥄 Provides beta-carotene, potassium, protein, B vitamins including folate, and zinc   ❄ Suitable for freezing

This combination of root vegetables and beef has a smooth consistency that appeals to young babies.

▶ Heat the butter in an oven-proof casserole, add the leeks, and sauté for 5 minutes, or until softened. Add the beef and sauté until browned.

▶ Add the carrots, parsnips, and potatoes to the casserole and cover

with beef or chicken stock. Bring the mixture to a boil.

▶ Transfer the casserole to the preheated oven and cook for 1¹/₂ –2 hours, or until the meat is soft. Blend to a purée of the desired consistency.

2 tbsp **butter**

³/₄ cup **leeks**, white part only, washed and sliced

¹/₂ lb **lean beef stewing steak**, cut into cubes

1 cup **carrots**, peeled and sliced

³/₄ cup **parsnips**, peeled and chopped

1¹/₂ cups **potatoes**, peeled and chopped

2 cups unsalted **chicken stock** (see opposite) or **beef stock**

9 to 12 months

Growing appetites

Solid foods should now be the focus of your child's meals. This is a time of growing independence, and your baby may insist on feeding himself. This may be a messy stage in his development, but the more you allow your baby to experiment, the quicker he will learn to feed himself. He will probably be much more proficient at chewing now, which means that chopped or mashed food can replace purées. Recipes from the previous chapter can still be served; simply adjust the texture as necessary.

Exploring texture

At this age, your baby may be on the way to eating three main meals a day, so that he receives a combination of starchy food, vegetable or animal protein, and fruit or vegetables. He will manage coarser textures (see pages 60–61), especially with the arrival of teeth to improve his chewing abilities (see page 58). He can master finger foods (see opposite), so keep up his energy levels between meals with healthy snacks of sandwiches or fruit or vegetable slices.

His diet can now include virtually all the foods the rest of the family eats, except lightly cooked eggs, unpasteurized or soft cheese, low-fat or high-fiber products, salt, and, until the age of one year, honey. Indeed, many dishes can be shared by the whole family as long as your baby's portion is unseasoned.

Keeping up his milk
Your baby may be drinking less milk as his appetite for solid food increases, but he still needs 17–27 fl oz (500–800ml) of his usual breast milk or formula per day (see page 30). If your baby has used bottles up to now, aim to decrease their use gradually, so that you can dispense with them altogether by the time he is one year old. It helps if you give most milk feedings in a cup, perhaps reserving a soothing bottle feeding for bedtime.

Once a bottle is no longer available, some babies aren't so excited about drinking milk. If this is the case with your baby, try to make sure that you give cereal with milk at breakfast, serve dairy foods such as milk and cheese, and make dishes such as rice pudding or cauliflower and cheese.

You may need to reduce the amount of milk you give your baby if he is not hungry at mealtimes. Although he still needs 17–27 fl oz (500–800ml) of milk a day, some of this can be given as dairy products such as yogurt or mini cheeses, which also make an excellent finger food. Make sure the milk and dairy products you offer your child are full-fat, not low-fat.

Maintaining his energy levels
Babies have small stomachs, so they cannot eat too much at mealtimes. Light meals that are full of protein and slow-release carbohydrates, such as vegetables or fish in cheese sauce, are ideal for fueling their rapid growth.

Snacks are also very important. Give your baby nutritious snacks such as cheese, carrot matchsticks, or rice cakes to supplement his small meals.

New independence

Your baby is now acquiring new physical skills: rolling, crawling, sitting, or even walking. Improved muscle power and hand-eye coordination skills allow him much more independent movement. Your baby will be delighted by the freedom his body is giving him and he will want to take the lead at mealtimes by feeding himself; he may even become impatient when you try to spoon-feed him, and prefer to be helped with just the occasional spoonful of food. He will probably be following a more predictable sleeping pattern, which helps to regulate mealtimes.

Encouraging self-feeding

Your baby will need progressively less help to eat, and may prefer to spoon soft foods up for himself. If more purée seems to go on the floor or his lap than in his mouth, you could use a two-spoon system: give him a spoon to hold so that he can make his own attempts at self-feeding, and use another spoon yourself to get some of the food into his mouth.

Experimentation

The more you allow your baby to experiment, the quicker he will learn to feed himself. It may be a messy procedure, but you should not discourage his

attempts, or worry that his table manners are less than perfect. He will be quick to pick up any anxieties on your part and could soon turn mealtimes into a battleground. Allow him to explore the feel of the food and take his time eating it.

"Your baby can now manage food with a lumpier texture, and he'll pick out some of the pieces himself to put in his mouth."

Remember

• Offer finger foods as part of your baby's meals to give him chewing practice and encourage him to eat independently.

• Do not offer your baby nuts, raw or lightly cooked eggs, soft or unpasteurized cheeses, or shellfish.

Finger foods

Finger foods are excellent for teaching self-feeding and should begin to play a useful part in your baby's diet; he will enjoy the freedom of movement they give him, and will appreciate the fact that he can eat this kind of food without adult intervention. Let him try steamed or raw vegetable sticks with a cold dip, or a favorite purée with bread sticks as finger foods. Remember that finger foods should be firm

"When he is teething, finger foods may be more appealing for your baby than eating from a spoon."

enough for your baby to pick up, yet tender enough for him to chew and swallow easily. Just because your baby has teeth, it doesn't mean that he instinctively knows how to use them for chewing—young babies are quite likely to bite off a piece of food, try to swallow it whole, and choke, so they must never be left unsupervised, even for a moment, when eating.

Ideal finger foods

• **vegetables** such as carrot or cucumber sticks, cauliflower, or green beans—at first, it is better to lightly steam vegetables or cook them in a little boiling water for a few minutes so that they are still a little crunchy but not completely hard; once your baby becomes more proficient at chewing, start giving him raw vegetables

• **fruit** such as banana chunks or apple or pear slices—introduce soft fruit such as banana or kiwi fruit slices to begin with if your baby finds it difficult to chew (some babies are allergic to kiwi fruit, so watch carefully for any adverse reaction the first time you give him this fruit)

• **dried fruit** such as apricots, figs, or apple pieces

• **toast fingers, rice cakes, or plain bread sticks**

• **mini sandwiches** with soft fillings, such as mashed bananas, cream cheese, or flaked tuna

• **cheddar cheese sticks, cheese slices, or mini cheeses**

• **dry cereals**

• **cooked pasta shapes**

• **small pieces of chicken or turkey**

• **mini meatballs or chicken balls**

BRUSHING YOUR BABY'S TEETH

Start brushing your baby's teeth as soon as they appear—at least twice a day, in the morning and at bedtime. Make tooth-brushing fun, perhaps by giving your baby his own toothbrush to hold while you brush your teeth. Bend down and show him what you are doing and encourage him to copy you. Of course, he won't do any useful brushing, but it will give him the right idea.

For most children, a mild-tasting fluoride toothpaste (varieties for children have a slightly lower fluoride content) and a good diet are sufficient to protect teeth. Too much fluoride is not good for your child and can result in discolored teeth. All you need is a pea-size amount of toothpaste and a soft brush to apply it with. Encourage your child to spit out the toothpaste instead of swallowing it.

Teething

During the three months leading up to your baby's first birthday, he may cut several teeth, so it is still important to offer textured foods that will encourage him to chew. Vegetable finger foods cooled in the refrigerator are especially soothing if your baby is teething. Chilled, peeled cucumber sticks are ideal. Semi-frozen banana chunks are also good for relieving sore gums. Keep a teething ring in the refrigerator for him to bite on when he's not hungry.

Opinions differ as to how far teething affects babies' well-being, but it is probable that it does cause some distress, and even makes them fussier than usual about their food. For a few days before each tooth breaks through the gum, you may notice a hard, whitish bump under the surface. Your baby might drool, so put a little petroleum jelly around his mouth and chin to help keep them from getting chapped. If his gums are particularly tender, he may reject being fed from a spoon. If this is the case, offer him finger foods to eat instead.

Preventing tooth decay

Children run a greater risk of tooth decay than adults because teeth are more vulnerable to acid when they are newly formed. In addition, during the first year or two after birth, the immune mechanism in the mouth is not fully developed.

To limit the possibility of tooth decay, never give your baby bottles filled with anything but milk or water. If your baby drinks fruit juice from a bottle, his teeth and gums will be in contact with damaging sugary and acidic fluids for prolonged periods of time. Always dilute fruit juice and give it to your baby only in a cup at mealtimes. Milk itself contains a form of sugar that would be corrosive if the teeth were never brushed, so be sure to brush your baby's teeth at bedtime. After brushing your baby's teeth at night, avoid giving him any sweet drinks or more food. At night, there is not enough saliva in the mouth to wash away harmful acid, so restrict nighttime drinks to water.

Remember

• There is no such thing as a "healthy" sugar. Honey, brown sugar, fruit sugars, and sucrose all rot teeth.

• As soon as teeth appear, buy a mild toothpaste designed for children and brush your baby's teeth morning and night.

• It is best to give your child sweet things to eat with meals, since the flow of saliva is greater when eating (saliva helps neutralize acid in the mouth). Diluted juice with meals is fine, but it is best to give only water or milk between meals.

• Encourage your baby to drink from a cup, and offer only water, diluted juice, or her usual milk.

• Try to dispense with bottles, except perhaps a bottle at bedtime, by the time your baby is one year old.

• When teething, it can be soothing for your baby to chew on a clean, wet washcloth that has been placed in the freezer for 30 minutes.

• Rubbing a sugar-free teething gel onto the gums may help ease pain, since these gels contain a local anesthetic. Alternatively, give your baby infant acetaminophen drops or try some homeopathic teething granules.

A varied menu

Toward the end of your baby's first year, solid food will replace much of her milk diet. It is important to introduce lots of different textures and flavors at this stage while your baby is so receptive to new foods. Offer some food mashed, some whole, some grated, and some diced: it's surprising what a few teeth and strong gums can manage. Finger foods that allow your baby to feed herself will become an increasingly important part of her daily diet, and will get her accustomed to independent eating and many new textures.

1 Cheesy pasta stars
Tiny stars or other soup pasta shapes make an ideal introduction to pasta. Here, they are combined with a tomato sauce enriched with grated cheddar cheese and sweetened with carrots. (See page 64 for recipe.)

2 Quick chicken couscous
Couscous, which is made from crushed semolina, has a mild taste and soft texture that is perfect for babies. It is also quick to cook and combines well with a variety of vegetables and even fruits. (See page 66 for recipe.)

3 Assorted dips
These colorful savory and sweet purées are served with toast, cheese shapes, fruit pieces, or raw vegetable sticks, which may be chilled to soothe gums made sore by teething. (See pages 62–63 for recipes.)

1

2

3

Creamy avocado dip & vegetable sticks

1 ripe **avocado**, halved and pitted

¼ cup **soft cream cheese**

1 tbsp snipped **chives**

1 ripe **tomato**, skinned, deseeded, and chopped

Steamed vegetable shapes

vegetables such as sweet potatoes, carrots, potatoes, or parsnips, washed and peeled

◷ Preparation: 10 minutes; cooking: 8 minutes   ⚘ Makes 4 portions
⚡ Provides folate, potassium, and vitamins A, C and E

An avocado has the highest protein content of any fruit, and babies like its mild creaminess. This dip also makes a good sandwich filling if mixed with grated cheese.

▶ Cut the vegetables into sticks or shapes, place in a steamer, and cook until tender, about 8 minutes.

▶ Scoop out the avocado flesh. Mash until smooth and mix with the remaining ingredients. (For adults, you can add lemon juice, seasoning, chopped cilantro, and maybe a little finely chopped chili.)

Red pepper dip & vegetable fingers

1 small **red pepper**, halved and deseeded

½ tbsp **vegetable oil**

1 **shallot**, finely chopped

1 ripe **tomato**, skinned, deseeded, and chopped

1¼ cups **soft cream cheese**

Raw vegetable shapes

vegetables such as carrots, celery, cucumbers, peppers, and kohlrabi or turnips, washed and peeled

TIP If your baby finds raw vegetables too hard, offer steamed cauliflower or root vegetables. Reduce the steaming time progressively.

◷ Preparation: 10 minutes; cooking: 10 minutes   ⚘ Makes 4 portions
⚡ Provides beta-carotene and vitamins A, B12, and C   ❄ Suitable for freezing

The vegetables for this dip should be cut into pieces small enough to be easily grasped, but not so tiny that they could be swallowed whole. You can also offer toast, pita fingers, or mild cheese shapes.

▶ To make the dip, roast the red pepper, then peel and roughly chop.
▶ Meanwhile, warm the oil in a small frying pan, add the shallot, and sauté until softened but not colored. Combine the red pepper with the shallot, tomato, and cream cheese, and blend together to make a smooth cream.

▶ Cut the raw vegetables into strips, or make fun shapes with miniature cookie cutters.

Easy mashed vegetable duo

1½ cups **rutabagas**, peeled and chopped

1¾ cups **parsnips**, peeled and chopped

1 cup **milk**

¼ cup grated **cheddar cheese**

◷ Preparation: 10 minutes; cooking: 22 minutes   ⚘ Makes 4 portions
⚡ Provides calcium, fiber, folate, potassium, protein, and vitamins A, B12 and C

This recipe makes both a good smooth purée and a slightly coarser-textured dish, as preferred.

▶ Place the vegetables in a saucepan with the milk. Bring to a boil, cover, and simmer for 20 minutes, or until soft.

▶ Remove the pan from the heat and stir in the cheese until melted. Mash to the desired consistency.

Fruity baby muesli

⏱ Preparation: 10 minutes, plus 2–12 hours soaking 🥄 Makes 2 portions
🥕 Provides fiber, iron, magnesium, B vitamins (except for B12), vitamin C, and zinc

Oats raise blood sugar levels relatively slowly, so oat-based breakfast cereals provide a more sustained energy boost than other cereals.

▶ Put the oats and wheat germ in a bowl with the dried apricot and raisins. Cover with grape juice. Leave to soak for at least 2 hours or overnight.

▶ Add the apple and grapes to the soaked cereal and blend. (Once your baby has mastered the art of chewing, there is no need to blend this muesli.)

1/3 cup **rolled oats**
1/4 cup **toasted wheat germ**
1 **dried apricot** or **pear**, chopped
1 tbsp **raisins**
2/3 cup **white grape juice** or **apple juice**
1/2 **red apple**, peeled and grated
3 **grapes**, halved and deseeded

Apple & date oatmeal

⏱ Preparation: 2 minutes; cooking: 12 minutes 🥄 Makes 2 portions
🥕 Provides calcium, fiber, and B vitamins including folate

▶ Put the apple and dates in a pan with the water and cook over medium heat for 5 minutes.
▶ Meanwhile, heat the milk in a pan, stir in the oats, bring to a boil, and simmer, stirring constantly, for 3–4 minutes, or until thickened. Mix with the fruit, then blend to the desired consistency.

1 **sweet eating apple**, peeled, cored, and chopped
3 tbsp pitted **dates**
4 tbsp **water**
2/3 cup **milk**
3 tbsp **rolled oats**

Exotic fruit salad

⏱ Preparation: 10 minutes 🥄 Makes 4 portions
🥕 Provides beta-carotene, fiber, folate, and vitamin C

If you can't find perfectly ripe, sweet exotic fruits, substitute peaches or strawberries.

▶ Finely chop all the fruit and simply combine with the orange juice.

1/2 **mango,** peeled and pitted
1/2 **papaya,** peeled and pitted
1 **kiwi fruit,** peeled
2 **lychees,** peeled and pitted
juice of 1 large **orange**

Raspberry, pear & peach purée

⏱ Preparation: 5 minutes; cooking: 5 minutes 🥄 Makes 4 portions
🥕 Provides fiber, folate, and vitamin C

This is very much a summer purée to be made when raspberries and peaches are ripe and sweet. It is also good mixed with baby rice cereal or mashed bananas.

▶ Place the fruit in a saucepan and simmer gently for about 5 minutes. Cool slightly, press through a sieve, and mix with the yogurt.

1 cup **raspberries**
2 ripe **pears**, peeled, cored and chopped
1 **peach**, pitted, peeled, and chopped
2 tbsp **Greek yogurt**

Butternut squash with alphabet pasta

3 cups **butternut squash**, peeled and cubed

2–3 tbsp **alphabet soup pasta**

2 tbsp **butter**

½ tbsp chopped **fresh sage**

1 tbsp freshly grated **Parmesan cheese** (optional)

⏱ Preparation: 5 minutes; cooking: 20 minutes Makes 4 portions
Provides beta-carotene and folate ❄ Suitable for freezing

► Put the squash in a steamer and cook until tender, about 15 minutes. Blend to a purée with 4–5 tbsp of water from the bottom of the steamer.
► Meanwhile, bring a pan of water to a boil, add the pasta, and cook until tender, about 5 minutes, then drain.
► Melt the butter in a pan, add the sage, and cook gently for 1 minute.
► Mix the sage, butter, and Parmesan cheese, if using, with the squash and pasta.

Cheesy pasta stars

1 cup **carrots**, peeled and sliced

1 cup **boiling water**

2 tbsp **butter**

1 cup **tomatoes**, skinned, deseeded, and chopped

⅓ cup grated **cheddar cheese**

2 tbsp **soup pasta stars (stelline)**

⏱ Preparation: 10 minutes; cooking: 25 minutes Makes 4 portions
Provides beta-carotene, calcium, folate, protein, and vitamins B12 and C
❄ Suitable for freezing

Tiny pasta stelline make a good introduction to pasta. The sweet taste of the carrots in this sauce is usually very appealing to babies.

► Place the carrots in a small pan, cover with the boiling water, and cook until tender, 15–20 minutes.
► Warm the butter in a separate pan, add the tomatoes, and sauté until mushy. Remove from the heat and stir in the cheese until melted.
► Meanwhile, bring a pan of water to a boil, add the pasta, and cook until tender, about 5 minutes, then drain.
► Mix together the cooked carrots with their cooking liquid and the cheese and tomato sauce. Blend to a purée and combine with the pasta stars.

Tomato & tuna pasta sauce

1 tbsp **olive oil**

1 small **onion**, peeled and finely chopped

1 **garlic clove**, peeled and crushed

1⅔ cups **canned chopped tomatoes**

1 tbsp **tomato purée**

½ tsp **balsamic vinegar**

½ tsp **superfine sugar**

¼ tsp **dried mixed herbs**

3½ oz **canned tuna in oil**

2 tbsp **soft cream cheese** or **mascarpone cheese**

⏱ Preparation: 5 minutes; cooking 20 minutes Makes 4 portions Provides beta-carotene, potassium, protein, and vitamins A, B12, C, D, and E ❄ Suitable for freezing

A simple but excellent standby, this dish always goes down well.

► Heat the oil in a saucepan, add the onion and garlic, and sauté for about 5 minutes, until softened.
► Add the remaining ingredients, except the tuna and cream cheese or mascarpone, and cook uncovered over medium heat for about 12 minutes.
► Drain and flake the tuna, add to the sauce, and heat through.
► Stir in the cream cheese or mascarpone until melted into the sauce.

Fillet of fish mornay with vegetables

⏱ Preparation: 10 minutes; cooking: 35 minutes   🔪 Makes 8 portions

🧪 Provides beta-carotene, calcium, protein, B vitamins including folate, and vitamin C

❄ Suitable for freezing

This tasty combination of white fish and vegetables in a mild cheese sauce is generally very popular with babies.

▶ Melt the butter in a saucepan, add the leeks, and sauté for 2–3 minutes. Add the carrots, cover with water, and cook for 10 minutes. Add the broccoli and cook for 5 minutes. Stir in the peas and simmer for a further 5 minutes, or until the vegetables are tender (adding a little more water if necessary).

▶ Meanwhile, put the fish in a pan with the milk, peppercorns, bay leaf, and parsley. Simmer for 5 minutes, or until the fish is cooked. Set aside, reserving the cooking liquid. Discard the flavorings.

▶ To prepare the sauce, melt the butter in a pan, stir in the flour, and cook for 1 minute. Gradually whisk in the fish cooking liquid, bring to a boil, and cook, stirring until the sauce has thickened. Remove from the heat, add the cheese, and stir until melted.

▶ Drain the vegetables and mix with the flaked fish and cheese sauce. Blend to a purée of the desired consistency for young babies. Provided the vegetables are tender, this can be mashed or chopped for older babies who are starting to chew.

1 tbsp **butter**

²⁄₃ cup **leeks,** washed and finely sliced

1 cup **carrots,** peeled and chopped

²⁄₃ cup **broccoli,** cut into small florets

¹⁄₃ cup **fresh** or **frozen peas**

¹⁄₄ lb **cod, hake, sole,** or **haddock fillets,** skinned

²⁄₃ cup **milk**

3 **peppercorns**

1 **bay leaf**

sprig of **parsley**

Sauce

1¹⁄₂ tbsp **butter**

1 tbsp **flour**

¹⁄₃ cup grated **cheddar** or **Edam cheese**

1/4 lb **cod fillet**, skinned

1/3 cup **milk**

2 tbsp **butter**

1 **shallot**, peeled and chopped

1/3 cup **zucchini**, chopped

2 cups **tomatoes**, skinned, deseeded, and chopped

1/2 cup grated **cheddar cheese**

TIP The cod can be microwaved on a high setting for 3 minutes.

Flaked cod with tomatoes & zucchini

⟳ Preparation: 10 minutes; cooking: 20 minutes ⚔ Makes 4 portions
↗ Provides beta-carotene, calcium, potassium, protein, B vitamins including folate, and vitamin C ❋ Suitable for freezing

▶ Place the fish in a saucepan, cover with the milk, and poach gently for about 6 minutes.
▶ Meanwhile, melt the butter in a pan, add the shallot, and cook slowly until softened. Add the zucchini and sauté for 5 minutes. Add the tomatoes and sauté for 5 minutes more, or until mushy. Remove the pan from the heat and stir in the cheese until melted.

▶ Flake the fish carefully with a fork, checking for and removing bones, and stir it into the tomato and zucchini sauce. For babies who don't yet like lumpy food, blend the final mixture until it reaches a smoother consistency.

---

2 oz boneless, skinless **chicken breast**, cooked

1 **tomato**, skinned, deseeded, and chopped

1/4 cup **avocado**

2 tbsp mild, full-fat **natural yogurt**

1 1/2 tbsp grated **cheddar cheese**

California chicken

⟳ Preparation: 10 minutes ⚔ Makes 1 portion ↗ Provides calcium, protein, B vitamins including folate, vitamins A, C, and E, and zinc

Use these ingredients to make yourself a salad or sandwich at the same time as a quick and easy meal for your baby. You can substitute Edam for cheddar cheese.

▶ Chop the chicken, then combine it with the remaining ingredients. Blend or chop the mixture to the desired consistency. If your baby prefers, you could leave out the cheese.

---

1 tbsp **butter**

2/3 cup **leeks**, white part only, washed and finely chopped

2 oz boneless, skinless **chicken breast**, diced

1/4 cup **parsnips**, peeled and diced

1/4 cup **carrots**, peeled and diced

1 cup unsalted **chicken stock** (see page 52)

1/2 cup **couscous**

Quick chicken couscous

⟳ Preparation: 10 minutes; cooking: 20 minutes ⚔ Makes 4 portions
↗ Provides beta-carotene, folate, iron, and protein

If you prefer, replace the chicken with extra seasonal vegetables.

▶ Warm the butter in a pan, add the leeks, and sauté for 5 minutes, or until softened. Add the chicken and sauté until just cooked through.
▶ Meanwhile, place the parsnips and carrots in a steamer, or in a saucepan with enough boiling water to cover, and cook until tender, about 10 minutes.

▶ Bring the stock to a boil in a pan. Stir in the couscous, remove the pan from the heat, cover, and leave for 5 minutes, or until the stock has been absorbed. Fluff with a fork and stir in the chicken and vegetables. Add extra stock or water if necessary.

Fruity chicken with carrots

⏱ Preparation: 10 minutes; cooking: 22 minutes 🔪 Makes 4 portions
🥄 Provides beta-carotene, niacin, protein, and vitamin B6 ❄ Suitable for freezing

Apple blends well with chicken to produce a great flavor in this quick-to-prepare dish. Well-cooked rice makes a good accompaniment.

▶ Heat the butter in a pan, add the onion, and sauté for 3–4 minutes. Add the chicken and sauté until it turns opaque. Add the carrots and cook for 2 minutes, then stir in the chopped apple and chicken stock.

▶ Bring the mixture to a boil, then cover and cook over a medium heat for about 15 minutes. Chop or purée to the desired consistency.

1 tbsp **butter**

3 tbsp **onion,** peeled and finely chopped

¼ lb boneless, skinless **chicken breast,** chopped

1 cup **carrots,** peeled and sliced

½ **dessert apple,** peeled, cored, and chopped

1¼ cups unsalted **chicken stock** (see page 52)

Creamy chicken & broccoli

⏱ Preparation: 5 minutes; cooking: 15 minutes 🔪 Makes 4 portions
🥄 Provides calcium, protein, B vitamins including folate and niacin, and vitamins A and C
❄ Suitable for freezing

You could add some small cooked soup pasta, such as stelline, to this recipe to make it more substantial.

▶ To prepare the cheese sauce, melt the butter in a saucepan, stir in the flour, and cook for 1 minute. Gradually whisk in the milk, bring to a boil, and cook until the sauce has thickened. Remove from the heat, add the cheese, and stir until melted.

▶ Meanwhile, steam the broccoli until tender. Combine the cheese sauce, chicken, and broccoli, then roughly chop up the mixture in a blender or by hand.

1 cup **broccoli,** cut into small florets

¼ lb boneless, skinless **chicken breast,** cooked and chopped

Mild cheese sauce

2 tbsp **butter**

2 tbsp **flour**

1¼ cups **milk**

½ cup grated **Edam** or **other mild cheese**

TIP If your baby doesn't like cheese, make a white sauce flavored with a pinch of nutmeg.

Baby's bolognese

⏱ Preparation: 10 minutes; cooking: 35 minutes 🔪 Makes 6 portions
🥄 Provides beta-carotene, iron, protein, B vitamins including folate, and zinc
❄ Suitable for freezing: sauce only

▶ Warm the oil in a pan, add the onion, garlic, and celery, and sauté for 3–4 minutes. Add the grated carrots and cook for 2 minutes.
▶ Add the ground beef and stir until browned. Stir in the tomato paste, fresh and sun-dried tomatoes, and stock. Bring the mixture to a boil, reduce the heat, cover, and cook for about 10 minutes. At this stage, you can chop the

meat in a food processor for just a few seconds to give it a slightly softer texture.
▶ Cook the spaghetti in boiling, lightly salted water according to the instructions on the package. Drain and chop into small pieces. Babies often dislike the chewy texture of red meat, so transfer the bolognese sauce to a blender and chop for a few seconds before combining it with the pasta.

1 tbsp **vegetable oil**

3 tbsp **onion,** peeled and finely chopped

1 small **garlic clove,** crushed

2 tbsp **celery,** finely chopped

¼ cup **carrots,** peeled and grated

¼ lb **lean ground beef**

½ tsp **tomato paste**

2 **tomatoes,** skinned, deseeded, and chopped

1 tbsp **sun-dried tomatoes,** chopped

⅓ cup unsalted **chicken stock** (see page 52)

2 oz **spaghetti**

12 to 18 months

Changing needs

"Establish the habit of eating five portions of fruit and vegetables a day now and you will have set up a healthy eating plan for life."

Your child can now enjoy a full, varied diet, and including her in family meals should be easier. Accordingly, the recipes in this chapter are designed to appeal to your toddler, but also to suit the tastes of the whole family. Toward the end of the first year, babies who have been good eaters can often become difficult and picky. At about this time, growth slows down dramatically, resulting in a natural decrease in appetite. In addition, your baby's newfound ability to walk and her increased independence mean that she may become reluctant to sit at the table for any length of time. Recognizing these changes will help you adapt to her needs.

Balancing a mixed diet

At around 12 months old, your baby may look quite chubby, but once she gets up on her feet, she will slim down. Toddlers are on the go all the time, and you will find that your child needs quick, energy-boosting snacks between meals.

In this and the following chapters, there are many suggestions for healthy snacks. Encourage your child to eat a variety of snacks, such as fruit, bites of cheese, or homemade cake, so they make up a useful part of her mixed diet.

Children's nutrition

Although your child will be joining in with family meals, the dietary advice that applies to you as an adult will not necessarily be appropriate for her. Young children have different nutritional needs and require more calories than adults to sustain the growth of muscle, tissue, and bone that takes place throughout childhood. Advice concerning adult fat and fiber intake, for example, does not apply to children under five.

While health experts tell us that adults and children over five should derive no more than 35 percent of their calories from fat, they also agree that we should not limit fat in the diets of children under two years of age. Due to the very fast rate of growth in the first two years of life, fat is needed because it is the most concentrated source of energy. Without enough fat in the diet, a child would need to burn protein for energy. Fat is also important for healthy development of the brain and nervous system. Unless you have been advised by a doctor to do so, don't give your child reduced fat products, such as low-fat milk. In fact, your child still needs about 14 fl oz (400ml) of milk a day, although now she can come off breast milk or formula and drink full-fat cow's milk.

A high-fiber diet, too, is still not appropriate for your child. Young children have small stomachs: fiber is low-calorie, bulky material that fills the stomach without meeting a toddler's high calorific needs, and it can even hinder the absorption of vital nutrients.

Keeping milk in the diet

If your child drinks milk only reluctantly and you are worried that she is not getting the recommended 14 fl oz (400ml) of milk per day, you can easily sneak milk into her meals without her noticing.

Yogurt or pasteurized cheese can be used as equivalents to milk. Alternatively, offer a fruity milkshake or smoothie (see page 112), make a cheese sauce (see page 65) for part of the main meal, mash some potatoes with plenty of milk, or whip half-set flavored gelatin with a can of evaporated milk for dessert.

Ideal dairy products

- whole-milk yogurt
- cheese: sliced, grated on pasta, or melted on toast
- macaroni and cheese • rice pudding • high-quality ice cream • fruit or chocolate smoothies or milkshakes

Rainbow of nutrition

Often, the stronger the color of a fruit or vegetable, the more nutritious it is. For instance, an orange-fleshed sweet potato contains more nutrients than an ordinary potato. Also, different-colored vegetables provide different nutrients, so try to include green, red, orange, yellow, dark blue, or purple fruits and vegetables in your child's diet.

The importance of fruit and vegetables

Health experts recommend we all try to include five portions of fruit or vegetables (not including potatoes) in our diet each day (see page 15). Do not be daunted by this—it is not as difficult as it sounds to incorporate five helpings of fresh fruit or vegetables in your child's daily diet.

Five-a-day eating plan

To incorporate five servings of fruit or vegetables into your child's daily diet, try the following eating plan.
- Serve some fresh or cooked fruit or diluted juice with breakfast.
- Add a serving of vegetables or salad to your child's lunch, and follow the savory course with a serving of fresh or cooked fruit.
- Provide a serving of vegetables at dinner time, followed by fresh fruit or a fruit dessert.

Vegetable rejection

Children often raise strong objections to eating vegetables, and only 1 in 5 children in North America eat enough vegetables. If your toddler is especially resistant to eating vegetables, try some of the following suggestions for

incorporating vegetables into her diet without her noticing.
- Sometimes children who don't like cooked vegetables do like eating them raw, so try giving carrot, red pepper, and cucumber sticks with a tasty dip, or find a salad dressing that your child loves and make interesting salads.
- If you do cook vegetables, they are much more nutritious and taste better if steamed instead of boiled.
- Chinese-style stir-fried vegetables with a touch of soy sauce and maybe some noodles or rice are popular with many children.
- Hide vegetables by blending them into pasta sauce or soup, as in my Pasta sauce with hidden vegetables (see page 78). Make oven-baked fries or mashed potatoes out of sweet potatoes instead of regular potatoes—sweet potatoes are rich in beta-carotene and thus more nutritious.
- Frozen vegetables are just as nutritious as fresh, and vegetables such as peas and sweet corn tend to be popular.
- If, after all your efforts, your child is still a confirmed veggie-hater, give her fruit instead, since it provides almost all the vitamins you get in vegetables.

Making meals fun

Young children, like adults, prefer to eat with company. If your toddler has cutlery she is able to use, is seated at the correct height, and has someone to share the meal with, mealtimes will be an enjoyable occasion for her.

You may find that she will eat things she has previously rejected, just because a sibling or friend who has come to play is eating it. Visiting a friend or relative's house often produces the same effect. The excitement of eating with other children, or in different surroundings, makes her adventurous enough to try new foods. In addition, when you and your child are with other people at a mealtime, you may both be more relaxed about the food you are eating.

"Eating as a family helps your child integrate into family mealtimes."

When you are on your own with her, you are probably more focused on what she is eating. There is a certain amount of unconscious pressure for your child if you are overseeing every mouthful she takes, and meals can become an ordeal for her. It is easy for both of you to forget that eating should be fun.

Eating sociably at home
Eating as a family will help your child to integrate into regular mealtimes as well as to learn some of your basic family rules about eating at the table. Even if the whole family cannot sit down together at meals during the week—perhaps because the meal is too late for your young child to join in more than occasionally—at least sit down beside her while she eats, or ask an older sibling or friend to join her.

Cooking for the family
By now, your toddler should be eating the same meals as the rest of the family. Life is too short to cook a different meal for each member of the family, and it is much easier to introduce new foods at this early age, when children's preferences (and prejudices) are not yet fixed. You can interest your child in food, perhaps by talking to her about its form, taste, or feel, or by adding a few presentational touches that will appeal to her.

Don't get anxious or angry if your toddler refuses to eat a new dish—it can take a few attempts for new foods to be accepted. Instead, make sure that the dessert is nutritious, so that you can relax in the knowledge that she is still eating a healthy diet, even if it's not in the traditional order. Remember that the "balance" of a diet should be assessed over a period of a few days to a week, rather than within a strict limit of 24 hours.

When your child is sick

When children are sick, they often lose their appetite. However, it is important to ensure that your child's fluid intake is maintained.

Diarrhea

Approximately 80 percent of a new baby is water (adults are around 70 percent water). Consequently, babies and young children are particularly vulnerable to dehydration during periods of diarrhea or vomiting. If a child is suffering from either of these problems, offer plenty of fluids. Special salt and sugar powders that are dissolved in water replace lost minerals and can be bought from pharmacies. Diluted fruit juices, freezer pops, or diluted, flat, caffeine-free soft drinks (take the bubbles out first with ice or a swizzle stick) are suitable for children with diarrhea. Milk is not suitable, but should soon be gradually reintroduced.

Monitor your child's fluid intake and urine output. Signs of dehydration are:
• less frequent urination
• more concentrated, dark yellow urine
• dry mouth and lips
• sunken eyes
• lethargic behavior.

Contact your doctor if your child shows these signs or if the diarrhea persists for more than 24 hours.

Upset stomach

If your child has an upset stomach, try the BRAT diet (see right). Offer small amounts of each of the foods. After 48 hours, introduce potatoes, cooked vegetables (especially root vegetables), and a boiled egg. Leave out dairy foods for a while, because an irritated gut can sometimes be aggravated by lactose in dairy foods.

Foods during illness

If your child loses her appetite but is not suffering from diarrhea or vomiting, give her nutritious liquids— milk, milkshakes (see page 112), fruit smoothies, or hot chocolate are good. Children who are reluctant to drink fluids are often willing to eat freezer pops. Give frozen juice bars or make your own from fresh fruit juice, puréed fruit, or yogurt (see page 177).

Offer simple, easily digested foods, such as chicken soup (see page 52), steamed fish with mashed potatoes, scrambled eggs on toast, or mashed bananas. Antibiotics kill the good bacteria in the body as well as the harmful ones. If your child is taking antibiotics, you could give her yogurt with live, active cultures to help restore the beneficial bacteria.

Constipation

If your child is constipated, give her plenty of water and diluted fruit juices. Cut down on sugary and fatty foods and offer fruit, vegetables, and whole-grain cereals, but do not overload the digestive system with fiber, because this is not a suitable way to relieve constipation in young children. Natural yogurt, prunes, and prune juice are more useful in gently relieving it.

Regression

Don't be surprised if your child reverts to more babyish feeding habits, even after she has recovered from her illness. While she is sick, she needs extra reassurance in the form of hugs, and she may want her drinks from a bottle again. Until her appetite returns, the memory of her more babyish comforts may make her want to eat the kinds of things you thought she had outgrown. (In fact, this may be the case throughout her early childhood whenever your child is sick.) Try not to worry—she'll soon be her old self, with a healthy appetite and ready to try new foods again.

Remember
• Keep your child's fluid intake high during illness.

• Recognize that she may revert to slightly babyish feeding habits for a short period of time.

The BRAT diet
• **Bananas** settle an acid stomach and provide potassium to regulate the body's mineral balance.

• **Rice** helps relieve diarrhea and provides the body with energy and protein.

• **Apples,** especially stewed apples, are a traditional cure for gastroenteritis.

• **Toast** (dry, white) helps settle the stomach and provides carbohydrates for energy.

Food for the senses

Your child can now enjoy a full, varied diet, and it should be easier to integrate him into family meals. The recipes in this section are designed to appeal to your toddler, but also to suit the tastes of the whole family. During this stage your child needs plenty of freedom to explore his food with his hands. Allowing him to do this will stimulate his interest in food and heighten his enjoyment of mealtimes. The foods on these pages are designed to appeal to the eye, to the senses of smell and touch, and, of course, to the taste buds.

1 Raspberry frozen yogurt
Scoops of frozen yogurt decorated with crisp wafers and chocolate chips make a mouthwatering, and tactile, dessert. (See page 84 for recipe.)

2 Yogurt pancakes
The contrast of sticky maple syrup, cool and juicy ripe summer fruits, and warm pancakes is tempting. (See page 84 for recipe.)

3 Root vegetable chips
The perfect finger food, these colorful and sweet-tasting chips are made from sweet potatoes, beets, and parsnips. They make an interesting, crunchy snack and are great for parties and picnics. (See page 76 for recipe.)

4 Chicken sausage snails
A simple dish of chicken sausages and mashed potatoes becomes, with the help of a little imagination, an eye-catching picture on a plate and an appealing meal. (See page 81 for recipe.)

Bananas with maple syrup

generous pat of butter

1 small **banana**, peeled and sliced

1 tbsp **maple syrup**

1/8 tsp **ground cinnamon**

Preparation: 3 minutes; cooking: 3 minutes   Makes 1 portion

Provides calcium, iron, protein, B vitamins including folate, and zinc

This makes a delicious breakfast or dessert served with a toasted fruit muffin, toasted raisin bread, pancakes, or waffles.

▶ Melt the butter in a saucepan. Add the sliced banana and cook, stirring occasionally, for one minute.

▶ Add the maple syrup and cinnamon and cook for one minute more.

Root vegetable chips

1 **sweet potato**, scrubbed

1 **parsnip**, peeled

2 **carrots** or 1 **raw beet**, peeled

can of **spray oil** for baking or **vegetable oil** for deep frying

freshly ground **sea salt** (optional)

TIP You can also make these chips using sliced plantain.

Preparation: 10 minutes; cooking: 15 minutes   400°F

Makes 4 portions   Provides beta-carotene, fiber, potassium, and vitamin E

Encourage your child to eat more vegetables by making these crunchy chips. They also make a healthy alternative to store-bought potato chips.

▶ Slice all the vegetables wafer-thin by hand or by using a slicing blade in a food processor. Spray some oil onto a couple of large baking sheets and brush to cover the surface. Heat the baking sheets for 5 minutes in the preheated oven.

▶ Place the vegetables on the baking sheets in a single layer and lightly spray with oil. Cook in the oven for 10–12 minutes, turning halfway through. Transfer to paper towels, sprinkle with sea salt, if desired, and serve cold.

▶ Alternatively, deep-fry the vegetables in a deep-fat fryer at 375°. Add each vegetable separately, and fry until crisp and golden, about 4–5 minutes.

Zucchini & tomato frittata

2 tbsp **vegetable oil**

1 **onion**, peeled and chopped

2/3 cup **zucchini**, thinly sliced

salt and freshly ground **black pepper**

2 **tomatoes**, skinned, deseeded, and chopped

4 **eggs**

1 tbsp **milk**

2 tbsp freshly grated **Parmesan cheese**

Preparation: 5 minutes; cooking: 30 minutes   Makes 8 portions

Provides calcium, protein, B vitamins including folate, and vitamins A and C

You can make this versatile frittata with a variety of ingredients. Served cold, it is perfect for taking on a picnic.

▶ Heat the oil in a 9-inch nonstick frying pan. Add the onion and zucchini, season lightly, and cook for about 15 minutes. Add the tomatoes and continue to cook for 3–4 minutes.

▶ Beat the eggs with the milk and pepper, and pour over the vegetables. Cook over medium heat for about 5 minutes, or until the eggs are set underneath. Preheat the broiler to high.

▶ Sprinkle the Parmesan over the frittata and cook briefly under the broiler until golden (if necessary, wrap pan handle with foil to prevent burning). Cut into wedges and serve hot or cold.

Variations

▶ Omit the zucchini and tomatoes. Instead, add 1/4 lb cooked diced ham and 1/2 cup peas to the beaten egg mixture.

▶ Omit the zucchini. Add one small diced and sautéed red pepper and 2 cubed boiled potatoes to the egg.

Mini veggie bites

↻ Preparation: 10 minutes; cooking: 10 minutes   ✎ Makes 8 fritters
✺ Provides beta-carotene, fiber, potassium, and vitamin C   ❄ Suitable for freezing

1 cup grated **carrots**

1 cup grated **zucchini**

²/₃ cup grated **potatoes**

salt and freshly ground **black pepper**

2 tbsp **flour**

vegetable oil for frying

Encourage your children to enjoy eating vegetables with this tasty recipe—the easy-to-hold fritters even taste good served cold.

▶ Squeeze out excess moisture from the grated vegetables. The best way to do this is to lay the vegetables on several sheets of paper towel and then cover the vegetables with more paper and press down to soak up the excess liquid.
▶ Mix the vegetables in a bowl with the seasoning and flour and form into 8 round fritters using your hands.
▶ Heat the oil in a frying pan and fry the fritters, gently flattening them with a spatula. Sauté for about 5 minutes, turning halfway through.
▶ Drain on paper towels. They should be golden and crisp on the outside and fully cooked inside.

Pasta cartwheels with cheese & broccoli

↻ Preparation: 10 minutes; cooking: 35 minutes   🔥 350°F
✎ Makes 4 portions   ✺ Provides calcium, protein, B vitamins including folate, vitamin A, and zinc   ❄ Suitable for freezing: sauce only

¼ lb **pasta cartwheels**

1¼ cups **broccoli,** cut into small florets

½ cup **frozen sweet corn**

Cheese sauce

2 tbsp **butter**

¼ cup **flour**

1¼ cups **milk**

pinch of **nutmeg**

½ cup grated **cheddar cheese**

salt and freshly ground **black pepper**

Topping

2 tbsp freshly grated **Parmesan cheese**

1½ tbsp **fresh bread crumbs**

▶ Cook the pasta in boiling, lightly salted water according to the instructions on the package. Drain and set aside.
▶ Meanwhile, place the broccoli and sweet corn in a steamer and cook for 4–5 minutes, or until tender. Cover to keep warm and set aside.
▶ To make the sauce, melt the butter in a small pan. Add the flour to make a paste and stir over a low heat for 1 minute. Gradually whisk in the milk, bring slowly to a boil, and cook until thickened, stirring constantly. Remove from the heat, add the nutmeg, stir in the cheddar cheese until melted, and season.
▶ Stir the vegetables into the sauce, then mix with the pasta. Pour the mixture into a greased gratin dish and sprinkle with the Parmesan cheese and bread crumbs. Bake in the preheated oven for about 15 minutes.

Variation

▶ To make macaroni and cheese, omit the vegetables and replace the cartwheels with ¼ lb of macaroni.

Pasta & sauce with hidden vegetables

🕐 Preparation: 10 minutes; cooking: 30 minutes   🍴 Makes 4 portions

🥄 Provides beta-carotene, folate, potassium, and vitamins C and E

❄ Suitable for freezing: sauce only

2 tbsp **olive oil**

1 small **onion,** peeled and chopped

1 **garlic clove,** peeled and crushed

2/3 cup **carrots,** peeled and chopped

3/4 cup **zucchini,** chopped

1 cup **mushrooms,** sliced

2 cups **canned chopped tomatoes**

1/2 cup **vegetable stock** (see page 47)

1/4 tsp **brown sugar**

salt and freshly ground **black pepper**

1/2 lb **pasta twists** (such as **rotini**)

If your baby is reluctant to eat vegetables, one solution is to resort to disguise. This sauce has lots of vegetables blended into it. Mix it with fun pasta shapes and you have a winner! A tablespoon of pesto makes a nice addition.

▶ Warm the oil in a pan, add the onion and garlic, and sauté for about 3 minutes. Add the carrots, zucchini, and mushrooms, and cook for about 15 minutes or until softened. Add the tomatoes, vegetable stock, and brown sugar, season to taste, and simmer for 10 minutes. Blend to a purée.

▶ Meanwhile, cook the pasta in boiling, lightly salted water according to the instructions on the package. Toss with the sauce and serve.

Rotini with quick-&-easy cheese sauce

🕐 Preparation: 5 minutes; cooking: 6 minutes   🍴 Makes 4 portions

🥄 Provides calcium, protein, B vitamins including folate, vitamin A, and zinc

1/2 lb **pasta twists** (such as **rotini**)

3/4 cup **frozen peas**

Sauce

2/3 cup **heavy cream**

1 cup grated **Gruyère cheese**

This is an easy recipe to make—the cheese is simply melted into the cream to make a tasty sauce. If your child prefers, leave out the peas and add some strips of ham instead.

▶ Cook the rotini in boiling, lightly salted water according to the instructions on the package. About 3 minutes before the pasta is done, add the frozen peas.

▶ Meanwhile, place the cream and cheese in a saucepan and cook over a gentle heat until the cheese has melted.

▶ Drain the pasta and peas and toss them with the cheese sauce.

Pasta salad with tuna & sweet corn

🕐 Preparation: 7 minutes; cooking: 12 minutes   🍴 Makes 2 portions

🥄 Provides protein, B vitamins, and vitamins C, D, and E

2 oz **pasta twists** (such as **rotini**)

3 1/2 oz **canned tuna in oil,** drained and flaked

1/3 cup **canned** or cooked **frozen sweet corn**

3 **cherry tomatoes,** quartered

1 **green onion,** finely chopped

Dressing

2 tbsp **mayonnaise**

1 tsp **lemon juice**

1 tsp **light olive oil**

If you like you could also add some avocado to this salad.

▶ Cook the pasta in boiling, lightly salted water according to the instructions on the package.

▶ Mix together the ingredients for the dressing.

▶ Mix the cooked pasta together with the tuna, sweet corn, tomatoes, and green onion, and toss in the dressing.

Orzo with colorful diced vegetables

⟳ Preparation: 10 minutes; cooking: 15 minutes   ✂ Makes 2 portions   ⚕ Provides beta-carotene, calcium, folate, protein, and vitamins A and C   ❄ Suitable for freezing

¼ lb **soup pasta** (such as **orzo**)

½ cup **carrots**, peeled and diced

½ cup **zucchini**, diced

⅔ cup **broccoli**, diced

2 tbsp **butter**

¼ cup freshly grated **cheddar** or **Parmesan cheese**

Orzo is the name given to tiny pasta shapes that resemble barley kernels (you can also find riso or puntalette—"grains of rice"). Its creamy, slightly chewy texture is very appealing to children.

▶ Put the pasta in a saucepan together with the diced vegetables. Cover with enough boiling water to cover the pasta and vegetables generously and cook for about 12 minutes, or until all the vegetables are tender. Drain thoroughly.

▶ Melt the butter in a large pan, stir in the drained pasta and vegetables, and remove from the heat.
▶ Add the grated cheese and toss until the cheese has completely melted.

Bow-tie pasta with ham & peas

⟳ Preparation: 5 minutes; cooking: 15 minutes   ✂ Makes 4 portions
⚕ Provides calcium, protein, B vitamins including folate, vitamin A, and zinc
❄ Suitable for freezing: sauce only

¼ lb **pasta bows (farfalle)**

½ **vegetable stock cube**

Sauce

1½ tbsp **butter**

2 tbsp **flour**

1¼ cups **milk**

¼ tsp **dry ground mustard**

½ cup **frozen peas**

½ cup grated **mature cheddar cheese**

2 oz **sliced cooked ham** or **prosciutto**, cut into strips

salt and freshly grated **black pepper**

Bow-tie pasta is a good shape for young children. Don't worry if they treat it as finger food—good manners will come in time! This is also successful made with green and white narrow pasta noodles (tagliolini or tagliarini).

▶ Cook the pasta in boiling, lightly salted water according to the instructions on the package.
▶ Meanwhile, make the sauce. Melt the butter in a small pan, stir in the flour to make a paste, and gradually whisk in the milk and mustard. Stir in the peas and cook for 3 minutes.
▶ Remove from the heat and stir in the cheese until melted. Add the ham, heat through, season, and toss with the pasta.

Variations

▶ To make a vegetarian version, omit the ham and add 1 cup sliced button mushrooms sautéed in a little butter until tender.
▶ Alternatively, omit the ham and add steamed small broccoli florets and diced carrots to the cheese sauce.
▶ You could also make this using a mixture of grated cheddar and Gruyère cheeses.

Joy's fish pie

↻ Preparation: 15 minutes; cooking: 50 minutes   🔺 350°F
✎ Makes 4 portions   🏃 Provides calcium, fiber, omega-3 fats, potassium, protein,
B vitamins including folate, vitamins A and D, and zinc   ❄ Suitable for freezing

*A good fish pie with creamy mashed potatoes makes a great meal for
kids. You can leave out the peas and sweet corn if you prefer and add
two chopped hard-boiled eggs instead.*

³/₄ lb **salmon fillets**, skinned

³/₄ lb **cod fillets**, skinned

2¹/₂ cups **milk**

4 **peppercorns**, 1 **bay leaf**, and a
parsley stalk

2 tbsp **butter**

1 **onion**, peeled and finely chopped

3 tbsp **flour**

¹/₂ tsp **dry ground mustard**

³/₄ cup **frozen peas**

³/₄ cup **canned** or **frozen sweet
corn**

1 tbsp snipped **chives**

¹/₂ cup grated **cheddar cheese**

salt and freshly ground **black pepper**

Mashed potatoes

2 lb **potatoes**, peeled and
cut into chunks

4 tbsp **milk**

1¹/₂ tbsp **butter**

salt and **white pepper**

1 beaten **egg white**

▶ For the mashed potatoes, boil some lightly salted water, add the potatoes, and boil until tender.

▶ Meanwhile, put the fish in a shallow pan with the milk, peppercorns, and herbs. Bring to a boil, then cover and cook for 5 minutes, or until the fish flakes easily. Remove the fish, strain the milk, and reserve. Flake the fish with a fork, checking carefully for bones, and set aside.

▶ Melt the butter in a small pan, add the onion, and sauté until softened. Stir in the flour to make a paste and cook for 1 minute. Gradually add the strained milk, stirring until the sauce thickens.

▶ Mix in the mustard, peas, sweet corn, chives, and cheddar cheese. Cook for 2 minutes. Season and add the fish. Spoon the mixture into a suitable ovenproof dish.

▶ Drain and mash the potatoes. Add milk, butter, and seasoning. Spread the potatoes over the fish, making peaks with a fork. Brush with beaten egg white and cook in the preheated oven for 25 minutes.

Rosti salmon cakes

↻ Preparation: 20 minutes; cooking: 40 minutes   ✎ Makes 8 fish cakes
🏃 Provides calcium, omega-3 fats, potassium, B vitamins, and vitamins A, C, D, and E
❄ Suitable for freezing

*Rosti is the name given to the grated potato cakes popular in Switzerland and
Germany. These salmon fish cakes are slightly crispy on the outside and moist
inside. They are the best I have ever eaten, and my children love them, too.*

1¹/₂ lb medium-size **starchy
potatoes such as russet or
fingerling**

³/₄ lb **salmon fillets**, skinned

²/₃ cup grated **Gruyère cheese**

2 medium **egg yolks**, lightly beaten

2 tbsp chopped **fresh parsley**

1 small **onion**, peeled and finely
chopped

salt and **white pepper**

¹/₃ cup **vegetable oil**

▶ Cook half the potatoes in their skins for 20 minutes in lightly salted water over medium heat. Drain and leave to cool.

▶ Meanwhile, cut the salmon into bite-size chunks and mix with the grated cheese, egg yolks, parsley, and chopped onion and season well. Peel and grate the cooked potatoes and stir into the salmon mixture.

▶ Peel and grate the uncooked potatoes, squeeze out the excess moisture, and season with salt and

ground white pepper. Using your hands, shape the salmon mixture into 8 round fish cakes and then press each fish cake into the raw grated potato until coated on both sides.

▶ Heat the oil in a large frying pan and cook the fish cakes a few at a time until golden and cooked through (about 4 minutes on each side). Drain any excess oil onto paper towels.

Chicken sausage snails

⟳ Preparation: 20 minutes; cooking: 1 hour 10 minutes

◔ Makes 4 portions ⚚ Provides iron, protein, B vitamins including folate, and zinc

❋ Suitable for freezing: chicken sausages only

With a little imagination, you can make succulent homemade chicken sausages into a fun and visually appealing meal.

▶ Put the chicken in a food processor with the onion, parsley, crumbled stock cube, apple, and bread crumbs. Chop for a few seconds, then season the mixture lightly.

▶ Form the mixture into four sausages each about 5 inches long. Spread the flour on a plate and use it to coat the sausages. Heat the vegetable oil in a frying pan, add the sausages, and sauté for about 15 minutes, turning occasionally, or until browned on all sides and cooked through.

▶ Meanwhile, place the potatoes in the bottom of a steamer, cover with lightly salted water, and cook until tender. Five minutes before the potatoes are done, put the vegetables for decorating in the top of the steamer and cook until tender. Mash the potatoes with the milk, butter, and seasoning.

▶ To assemble, form the potato into four dome shapes using an ice-cream scoop and decorate with a ketchup spiral to create a snail-shell effect (you can use a piping bag with a small nozzle for this, or cut a small hole in the corner of a freezer bag and use that). Put a sausage underneath each dome of potato. Use the steamed carrot sticks and peas to make the snail's feelers, and arrange the cabbage as grass.

Chicken sausages

³/₄ lb boneless, skinless **chicken breast**, cubed

1 medium **onion**, peeled and finely chopped

1 tbsp chopped **fresh parsley**

1 **chicken stock cube** dissolved in 1 tbsp **boiling water**

1 large **apple**, peeled and grated

2 tbsp **fresh bread crumbs**

salt and freshly ground **black pepper**

flour for coating

vegetable oil for frying

Mashed potatoes

1 lb **potatoes**, peeled and cut into chunks

2 tbsp **milk**

2 tbsp **butter**

salt and **white pepper**

To decorate

shredded **savoy cabbage**

1 **carrot**, peeled and cut into sticks

16 **frozen peas**

ketchup

Turkey meatballs

1 lb **ground turkey**

1 **onion**, peeled and finely chopped

1 small **apple**, peeled and grated

3 tbsp **fresh bread crumbs**

1 **egg**, lightly beaten

2 tbsp chopped **fresh sage** or **thyme**

salt and freshly ground **black pepper**

flour for coating

2 tbsp **vegetable oil** for frying

Red pepper sauce

1½ tbsp **vegetable oil**

2 **shallots**, peeled and finely chopped

1½ **red peppers**, deseeded and chopped

1 tsp **tomato purée**

3 tbsp chopped **fresh basil**

1¾ cups **vegetable stock** (see page 47)

salt and freshly ground **black pepper**

TIP *These can be made ahead and frozen, then simply defrosted and reheated in a microwave (just make sure you test the temperature before giving them to your child).*

Turkey balls & pepper sauce

Preparation: 20 minutes; cooking: 40 minutes   350°F

Makes 8 portions   Provides beta-carotene, iron, protein, B vitamins including folate, vitamins C and E, and zinc   Suitable for freezing

Served with rice or spaghetti, these little meatballs make a great lunch. If you have time, roast and skin the peppers for the sauce, which can also be made with chicken stock (see page 52).

▶ To make the red pepper sauce, heat the oil in a frying pan, add the shallots and red peppers, and sauté until softened. Stir in the remaining ingredients and season to taste. Bring to a boil and simmer for 15–20 minutes. Blend until smooth.

▶ Mix together all the ingredients for the meatballs, seasoning to taste. Use your hands to form the mixture into about 24 walnut-size balls. Spread the flour on a plate and use it to coat the meatballs. Heat the oil in a frying pan, add the balls, and sauté, turning until they are golden all over.

▶ Transfer the meatballs to a casserole, cover with pepper sauce, and cook in the preheated oven for about 20 minutes, or until the meatballs are cooked through and well browned.

Finger-licking chicken & potato balls

⟳ Preparation: 10 minutes; cooking: 40 minutes ⚷ Makes 8 portions

⚶ Provides beta-carotene, folate, potassium, protein, and vitamin E

❄ Suitable for freezing

Mashed potatoes and parsnips give these balls a soft texture and a hint of sweetness, and they are just the right size for picking up and nibbling.

▶ Put the potatoes and parsnips in a pan, cover with water, bring to a boil, and simmer, covered, for 12–15 minutes or until tender.

▶ Meanwhile, heat 1 tbsp of oil in a frying pan, add the onion and carrot, and sauté for 4–5 minutes. Add the chicken and continue to sauté for about 10 minutes or until cooked through.

▶ Drain the potatoes and parsnips and mash with half the butter until smooth. Finely chop the chicken, onion, and carrot in a food processor and mix with the mashed vegetables.

▶ Form the mixture into 24 walnut-size balls. Spread the flour on a plate and use it to coat them. Heat the remaining oil and butter in a frying pan, add the meatballs, and sauté until golden.

¾ cup **potatoes**, peeled and chopped

¾ cup **parsnips**, peeled and chopped

3 tbsp **vegetable oil**

½ small **onion**, peeled and finely chopped

1 **carrot**, peeled and grated

¼ lb boneless, skinless **chicken breast**, cut into chunks

large pat of **butter**

flour for coating

Shepherd's pie

⟳ Preparation: 5 minutes; cooking: 1 hour 10 minutes 🔥 350°F

⚷ Makes 8 portions ⚶ Provides beta-carotene, iron, potassium, protein, B vitamins including folate, vitamin C, and zinc ❄ Suitable for freezing

If you prefer, you can make the shepherd's pie in individual ramekins and decorate with vegetable faces (see page 164).

▶ Warm the oil in a pan, add the onion, red pepper, and garlic, and sauté until softened. Add the meat and sauté until browned. If desired, transfer the cooked mixture to a food processor and chop for a few seconds on the pulse setting.

▶ Transfer the meat to a saucepan and add the stock, parsley, tomato purée, Worcestershire sauce, and mushrooms. Cook over a medium heat for about 20 minutes.

▶ Meanwhile, boil the potatoes in lightly salted water until tender, then drain and mash with 2 tbsp of butter and the milk. Season to taste.

▶ Arrange the meat either in one large dish or in individual ramekins, cover with the mashed potatoes, and dot the topping with the remaining butter. Cook in the preheated oven for 20 minutes.

Variation

▶ To make cottage pie, replace the ground lamb with the same quantity of lean ground beef. For the topping, omit the mashed potatoes and replace with 7 cups boiled and mashed rutabagas, or use a combination of mashed rutabagas and potatoes.

1½ tbsp **vegetable oil**

1 large **onion**, peeled and chopped

1 small **red pepper**, finely chopped

1 **garlic clove**, peeled and crushed

1 lb **lean ground lamb**

1¼ cups **chicken stock** (see page 52) or **beef stock**

1 tbsp chopped **fresh parsley**

1 tbsp **tomato purée**

1 tsp **Worcestershire sauce**

2½ cups **mushrooms**, sliced

Mashed potatoes

2 lb **potatoes**, peeled and roughly chopped

2½ tbsp **butter**

4 tbsp **milk**

salt and **white pepper**

TIP To make ground meat more palatable to young children, cook it first and then chop it in a food processor.

Raspberry frozen yogurt

⟳ Preparation: 2 minutes; cooking: 35 minutes, including 20 minutes freezing

✎ Makes 8 portions ⚡ Provides calcium, protein, and vitamins B12 and C

This frozen yogurt recipe can also be made with a mixture of berries—perhaps strawberries, blackberries, and raspberries. A few minutes before you want to eat it, take it out of the freezer and allow to soften slightly. Serve plain or with some fresh raspberries.

2 cups **frozen** or **fresh raspberries**

4 tbsp **superfine sugar**

½ cup **water**

1¼–1½ cups mild, full-fat **natural yogurt**

6 tbsp **sour cream**

2–3 tbsp **confectioner's sugar**

TIP *If you don't have an ice-cream maker, place the mixture in a plastic tub and freeze for about 1 hour. Then beat by hand or in a food processor to break up the ice crystals. Freeze again, repeating the beating procedure once or twice during freezing.*

▶ Put the raspberries in a saucepan with the sugar and water. Bring to a simmer, then cook for 5 minutes. Purée using a handheld blender, then strain through a sieve to get rid of the seeds. Leave to cool.

▶ Stir the yogurt and sour cream into the raspberry purée and add just enough confectioner's sugar to sweeten. Transfer to an ice-cream maker and freeze for about 20 minutes.

Variation

▶ Mix 1½ cups cherry yogurt with 6 tbsp of sour cream. Stir in ⅔ cup canned pitted black cherries, ⅓ cup maple syrup, and ¼ cup grated semi-sweet chocolate. Transfer mixture to an ice-cream maker, and freeze as described above.

Yogurt pancakes

⟳ Preparation: 2 minutes; cooking: 10 minutes ✎ Makes 8 portions

⚡ Provides calcium, protein, and vitamins B2, B12, and C (served with fruit)

❄ Suitable for freezing (see tip, left)

Mini pancakes are delicious served with fresh fruit and maple syrup. You could also add a few raisins to a maple-syrup-sweetened batter to make raisin pancakes.

1 **egg**, lightly beaten

⅔ cup mild, full-fat **natural yogurt**

⅔ cup **milk**

1¼ cups **self-raising flour**

¼ tsp **salt** or 2 tbsp **maple syrup** (for a sweeter version)

vegetable oil for frying

To accompany

pure maple syrup

fresh fruit, such as strawberries, raspberries, or sliced peaches

TIP *These pancakes can be layered between pieces of waxed or greaseproof paper and then frozen. Reheat in a toaster.*

▶ Mix together the beaten egg and the yogurt, then stir in the milk, flour, and salt or maple syrup. Mix until you have a smooth batter.

▶ Heat a little oil in a frying pan until sizzling hot. Drop heaped tablespoons of batter into the pan, leaving plenty of space around each one, and flatten slightly with a spatula. They should spread to about 2½ inches across. Cook for 1–2 minutes until lightly browned, then turn and cook for a further 1–2 minutes until browned on the other side and set in the center.

▶ Drizzle maple syrup over the pancakes and serve sprinkled with fruit.

Raisin toast fingers

⏱ Preparation: 10 minutes ⚬ Makes 1 portion 🥕 Provides magnesium and potassium

1 slice **raisin bread**

½ tbsp **creamy peanut butter** or **cream cheese**

½ small **banana**, peeled and sliced

Simple to prepare, this filling snack or dessert is an appealing mix of sweet and savory tastes.

▶ Toast the raisin bread and spread with peanut butter or cream cheese.

▶ Arrange the sliced banana on top and cut into fingers, squares, or triangles.

Gelatin boats

⏱ Preparation: 5 minutes; cooking: 10 minutes plus 1 hour 45 minutes setting
⚬ Makes 8 portions 🥕 Provides vitamin C if using added fruit

2 large **oranges**, halved

1 package (4-serving size) **fruit-flavored gelatin**, such as strawberry or orange

1 small can **mandarin orange segments** (optional)

1 half-pint **fresh raspberries** (optional)

Of all the foods I make for parties, these ingeniously simple flavored gelatins are perhaps the most popular.

▶ Squeeze the juice from the orange halves (keep it to drink) without breaking the skins. Carefully scrape out the membrane and discard.

▶ Make the gelatin according to the instructions, reducing the amount of water specified by a quarter if using fruit. Divide the fruit, if using, between the orange halves, then fill with gelatin and refrigerate until set.

▶ Take a wet knife and cut each orange half in half again. Thread a cocktail stick down the center of each rice-paper triangle, then set the sail in the gelatin.

Variation

▶ Choose three contrasting-colored gelatins and set each layer separately in a tall glass. Set the first layer of gelatin in the refrigerator with the glass at an angle so that the gelatin sets diagonally. Do the same with the second layer of gelatin. Pour in the last layer of gelatin and set with the glass standing upright.

To decorate

8 small **rice paper** triangles

8 **cocktail sticks**

NOTE These gelatin boats use cocktail sticks. For young children, place the boats on each child's plate, then remove the cocktail sticks before they begin to eat.

18 months to 2 years

The active toddler

Food tastes are decided early in life, so you should try to establish a varied, healthy diet for your child while he is still receptive to new foods and before peer pressure and TV advertising take their toll. However, despite your best efforts, your plans may be derailed by a period of picky or erratic eating and you may have to use a little ingenuity to stimulate his appetite. This chapter is full of ideas for healthy "fast foods" and easy ways to prepare some all-time favorite children's recipes to tempt even the most reluctant child.

Busy bodies

As your child nears his second birthday, his growth rate slows down substantially. At the same time, his levels of activity are on the increase because he has greater physical competence and probably a busier, more active daily schedule. As a result, your rounded baby will become a slimmed-down, active toddler, losing much of his baby fat.

Although he has high energy requirements, his small stomach will probably cope best with light meals interspersed with snacks. Remember that toddlers are not conditioned to eat by the clock, and, quite sensibly, will tend to want to eat only when they are truly hungry.

By this age, they will be fairly vocal in their preferences, and you will want to give your child easily prepared food that you can prepare quickly (see pages 92–93), before his hungry demands become furious outbursts. Of course, you will want to create some structure and routine for family mealtimes, but be flexible. The last thing you want to do is make an issue over "correct" mealtimes, turning your child into a resentful eater. Ninety percent of children are picky eaters at some point during their childhood.

Tantrums

Remember that your child is entering the stage of toddler tantrums, when the frustrations he encounters can make him explode with rage. It is hard for you, too, and you may need to try out a number of ways to encourage him to eat (see page 91). Avoid using bribes, however, because you will only encourage bad behavior.

GRAZING HABITS

Snacks are an important part of a child's diet, and you should try to ensure that there are plenty of healthy and tasty snacks available, instead of letting your child eat candy, cookies, or chips between meals. Prepare a selection of cut-up fresh fruit or vegetables and leave them in the refrigerator for when she is hungry.

If you are worried that your child's food intake is low, and that the amounts of food she consumes at mealtimes are minuscule, keep a diary of her total food intake over a period of a few days or a week. Many children have the habit of "grazing"—nibbling a little food here and there—and if you add up all these snacks, you may find that your child's diet is reasonably substantial and balanced.

Limiting sugary foods

As toddlers are exposed to an increasingly varied diet, they may be quick to acquire a sweet tooth. Since they are most likely to pick up their eating habits from the immediate family, you may need to be strong-minded yourself if you want your child to have a low sugar intake.

It is not just the amount of sugar we eat that harms our teeth, but also the frequency with which we put sugary foods in our mouth: each time we eat sugary foods, the bacteria in dental plaque produce acids that attack tooth enamel and can cause tooth decay. Consequently, a candy bar consumed all at once does less harm than eating the same treat over a more prolonged period of time.

Try to confine sugary foods to mealtimes, not only to reduce the frequency of eating sugary foods but also because eating other foods at the same time dilutes the acid and reduces the harmful effects of the sugar. At mealtimes, there is also more saliva in the mouth to wash away acids. Cheese is particularly beneficial at the end of a meal because it is alkaline and helps to neutralize the harmful acid that causes tooth decay.

Do not let candy and desserts become synonymous with rewards: try to offer other treats, such as stickers or comics. Consider making a rule that sweet foods are allowed only at certain times, perhaps once a week.

Sweet drinks

Even pure fruit juices contain fructose (a natural sugar), which can cause tooth decay, so confine diluted fruit juices to mealtimes, where they can also benefit your child by increasing the absorption of iron from food. Read labels carefully; sugar can be disguised under other names, such as glucose, maltose, or dextrose. Some individual cartons of fruit juice contain as much as six teaspoons of sugar. Diet soft drinks are no kinder to teeth—they also contain acids that attack tooth enamel. Sweet drinks at bedtime are not a good idea, since saliva won't wash away the acid during the night and you'll undo all the good done by tooth-brushing.

Pick-me-up foods
For a quick spurt of energy:
• bowl of corn flakes
• pieces of fruit, fresh or dried
• yogurt with honey
For a steady stream of energy:
• raw vegetables with dips
• bread with ham, tuna, or cheese
• baked potato with filling
• baked beans on toast
• salad with hard-boiled egg
• oatcakes with cheese
• freshly made fruit milkshakes

Remember
• The stickier the food, the more likely it is to cause tooth decay. Even seemingly healthy foods, such as raisins or chewy cereal bars, can harm your child's teeth if eaten too often between meals.

• Fruits such as bananas, apples, pears, tangerines, and grapes make good snacks. They contain slow-release sugars that give your child energy as well as vital vitamins.

Tooth-friendly snacks
• vegetable sticks, such as carrot, cucumber, sweet pepper, or celery, on their own or with a dip • cheese • cheese on toast • lightly salted popcorn • toasted seeds • toast fingers • cream cheese with mini bread sticks • rice cakes • mini sandwiches with egg salad, or cream cheese and cucumber • mini pita pockets filled with tuna salad • mini salads, such as mozzarella and tomato or pasta with tuna • fresh fruit

The picky eater

"A picky diet may be nutritious yet unconventional—no young child ever starves himself! Remember, it is the balance of his diet over several days that really matters."

Refusing food is one of the first ways young children can flex their muscles and assert their independence. It doesn't take them long to realize how easy it is to manipulate you at the dinner table. Indeed, battles at mealtimes are often one of the most stressful aspects of early parenthood. Cajoling a child to eat —whether in the form of bribery or threats—is usually counterproductive.

Keeping calm

However unreasonable your child's eating habits seem to be, try to respond calmly. The aim is to help your child fit into normal family eating, not to force him into cooperation. Don't put pressure on your child to eat the foods you want him to eat. Try to keep the emotional temperature down; food shouldn't be used as a means to teach a child to do as he is told.

Unfortunately, many children seem to enjoy stretching their parents' patience to the limit; after all, refusing to eat makes them the center of attention. Refuse to be riled; simply take the rejected meal away, and don't offer unhealthy alternatives. Attempting to induce guilt won't work, either; telling a child that he has a moral duty to leave a clean plate is unlikely to motivate a two-year-old to finish his dinner.

No young child ever starves himself, and his picky diet may be nutritious even if it is unconventional. Remember that it is the balance of his diet over several days that really matters.

STRATEGIES FOR COPING WITH A PICKY EATER

- Limit empty-calorie snacks, such as chips or chocolate, and keep a supply of healthy snacks available—for example, keep a low shelf in the refrigerator stocked with cut-up fresh fruit and other healthy foods. When children are hungry, they won't wait.

- If your child will not eat vegetables on his own, create recipes that vegetables can be blended into, such as tomato and vegetable sauce for pasta, or creamy tomato soup made with carrots and onions. What children cannot see, they cannot pick out. Also, many children who do not like cooked vegetables will eat the raw versions, such as carrot sticks or bell pepper strips with a tasty dip.

- Only buy the foods that you want your child to eat.

- It's important to introduce as many foods as possible at an early age. You could try making a game out of this by blindfolding your child before introducing a new food and asking him to guess what it is.

- Without going to unnecessary lengths, try to make sure your child's food not only tastes good, but looks good, too. Choose colorful food and arrange it in an interesting pattern on the plate.

- Mealtimes are social occasions, so set a good example by eating with your child as often as possible. You cannot expect your child to realize that mealtimes involve sitting down and staying in one place unless he sees you and the rest of the family doing so. Try to avoid distractions such as watching television at mealtimes.

- Inviting another child over for dinner—preferably a child with a good appetite—is a handy trick. Invariably, you will find that your child eats whatever his friend is eating!

- Once a child's palate has become accustomed to the intense sweetness of refined, sugary foods, it is harder for him to appreciate the more gentle, natural sweetness of fruit. So if you want your child to enjoy fresh fruit, restrict his intake of sugary foods.

- If your child is underweight and not eating well, he needs as much energy (calories) as possible. Offer full-fat dairy products, such as cheese, milkshakes, or good-quality ice cream, and avoid using low-fat dairy products. Make sure he isn't filling up on drinks, candy, or too much milk.

- Too much food on a plate can be discouraging. Keep portions small and give second helpings if requested. Children tend to find individual portions of food— shepherd's pie in ramekin dishes, for example—much more appealing than a dollop of food on a plate.

- Give your child room to assert his independence, perhaps by letting him choose two out of the three vegetables offered to him.

- After a period of time, try reintroducing foods that your child once refused.

- Do not give the same recipe to your child over and over again just because you know he likes it. He will probably become bored with it and refuse to eat it after a while.

"Food fads"

Occasionally, children go through periods of eating only a few specific foods. Don't worry too much. Children can thrive on quite a limited range of foods and, except in rare cases, will eventually get bored with a monotonous diet. If, for example, your child wants only peanut-butter sandwiches at every meal, make sure the bread is whole-wheat and give him a milkshake or glass of milk to accompany the sandwich. At the same time, offer tasty and nutritious alternatives.

Sometimes fads may appear even more irrational; your child might refuse foods that have come in contact with each other on his plate, for instance. In this case, a sectioned plate may provide the solution.

Rejecting specific foods

If your child repeatedly rejects a particular food, you can assume that he really doesn't like it. Try to recognize when your child is being stubborn and when he has a genuine dislike of a particular food.

If vegetables are a problem, there are many ways to disguise them in the diet (see page 71). Meat is another food that is often rejected. A healthy diet need not include meat as long as your child's diet includes milk and dairy products, beans and legumes, or soy-based products, which will provide adequate quantities of protein, iron and B vitamins (see page 13). However, it is often the texture rather than the taste of meat that children object to. If your child dislikes lumps of meat, try giving him dishes such as spaghetti bolognese (see page 67) or shepherd's pie (see page 83), blending the meat until fairly smooth. Alternatively, make bite-size meatballs (see page 103) and serve them with ketchup, or moisten finely ground meat with gravy and mix it into a combination of mashed potatoes and carrots.

Remember

• Avoid empty calories, as in soft drinks or candy; keep a supply of healthy snacks.

• Offer full-fat milk, yogurt, and cheese. Low-fat milk should not be offered as a drink until your child is at least two years old.

• If your child likes to play with his food before eating it, let him, and forget about perfecting table manners for the time being.

• Provide small servings or make individual portions of food; these are more appealing and allow your child some control over how much food he eats.

• Serve an occasional meal in a different place—even a picnic lunch on the floor may work.

Fast food for toddlers

The active toddler's hunger rarely coincides with regular mealtimes. Because she uses up energy so quickly with her new-found independence, light, frequent snacks may best suit her needs. She is also too young to wait patiently for meals, so it's a good idea to be able to offer easy-to-prepare, healthy "fast foods." All the foods shown here are visually appealing and have interesting textures and vibrant flavors—and all can be eaten on the run.

1 Pinwheel sandwiches

The most versatile of fast foods, shaped sandwiches make savory mouthfuls. Toddlers will adore these sticky spirals of soft brown bread rolled with their favorite fillings. (See page 95 for recipe.)

2 Chunky tomato & cream cheese dip

Children often prefer vegetables raw, especially if cut to form whimsical shapes, and they love dunking them into dips. This ensemble makes a nutritious between-meals snack. (See page 94 for recipe.)

3 Kebabs in pita pockets

Miniature kebabs can be grilled, taken off the skewers, and stuffed into warm pita bread pockets with some colorful salad leaves. Chicken with tomatoes and tofu with chunky vegetables are two delicious combinations. (See pages 98 and 102 for recipes.)

1

2

3

2 **eggs**

1 tbsp **milk** or **heavy cream**

salt and freshly ground **black pepper**

1 tbsp **butter**

1 **tomato**, skinned, deseeded, and chopped

2 tbsp grated **Gruyère cheese**

Scrambled eggs with cheese & tomatoes

Preparation: 2 minutes; cooking: 6 minutes   Makes 2 portions

Provides calcium, iron, protein, B vitamins, and vitamins A and E

Scrambled eggs make a quick and nutritious family breakfast. Serve them with a toasted bagel or buttered toast. For a special breakfast or brunch, add strips of smoked salmon.

▶ Beat the eggs with the milk and season lightly. Melt the butter in a saucepan over a low heat, add the chopped tomato, and sauté for 1 minute.

▶ Add the egg mixture and heat, stirring continuously with a wooden spoon, until the eggs start to cook. Add the cheese and continue to stir until the eggs are set.

$\frac{1}{2}$ cup each chopped **dried mangoes** and **apricots**

3 tbsp **raisins**

$1\frac{1}{2}$ cups **muesli mix**, or $\frac{3}{4}$ cup each of **oat flakes** and **wheat flakes**

$\frac{1}{4}$ cup finely chopped **hazelnuts** (optional)

$1\frac{1}{2}$ cups **apple and mango juice** or plain **apple juice**

$\frac{1}{2}$ **red apple**, cored and chopped

extra **fresh fruit**, such as banana or raspberries (optional)

NOTE This recipe contains nuts. Omit the nuts if there is a family history of nut allergy.

Apple, mango & apricot muesli

Preparation: 5 minutes, plus overnight soaking   Makes 4 portions   Provides beta-carotene, fiber, iron, potassium, protein, B vitamins including folate, vitamin A, and zinc

Unfortunately, many breakfast cereals designed for children are low in nutrients and high in sugar. I make a healthy, Swiss-style muesli for my family, using a store-bought muesli mix—a blend of rolled oats, wheat, barley, and rye flakes—and fresh fruit. This mix, without the added fresh fruit, can be kept refrigerated for several days.

▶ Soak the dried fruit, muesli mix, and nuts in the juice overnight or for several hours. In the morning, stir in the apple and your chosen extra fresh fruit and serve with milk, if desired.

Variation

▶ Make a deliciously unusual muesli by substituting grape juice for the apple juice and using chopped dried peaches instead of mangoes and apricots.

$\frac{3}{4}$ cup **soft cream cheese**

3 tbsp **mayonnaise**

1 tbsp **ketchup**

1 tsp **fresh lemon juice**

$\frac{1}{4}$ tsp **Worcestershire sauce**

$\frac{1}{4}$ tsp **soy sauce**

$\frac{1}{2}$ tbsp snipped **chives**

2 **tomatoes**, skinned, deseeded, and chopped

TIP This dip can also be made with low-fat dairy products, but only for older children.

Chunky tomato & cream cheese dip

Preparation: 10 minutes, plus overnight soaking   Makes 8 portions

Provides vitamins A, B12, and E

Serve this appealing dip with raw and cooked vegetables, bread sticks, or toasted pita bread for a tasty and energizing snack.

▶ Simply mix all the ingredients together, blending them thoroughly, and serve.

Variation

▶ To make a cream cheese and chive dip, mix together the same quantities of soft cream cheese and mayonnaise with 3 tbsp of milk. Mix in 1 tsp of Dijon mustard, 2 tbsp of snipped chives, a pinch of sugar, and freshly ground pepper to taste. Blend and serve.

Shaped sandwiches

Sandwiches make a quick snack that can be eaten on the run, and you can use all sorts of fillings and breads. Try to use foods from each of the main groups—bread, fruit and vegetables, meat and alternatives, and dairy products—to make sandwiches that are nutritious alternatives to cooked meals.

Open sandwiches

Cut slices of bread into simple shapes, or into animal shapes using cookie cutters. Butter and then spread with filling. Try cottage-cheese or egg-salad sheep or ducks or cheddar-cheese butterflies; geometric shapes spread with a favorite filling, such as diamond-shaped bread kites spread with mashed avocadoes, or with thinly sliced ham, turkey, or chicken; or bread and cheese squares decorated to look like presents with red pepper, tomato, or chive ribbons.

Double-decker sandwiches

Take three slices of buttered brown or white bread, with the center slice buttered on both sides. Sandwich together with two complementary but contrasting fillings, such as sliced bananas and strawberry jam; grated cheese, shredded lettuce and yeast extract; or egg salad and tuna with mayonnaise. Cut into strips.

Pinwheel sandwiches

Trim the crusts off two thin slices of bread. Overlap the edges slightly and flatten with a rolling pin so that they join together. Butter and spread the flattened bread with a colorful filling and roll up, jelly-roll style. Cut across into thin rounds. Suggested fillings include peanut butter and jelly; cream cheese and mashed avocadoes; egg salad; or ham or turkey slices.

Mini pita bread pockets

Warm a small pita bread, cut it in half, and fill with a mix such as tuna and mayonnaise with salad; grated cheese or shredded chicken or ham with salad; sliced hard-boiled eggs with lettuce; or mashed sardines and sliced tomatoes.

Tortilla wraps

Wraps make a good alternative to sandwiches. Warm small flour tortillas and fill with thin slices of turkey, shredded lettuce, and grated cheese with a little mayonnaise. Or try chicken and salsa or tuna salad.

2 tbsp **vegetable oil**

1 **onion,** peeled and finely chopped

1 cup **carrots,** peeled and diced

$^1\!/_2$ **celery stalk,** finely chopped

$^1\!/_3$ cup **leeks,** white part only, washed and finely chopped

$^3\!/_4$ cup **potatoes,** peeled and chopped

$^1\!/_2$ cup **zucchini,** diced

2 ripe **tomatoes,** skinned, deseeded, and chopped

3 pints **chicken stock** (see page 52)

2 tsp **tomato purée**

$^1\!/_3$ cup **frozen peas**

2 oz **alphabet pasta**

salt and freshly ground **black pepper**

TIP This soup can also be made with vegetable stock (see page 47).

Alphabet pasta minestrone

↻ Preparation: 10 minutes; cooking: 45 minutes   ✑ Makes 8 portions

🥄 Provides beta-carotene, fiber, folate, potassium, and vitamins C and E

❄ Suitable for freezing

Homemade minestrone makes a nutritious soup for children, and also becomes a satisfying family meal if supplemented with bread and salad. You can add shredded cabbage (about 2 cups) to make it even more substantial, if you like. The tiny alphabet pasta shapes appeal to children.

▶ Heat the oil in a large pan, add the onion, and sauté for about 5 minutes. Add the carrots, celery, and leeks, and sauté until they begin to soften, about 5 minutes. Add the potatoes and zucchini and sauté for 2–3 minutes.

▶ Stir in the chopped tomatoes, stock, and tomato purée. Bring to a boil, then cover and simmer for 20 minutes. Add

the frozen peas, return the soup to a boil, and cook for 5 minutes.

▶ Stir in the alphabet pasta, return the soup to a boil, then simmer for about 5 minutes. Taste and season lightly.

$^1\!/_4$ lb **pasta bows (farfalle)**

Sauce

2 tbsp **butter**

$^1\!/_3$ cup **leeks,** washed and finely chopped

$^1\!/_2$ cup **carrots,** peeled and diced

$^1\!/_2$ cup **zucchini,** diced

$^2\!/_3$ cup **broccoli,** cut into very small florets

salt and freshly ground **black pepper**

$^2\!/_3$ cup **heavy cream**

$^1\!/_3$ cup freshly grated **Parmesan cheese**

Bow-tie pasta with spring vegetables

↻ Preparation: 10 minutes; cooking: 20 minutes   ✑ Makes 4 portions

🥄 Provides beta-carotene, calcium, fiber, folate, protein, and vitamins A, B12, and C

❄ Suitable for freezing: sauce only

This dish is simple to prepare but never fails to please. You can use other pasta shapes, such as tagliatelle or penne, with the creamy sauce, and you can use other vegetables depending on what your child likes. Try broccoli, sweet corn, and peas.

▶ Cook the pasta in boiling, lightly salted water according to the instructions on the package.

▶ Meanwhile, melt the butter in a heavy-bottomed saucepan, add the leeks and carrots, and sauté for about 5 minutes. Add the diced zucchini and broccoli and cook for about 7 minutes, or until all the vegetables are tender. Season to taste.

▶ Pour in the cream and cook, stirring, for 1 minute. Remove from the heat and stir in the Parmesan. Toss the pasta with the sauce, and serve.

Pasta twists, broccoli, bean sprouts & baby sweet corn

⟳ Preparation: 5 minutes; cooking: 12 minutes   ✂ Makes 4 portions
🥕 Provides folate, potassium, protein, and vitamins A and C

▶ Cook the pasta in boiling, lightly salted water according to the instructions. Steam the broccoli and baby sweet corn for 4 minutes, then set aside.
▶ Put the butter and oil in a wok and sauté the onion and garlic for 3 minutes.

Add the bean sprouts and sauté for 3 minutes more. Add the steamed broccoli and baby sweet corn and stir-fry for 1 minute.
▶ Stir in the chicken stock, add the cooked, drained pasta, and heat through.

$1/2$ lb **pasta twists** (such as **rotini**)

$1^1/_3$ cups **broccoli**, cut into florets

1 cup **baby sweet corn**, cut into quarters

2 tbsp **butter**

$1/2$ tbsp **sunflower oil**

1 **onion**, peeled and finely chopped

1 **garlic clove**, peeled and crushed

$1^3/_4$ cups **bean sprouts**

1 **chicken stock cube**, dissolved in $1/3$ cup **boiling water**

Mini pizzas

⟳ Preparation: 10 minutes; cooking: 15 minutes   ✂ Makes 4 portions
🥕 Provides calcium, protein, B vitamins, and vitamin A

Adding a selection of colorful vegetables to mini pizzas is a great way to encourage your child to eat more vegetables. For a special occasion, you might like to make an animal-face design as shown below.

▶ To make the topping, warm the butter in a pan, add the green onion, and sauté for 1 minute. Add the zucchini and mushrooms and sauté until just tender, about 4 minutes. Season to taste. Preheat the broiler to high.
▶ Lightly toast the muffins or bread. Divide the tomato sauce between each of the cut sides of muffin or bread, spread evenly, and sprinkle with cheese.
▶ Top with cooked vegetables, perhaps making patterns or animal faces, then cook under the broiler until the cheese is bubbling and golden.
▶ To create a mouse face (see right, bottom), use steamed zucchini pieces for the ears, stuffed olive slices for the eyes, a black olive for the nose, strips of carrot for the whiskers, and two sweet corn kernels for the teeth.

▶ To make a bear face (see right, top), use sliced carrot for the ears, oval shapes cut from a slice of cheese, sliced mushrooms sautéed in a little butter and sliced, pitted black olives for the eyes, pitted black olives for the nose and mouth, and fine strips of red pepper for whiskers.

Variation

▶ For a nonvegetarian mini pizza, top with diced ham or, if your child prefers, pepperoni, in addition to, or instead of, the cooked and raw vegetables.

2 **muffins**, split in half, or 1 small **baguette**, cut in half

4 tbsp good **tomato sauce** (homemade or store-bought)

$1/2$ cup grated **cheddar**, **Gruyère**, or **mozzarella cheese**

Topping

1 tbsp **butter**

1 tbsp chopped **green onion**

$1/2$ cup **zucchini**, thinly sliced

$3/4$ cup **mushrooms**, sliced

salt and freshly ground **black pepper**

2/3 cup **basmati rice**

1½ tbsp **vegetable oil**

1 **onion**, peeled and cut into rings

1 **garlic clove**, peeled and crushed

1 cup **baby sweet corn**, cut into quarters

½ cup **carrots**, peeled, sliced thinly, and cut into shapes with a tiny cookie cutter

1 cup **broccoli**, cut into small florets

1 cup **bean sprouts**

½ cup **red pepper**, cored, deseeded, and cut into strips

1 **green onion**, finely chopped

pinch of **black pepper**

Sweet & sour sauce

¾ cup **vegetable stock** (see page 47)

½ tbsp **cornstarch** blended with 1 tbsp **cold water**

2 tsp **soft brown sugar**

½ tbsp **soy sauce**

Sweet & sour vegetable stir-fry

↻ Preparation: 15 minutes; cooking: 15 minutes   ✂ Makes 4 portions

🖊 Provides beta-carotene, fiber, folate, and vitamins C and E

You can encourage your child to eat vegetables by appealing to her visual senses with this colorful stir-fry. It's important to ensure that the vegetables remain crisp to retain their flavor and nutrients.

▶ Rinse the rice, then cook it in boiling, lightly salted water, according to the instructions on the package.

▶ For young children, blanch the carrots and broccoli to make them easier to chew.

▶ Heat the oil in a wok or frying pan. Add the onion and garlic and sauté until softened, about 5 minutes. Add the sweet corn, carrots, and broccoli, and stir-fry for a further 3 minutes.

▶ Add the bean sprouts, red pepper, and green onion and stir-fry for a further 3 minutes. Season with black pepper.

▶ To make the sauce, blend the vegetable stock with the cornstarch paste in a small pan. Mix in the brown sugar and soy sauce. Set over a high heat, bring to a boil, and simmer for about 2 minutes, until the sauce is thickened.

▶ Toss the hot vegetables with the sauce, and heat through in the wok. Serve on a bed of fluffy white rice.

½ lb **firm tofu**, cubed

6 cobs **baby sweet corn**, halved

1 **zucchini**, trimmed and sliced into round chunks

8 **cherry tomatoes**

4 **mini pitas**, split in half

salad leaves, to garnish

Marinade

1½ tbsp **soy sauce**

1½ tbsp **honey**

1½ tbsp **Chinese plum sauce**

1 tbsp **vegetable oil**

1 **green onion**, finely chopped

TIP The sweet corn and zucchini may be parboiled before skewering, if preferred.

Sweet corn, cherry tomato & tofu kebabs

↻ Preparation: 1 hour 5 minutes, including 1 hour marinating; cooking: 6 minutes

✂ Makes 4 portions   🖊 Provides calcium, fiber, folate, omega-3 fats, protein, and vitamins C and E

Tofu (soybean curd) is a nutritious alternative to meat. Although naturally bland, it is delicious marinated because it soaks up flavors well, and its soft texture appeals to children.

▶ Combine the ingredients for the marinade in a small jug. Put the tofu in a shallow bowl and pour on the marinade. Cover and leave to soak for about 1 hour. While the tofu marinates, soak four wooden skewers in water to stop them from burning under the broiler.

▶ Thread the tofu cubes and vegetable pieces alternately onto the skewers. Brush with some of the marinade. Cook under a hot broiler or on the grill for about 3 minutes

on each side, basting occasionally, or until the vegetables are tender and the tofu is nicely browned.

▶ Slide the kebabs off the skewers, arrange in the pita pockets, and garnish with salad leaves.

Annabel's vegetable fritters

⏱ Preparation: 25 minutes; cooking: 10 minutes   ✂ Makes 4 portions

🍴 Provides beta-carotene, calcium, fiber, iron, B vitamins, and vitamins C and E

❄ Suitable for freezing

These fritters are tasty eaten hot or cold and are ideal for a lunchbox or picnic.

▶ Grate the sweet potatoes, squash, and potatoes. Squeeze out some of the excess moisture from the grated pulp.

▶ In a mixing bowl, combine all the vegetables with the parsley, bread crumbs, soy sauce, and beaten egg. Season to taste.

▶ Form the mixture into about 12 walnut-size fritters. Spread the flour out thinly on a plate and use it to coat the fritters lightly.

▶ Heat the oil in a large frying pan, add the fritters, and sauté over a medium heat for 8–10 minutes, turning, until golden on the outside and cooked through.

1$\frac{1}{3}$ cups **sweet potatoes**, peeled

1 cup **butternut squash** or **pumpkin**, peeled

1 cup **potatoes**, peeled

$\frac{3}{4}$ cup **leeks**, white part only, washed and finely chopped

2 cups **mushrooms**, chopped

2 tbsp chopped **fresh parsley**

1$\frac{1}{4}$ cups **fresh bread crumbs**

$\frac{1}{2}$ tbsp **soy sauce**

$\frac{1}{2}$ lightly beaten **egg**

salt and freshly ground **black pepper**

flour for coating

vegetable oil for frying

TIP This recipe is best made with soft white bread crumbs, but you can use whole-wheat bread crumbs.

Vegetarian croquettes

⏱ Preparation: 10 minutes; cooking: 30 minutes   🌡 350°F

✂ Makes 8 portions   🍴 Provides beta-carotene, calcium, fiber, folate, protein, and vitamins B12 and C   ❄ Suitable for freezing

▶ Bring a large pan of lightly salted water to a boil, add the potatoes, and cook until tender. Drain and mash with the butter and seasoning.

▶ Meanwhile, place the vegetables in a steamer and cook until tender, about 6–7 minutes.

▶ Mix into the mashed potatoes and season to taste.

▶ Cut the cheese into eight sticks. Use your hands to shape the potato and vegetable mixture around the cheese to form eight sausage-shaped croquettes.

▶ Roll the croquettes in the crushed potato chips until well coated and place on a baking sheet. Transfer to the preheated oven and bake for 15 minutes.

1 lb **potatoes**, peeled and roughly chopped

pat of **butter**

salt and **white pepper**

$\frac{3}{4}$ cup **broccoli**, cut into small florets

$\frac{2}{3}$ cup **carrots**, peeled and chopped

$\frac{1}{3}$ cup **frozen sweet corn**

$\frac{1}{2}$ cup **cheddar cheese**

1 cup **potato chips**, crushed

Salmon starfish

1 lb **potatoes**, mashed and chilled

2 tbsp **ketchup**

1 tsp **Worcestershire sauce**

1 **egg**, lightly beaten

2 tbsp chopped **chives**

¾ lb cooked **salmon fillets**, flaked

3 tbsp **fresh bread crumbs**, plus extra for coating

a little melted **butter**

TIP These fish cakes can be shallow-fried instead of oven-baked.

⏱ Preparation: 20 minutes; cooking: 8 minutes   🔥 350°F

🍳 Makes 8 portions   📝 Provides omega-3 fats, protein, B vitamins including folate, and vitamin D   ❄ Suitable for freezing

I serve these fish cakes with shredded green-bean "seaweed" and Special tomato sauce (see page 153).

▶ Mash the potatoes with the ketchup, Worcestershire sauce, beaten egg, and chives. Mix in the salmon and 3 tbsp of bread crumbs. Shape the mixture into flat fritters.

▶ Use a large star-shaped cookie cutter to cut eight starfish shapes. Gently pull out the points of the stars.

Coat with bread crumbs and brush with melted butter.

▶ Set the fish cakes on a lightly greased baking sheet. Transfer to the preheated oven and cook for 4 minutes on each side.

Mini golden fish balls

vegetable oil for shallow frying

pat of **butter**

1 **onion**, peeled and finely chopped

1 lb ground or finely chopped **fish**, such as haddock, bream, whiting, cod, or hake

½ cup **carrots**, peeled and finely grated

1 tbsp chopped **fresh parsley**

2 tsp **superfine sugar**

½ lightly beaten **egg**

1 tbsp **flour**

salt and freshly ground **black pepper**

⏱ Preparation: 5 minutes; cooking: 20 minutes   🍳 Makes 8 portions

📝 Provides beta-carotene, protein, B vitamins, and vitamin E   ❄ Suitable for freezing

These fish balls are just the right size for toddlers to pick up. They are not at all fishy and have a slightly sweet taste. Make your own mixture of ground fresh fish in a food processor.

▶ Heat a tbsp of vegetable oil and the butter in a small frying pan. Add the onion and sauté for about 5 minutes, or until just softened.

▶ Put the ground fish in a mixing bowl and stir in the onion, carrots, parsley, sugar, beaten egg, and flour. Season to taste, then form the mixture into about 24 balls, each about the size of a large cherry tomato.

▶ Heat a further 3 tbsp of vegetable oil in the frying pan. Add the fish balls and fry for about 10 minutes, until golden brown all over. Drain on paper towels. Serve with ketchup.

Chicken & tomato sauce with rice

⏱ Preparation: 10 minutes; cooking: 30 minutes   🍴 Makes 6 portions   📈 Provides beta-carotene, protein, B vitamins, and vitamins C and E   ❄ Suitable for freezing

Unlike a real risotto, which needs a lot of attention, this tasty and comforting rice dish is easy to make.

▶ Cook the rice in boiling, lightly salted water, according to the instructions on the package.
▶ Heat the oil in a fairly large saucepan and sauté the onion, garlic, and carrot for 7 to 8 minutes. Add the chopped chicken and sauté, stirring occasionally, until it is cooked through. Add the remaining ingredients except for the peas and cook, covered, for 15 minutes. Add the frozen peas and cook for 3 minutes.
▶ Drain the rice when cooked and mix with the chicken and tomato sauce.

1 cup **long-grain white rice**
2 tbsp **olive oil**
1 **onion,** peeled and chopped
1 **garlic clove,** peeled and crushed
1 medium **carrot,** peeled and diced
1/2 lb **chicken breast fillet**
1 1/4 cups **tomato purée**
1 **chicken stock cube** dissolved in 1/3 cup boiling water
few drops **Worcestershire sauce**
1 tbsp chopped **fresh parsley**
1/2 tsp **superfine sugar**
salt and freshly ground **black pepper**
2/3 cup **frozen peas**

Crunchy chicken fingers

⏱ Preparation: 5 minutes; cooking: 13 minutes   🍴 Makes 2 portions   📈 Provides iron, protein, B vitamins including folate, and vitamin E   ❄ Suitable for freezing: before cooking

Served with a little bowl of ketchup for dunking, these crunchy chicken pieces make a tasty finger food.

▶ Lightly season the flour and put into a plastic bag. Add the chicken pieces and shake until coated.
▶ Dip the chicken fingers in beaten egg, then roll them in the corn flakes.
▶ Heat the oil in a frying pan, add the chicken, and sauté for about 6 minutes on each side, or until crunchy on the outside and cooked through.

salt and freshly ground **black pepper**
1/4 cup **flour**
1 **chicken breast fillet** (about 1/4 lb), cut into 6 strips
1 small **egg,** lightly beaten
1 2/3 cups **corn flakes,** crushed with a rolling pin
2 tbsp **vegetable oil**

Honey chicken

⏱ Preparation: 1 hour 5 minutes, including 1 hour marinating; cooking: 15 minutes
🍴 Makes 2 portions   📈 Provides beta-carotene, potassium, protein, B vitamins including folate, and vitamins C and E

Marinating chicken gives it a wonderful flavor. Use any combination of your child's favorite vegetables to make this recipe.

▶ Mix together the ingredients for the marinade and marinate the chicken for 1 hour or, if you prefer, overnight.
▶ Cook the rice in boiling, lightly salted water according to the instructions on the package, adding the broccoli to the boiling water 5 minutes before the end of the rice cooking time. While the rice is cooking, heat the sunflower oil in a nonstick saucepan.
▶ Drain the marinade from the chicken, remove the garlic, and reserve.
▶ Brown the chicken in the heated oil for about 3 minutes. Add the red pepper and continue to sauté until the chicken and red pepper start to caramelize.
▶ Put the reserved marinade in a small saucepan and bring to a boil. Drain the rice and combine with the chicken, red pepper, and marinade. Season to taste.

1 large **chicken breast fillet** (about 1/2 lb) cut into thin strips
1/2 cup **parboiled** or **basmati rice**
1/2 cup **broccoli,** cut into small florets
1 tbsp **sunflower oil**
3 tbsp **red pepper,** cut into thin strips
salt and freshly grated **black pepper**

Marinade
1 tbsp **olive oil**
1 tbsp **lemon juice**
1 small **garlic clove,** peeled and sliced
1 tbsp **soy sauce**
1 tbsp **honey**
freshly grated **black pepper**

1 **boneless chicken breast** (about $1/4$ lb) and 4 **thighs**, skinned and trimmed, or 2 **chicken breasts**

$1/2$ **red pepper**, cut into chunks

$1/2$ small **onion**, peeled and cut into chunks

4 **mini pitas**, split in half

salad leaves, to garnish

Marinade

1 tbsp **soy sauce**

1 tbsp **honey**

1 tbsp each freshly squeezed **lemon juice** and **orange juice**

1 tsp **vegetable oil**

TIP Add $1/2$ tbsp of sesame seeds to the marinade for extra flavor.

Chicken kebabs with honey & citrus marinade

Preparation: 35 minutes including 30 minutes marinating; cooking: 10 minutes

Makes 4 portions   Provides beta-carotene, iron, protein, B vitamins, and vitamin C

You can use your own choice of vegetables to make these tasty kebabs. Mushrooms and zucchini are a good option.

▶ Combine the marinade ingredients in a bowl. Cut the chicken into small chunks and add to the marinade with the pepper and onion. Cover and leave for at least 30 minutes. Meanwhile, soak four wooden skewers in water to keep them from burning under the broiler.

▶ Preheat the broiler to high. Thread alternate pieces of chicken, pepper, and onion onto the skewers. Transfer to a hot broiler or grill and cook for about 5 minutes on each side, or until they are cooked through and nicely browned. Toast the pita bread.

▶ Slide the kebabs off the skewers, arrange alternate pieces of chicken and vegetable in the pita bread pockets, and garnish with salad leaves.

---

2 tbsp **vegetable oil**

1 large **shallot**, peeled and finely chopped

1 **garlic clove**, peeled and crushed

1 **leek**, washed, trimmed and sliced

1 lb **ground chicken**

1 **carrot**, peeled and diced

$12/3$ cups **canned chopped tomatoes**

$1/2$ cup **water**

1 tsp **superfine sugar**

2 tsp **ketchup**

2 tsp **fresh thyme leaves**

salt and freshly ground **black pepper**

$3/4$ lb **spaghetti** or **tagliatelle**

Chicken bolognese

Preparation: 5 minutes; cooking: 30 minutes   Makes 8 portions

Provides beta-carotene, potassium, protein, B vitamins including folate, and vitamin E

Suitable for freezing

You can use ground chicken or turkey to make a delicious pasta sauce. This version would make a good cannelloni filling. If you don't have fresh thyme, substitute half a teaspoon of dried thyme.

▶ Warm the vegetable oil in a frying pan, add the shallot and garlic, and sauté over a low heat for 2–3 minutes. Add the leek and sauté for about 3 minutes, until it begins to soften.

▶ Add the chicken, breaking it up with a fork so that it does not stick together, and sauté for about 3 minutes. At this stage, you can transfer the cooked chicken to a blender and process for a few seconds so that it has a smoother texture. Add the diced carrot and then stir in the remaining ingredients.

▶ Bring the mixture to a boil and then simmer for about 20 minutes, stirring occasionally, until the vegetables are tender and the chicken is cooked through.

▶ Meanwhile, cook the spaghetti or tagliatelle in boiling, lightly salted water according to the instructions on the package.

▶ Lightly season the chicken bolognese and serve with the pasta.

Lamb meatballs with a sweet & sour sauce

⟳ Preparation: 20 minutes; cooking: 25 minutes ⚬ Makes 8 portions 🖌 Provides iron, protein, B vitamins including folate, vitamin C, and zinc ❄ Suitable for freezing

These light and succulent meatballs in a tangy tomato-based sauce are delicious served with rice or pasta. They also make a good finger food served with ketchup.

▶ Mix together all the ingredients for the meatballs, seasoning to taste, then form the mixture into about 16 small balls. Spread the flour on a plate and use it to coat the meatballs on all sides.
▶ Heat the vegetable oil in a frying pan, then add the meatballs and sauté for 10–15 minutes, turning them occasionally, until browned and almost cooked through.

▶ Meanwhile, mix together all the ingredients for the sauce in a small pan set over a medium-high heat and cook for 4 minutes. Taste and season if necessary.
▶ Pour the sauce over the meatballs in the frying pan and cook over a medium heat for about 10 minutes, or until the sauce has thickened and the meatballs are cooked through.

Meatballs

1/2 lb **ground lamb**

1 **onion**, peeled and finely chopped

1/2 **red pepper**, finely chopped

1 tbsp finely chopped **fresh parsley**

1 small **apple**, peeled and grated

salt and freshly ground **black pepper**

flour for coating

2 tbsp **vegetable oil** for frying

Sweet & sour sauce

1 2/3 cups **canned chopped tomatoes**

1 tbsp **vinegar**

1 tbsp **brown sugar**

1 tbsp **ketchup**

dash of **Worcestershire sauce**

Couscous with ham & peas

⟳ Preparation: 5 minutes; cooking: 10 minutes ⚬ Makes 4 portions
🖌 Provides beta-carotene, potassium, and B vitamins including folate

Couscous is a grain made from wheat and is a staple of Middle Eastern cuisine. You can find it in most supermarkets next to the rice section. Very quick and easy to prepare, it combines well with both savory and sweet foods. This meal can be eaten hot or cold.

▶ Bring the chicken stock to a boil, then pour it over the couscous. Stir with a fork and set aside for about 6 minutes.
▶ Meanwhile, melt the butter in a saucepan and sauté the onion for 2–3 minutes until softened. Add the peas, a generous pinch of sugar, a little salt, and the water. Lower the heat, cover, and cook for 3 minutes more.

▶ Fluff up the couscous with a fork, stir in the onion, peas, and diced ham, and season to taste.

1 cup **chicken stock** (see page 52)

1/2 cup **instant couscous**

1 tbsp **butter**

1/2 small **onion**, peeled and finely chopped

1/2 cup **frozen peas**

pinch of **sugar**

pinch of **salt**

3 1/2 tbsp **water**

1/4 cup diced **ham**

salt and freshly ground **black pepper**

The picky eater

The most rapid rate of growth in a child's life is between birth and one year; then, after the first year, the child's growth slows down dramatically. This is one of the reasons why toddlers become more exacting food critics, with "fads" such as eating only plain pasta, not eating yogurt with chunks, or refusing any dish with visible onions. You will need all your patience at this very trying time. In this chapter, I have put together a selection of favorite recipes with that magical ingredient—"child appeal."

1 Chicken chow mein
A tasty combination of tender marinated chicken strips, crisp stir-fried vegetables, and Chinese noodles. Even confirmed vegetable-haters are often tempted to eat vegetables such as baby sweet corn and sugar-snap peas when they are stir-fried with noodles and soy sauce. (See page 111 for recipe.)

2 Cream of tomato soup
This tasty tomato soup, made with fresh tomatoes, carrots, and onions, is popular with children. Blending vegetables into a soup is a good way to encourage your child to eat more vegetables. (See page 106 for recipe.)

3 Tomato & mascarpone pasta sauce
When all else fails, picky children can usually be relied on to eat pasta. This tomato sauce enriched with mascarpone—Italian cream cheese—is quick and easy to prepare. (See page 107 for recipe.)

Sweet potato & carrot soup with ginger & orange

2 tbsp **vegetable oil**

2 **onions**, peeled and chopped

1 **garlic clove**, peeled and crushed

2 tsp grated fresh **ginger root**

3½ cups **carrots**, peeled and chopped

1½ cups **sweet potatoes**, peeled

1 quart **chicken stock** (see page 52) or **vegetable stock** (see page 47)

3½ tbsp freshly squeezed **orange juice**

salt and freshly ground **black pepper**

⅓ cup **coconut cream** or **coconut milk**

chopped **parsley** to garnish

Preparation: 10 minutes; cooking: 30 minutes   Makes 6 portions

Provides beta-carotene, folate, potassium, and vitamins C and E   Suitable for freezing

▶ Heat the oil in a large pan and sauté the onions and garlic for about 5 minutes or until softened.

▶ Chop the carrots and sweet potatoes. Add the grated ginger, carrots, and sweet potatoes to the pan and cook for about 5 minutes, stirring occasionally. Add the stock, cover and simmer for 20 minutes, or until the vegetables are tender.

▶ Purée the soup in a food processor or blender. Stir in the orange juice and season to taste. Then swirl in the coconut cream and garnish with chopped parsley to serve.

Cream of tomato soup

2 tbsp **olive oil**

1 **onion**, peeled and diced

1⅔ cups **carrots**, peeled and diced

1 lb ripe **plum tomatoes**, skinned and roughly chopped

⅔ cup **tomato purée**

1¾ cups **chicken stock** (see page 52) or **vegetable stock** (see page 47)

1 **bay leaf**

sprig of **fresh thyme**

⅓ cup **heavy cream**

salt and freshly ground **black pepper**

Preparation: 10 minutes; cooking: 45 minutes   Makes 5 portions

Provides beta-carotene, potassium and vitamins A, C and E   Suitable for freezing

A really good homemade tomato soup is usually a hit with children. Pour this one into a thermos flask with a top that doubles as a mug, and take it along on your cold-weather excursions.

▶ Heat the oil in a large saucepan. Sauté the onion and carrots for 5–6 minutes. Stir in the tomatoes, tomato purée, stock, bay leaf, and thyme and bring to a simmer. Cover and cook for 35–40 minutes.

▶ Remove the bay leaf and the stalk from the thyme, returning the thyme leaves to the pot. Blend in a food processor until smooth. Stir in the cream, and season with salt and pepper.

Cream of chicken soup with sweetcorn

½ cup **chicken stock** (see page 52)

1 **bay leaf**

2 skinless, boneless **chicken breasts** (about ¾ lb)

3 tbsp **butter**

1 stalk **celery**, chopped

1 **onion**, peeled and chopped

⅓ cup **flour**

1¼ cups **hot milk**

1¾ cups **canned sweet corn**

salt and freshly ground **black pepper**

TIP This tasty and nutritious soup is a meal in itself. Serve with carrot and cucumber sticks and fresh bread.

Preparation: 10 minutes; cooking: 35 minutes   Makes 6 portions   Provides potassium, protein, B vitamins including folate, and vitamin C   Suitable for freezing

▶ Bring the stock and bay leaf to a simmer and place the chicken breasts in the stock. Simmer for 10 minutes. Remove the chicken with a slotted spoon and set aside until cool enough to handle. Reserve the stock and bay leaf.

▶ Melt the butter in a large saucepan and cook the celery and onion for 6–7 minutes. Stir in the flour and cook for 1–2 minutes. Pour in the hot milk and stir until thickened. Add the stock and bay leaf and bring to a simmer.

▶ Tear the cooked chicken into pieces and add to the pan. Simmer for 10–15 minutes, adding the sweet corn for the last 3 minutes. Season with pepper.

▶ Remove the bay leaf and blend in a food processor or blender. For a smoother texture, push the mixture through a sieve or purée in a food mill.

Macaroni & cheese

⟳ Preparation: 10 minutes; cooking: 12 minutes 🌡 350°F 🍴 Makes 6 portions
🥄 Provides calcium, protein, B vitamins, and vitamin A ❄ Suitable for freezing

When all else fails, most picky eaters can be relied upon to eat pasta with grated cheese. Here's a slight variation that should have nearly universal appeal. The crunchy ciabatta topping is optional.

▶ Cook the macaroni until *al dente* (still slightly firm to the bite). Melt the butter in a saucepan and stir in the flour. Cook for 1–2 minutes, stirring continuously.
▶ Gradually add the milk, bring to a simmer, and cook until thickened. Add the cheese and mustard and stir until the cheese has melted. Mix in the macaroni, season to taste, and transfer to an ovenproof dish.
▶ Mix the crumbled ciabatta with the olive oil and Parmesan cheese. Sprinkle over the top of the pasta and bake in the preheated oven for 10 minutes.

½ lb **macaroni**

2 tbsp **butter**

¼ cup **flour**

1¾ cups **milk**

⅔ cup grated **cheddar cheese**

⅔ cup grated **Gruyère cheese**

½ tsp **ground dry mustard**

salt and freshly ground **black pepper**

½ cup **ciabatta loaf crumbs** or **toasted white bread crumbs**

½ tbsp **olive oil**

2 tbsp freshly grated **Parmesan cheese**

Tomato & mascarpone pasta sauce

⟳ Preparation: 5 minutes; cooking: 20 minutes 🍴 Makes 4 portions
🥄 Provides beta-carotene, potassium, and vitamins A, B12 and E ❄ Suitable for freezing

Penne goes well with this creamy tomato sauce. Some children don't like to see green things in the sauce, so you can leave out the basil and use a fourth of a teaspoon of mixed herbs instead.

▶ Heat the olive oil in a saucepan and sauté the onion and garlic for 7–8 minutes. Stir in the tomato purée and sugar, and simmer for 10 minutes with the lid on, stirring occasionally.
▶ Remove from the heat, add the basil, and blend in a food processor. Return to the pan and add the mascarpone. Stir until melted and simmer for 1–2 minutes. Season to taste.

1 tbsp **olive oil**

1 **red onion**, peeled and chopped

1 **garlic clove**, peeled and crushed

1⅔ cups **tomato purée**

pinch of **sugar**

2 tbsp torn **basil leaves**

½ cup **mascarpone** or **cream cheese**

salt and freshly ground **black pepper**

Spaghetti bolognese

⟳ Preparation: 8 minutes; cooking: 27 minutes 🍴 Makes 6 portions
🥄 Provides beta-carotene, iron, potassium, protein, B vitamins, vitamins C and E, and zinc
❄ Suitable for freezing: sauce only

▶ Heat the oil in a saucepan, stir in the onion, garlic, and carrot, and sauté for 2 minutes. Add the ground beef and cook for about 5 minutes until browned. For a smoother consistency, transfer the sautéed meat and vegetables to a food processor and chop for a few seconds.
▶ Stir in the chopped tomatoes, milk, bay leaf, thyme, salt, and pepper. Cover and simmer for 15–20 minutes.
▶ Meanwhile, cook the pasta in boiling, lightly salted water according to the instructions on the package. Drain and mix with the sauce. If the sauce is too thick, you can add a little of the pasta cooking water to thin it out.

1 tbsp **olive oil**

1 **onion**, peeled and chopped

1 **garlic clove**, peeled and crushed

1 medium **carrot**, peeled and grated

¾ lb **lean ground beef**

2¼ cups **canned chopped tomatoes**

½ cup **milk**

1 **bay leaf**

1 tsp **fresh thyme leaves** or ½ tsp **dried thyme**

salt and freshly ground **black pepper**

½ lb **spaghetti**

1 medium **sweet potato,** scrubbed

1 tbsp **oil**

salt

Sweet potato oven wedges

Preparation: 5 minutes; cooking: 40 minutes ◉ 400°F

Makes 2 portions ✎ Provides potassium and vitamins C and E

▶ Cut the sweet potato lengthwise into wedges. Place on a baking tray and lightly brush with the oil. Season with a little salt and bake in the preheated oven for 35–40 minutes, turning occasionally until soft inside and golden brown on the outside.

1 lb **zucchini**

salt and freshly ground **black pepper**

$1/2$ cup **flour**

$1/3$ cup **cornstarch**

1 tsp **salt**

$2/3$ cup **ice-cold water**

vegetable oil for frying

TIP You can cook other vegetables in this batter—try sweet potatoes, cauliflower, or broccoli.

Zucchini fritters

Preparation: 10 minutes; cooking: 10 minutes ◉ Makes 4 portions

✎ Provides fiber, folate, magnesium, and potassium

Try these if your child isn't eager to eat vegetables. They are delicious and were very popular with my tasting panel—even the confirmed veggie haters.

▶ Wash and dry the zucchini and trim off the ends. Cut into sticks about $2^1/2$ inches long and $1/2$ inch wide, and season with a little salt and pepper.
▶ In a bowl, mix together the flour, cornstarch, salt, and pepper. Stir in the ice-cold water until the mixture is slightly thicker than the consistency of heavy cream.
▶ Heat the oil in a deep-fat fryer to 400°F. Alternatively, use a wok or deep

frying pan filled to about $2^1/2$ inches with oil. You can tell when the oil is hot enough for frying if a piece of vegetable sizzles as it touches it.
▶ Dip the zucchini sticks into the batter and fry them until crispy and golden. Don't fry too many at a time or you will reduce the temperature of the oil. Lift out the basket or remove the zucchini fritters with a slotted spoon. Drain on paper towels and serve immediately.

1 lb **carrots,** peeled and thinly sliced

1 small **onion,** peeled and finely chopped

3 tbsp **butter**

$2^1/2$ tbsp **flour**

$1^1/4$ cups **milk**

$1/2$ cup grated **Gruyère cheese**

salt and **white pepper**

1 tbsp chopped **fresh parsley**

$2^1/2$ cups **corn flakes,** crushed

Carrots with a crunchy corn-flake topping

Preparation: 10 minutes; cooking: 30 minutes ◉ 350°F

Makes 4 portions ✎ Provides beta-carotene, calcium, iron, protein, B vitamins including folate, and vitamins A and D

Surprisingly, carrots are more nutritious eaten cooked than raw. This is because the cooking process helps our bodies to absorb the beta-carotene.

▶ Cook the sliced carrots in lightly salted water (or steam) until just tender.
▶ Meanwhile, sauté the chopped onion in half the butter until softened. Remove from the heat, stir in the flour, and cook for 1 minute. Gradually whisk in the milk. Return to the heat and stir until thickened and smooth. Take off the heat and stir in

the cheese until melted. Season to taste.
▶ Combine the cooked carrots and parsley with the cheese sauce, and spoon into a suitable ovenproof dish. Melt the remaining butter and stir in the crushed corn flakes. Arrange the corn flakes over the carrots and cook in the preheated oven for 20 minutes.

Tuna melt

⟳ Preparation: 5 minutes; cooking: 2 minutes ⚔ Makes 2 portions
⚕ Provides iron, potassium, protein, B vitamins including folate, and vitamins A, D, and E

▶ Preheat the broiler to high. Mix the tuna, mayonnaise, green onion, and lemon juice. Toast the bread and spread with a little butter or margarine. Divide the tuna filling between the two slices of bread. Cover with the cheese slices.
▶ Place under the broiler until the cheese begins to melt and turn golden. Cut each sandwich into squares, fingers, or triangles, or serve on toasted muffins.

3½ oz **canned tuna in oil**, drained
1½ tbsp **mayonnaise**
1 tbsp finely sliced **green onion**
1 tsp **lemon juice**
2 slices **whole-wheat bread** or **English muffin**, toasted
butter or **margarine**
2 slices **Emmental** or **Gruyère cheese** (about ⅓ cup)

Honey & soy salmon skewers

⟳ Preparation: 1 hour 10 minutes, including 1 hour marinating; cooking: 5 minutes
⚔ Makes 2 portions ⚕ Provides omega-3 fats, potassium, protein, B vitamins, and vitamins D and E

This is a really delicious way to cook salmon, and the marinade makes a glossy, caramelized coating. Serve the kebabs with rice.

▶ Mix together the ingredients for the marinade in a shallow dish and stir in the cubes of salmon, making sure they are well coated. Leave to marinate for about 1 hour, turning occasionally. Meanwhile, soak two bamboo skewers in water to stop them from burning under the broiler.
▶ Preheat the broiler to high. Line a broiler pan with foil, thread the cubes of salmon onto the skewers, and place on the foil. Brush the salmon with the marinade and broil for about 5 minutes, basting with the marinade and turning occasionally, until golden on the outside but still moist and juicy inside.
▶ Put the remaining marinade in a small pan and simmer for a few minutes until reduced. Serve the kebabs with rice, and spoon the reduced marinade over the salmon.

¼ lb **salmon fillet**, skinned and cut into ¾-inch cubes

Marinade
1 tbsp **honey**
1 tbsp **soy sauce**
1 tbsp **light olive oil** or **vegetable oil**

TIP Ensure you remove the skewers before giving the salmon cubes to toddlers.

1 tbsp **olive oil**

1 large **onion**, peeled

1 **garlic clove**, peeled and crushed

1½ slices **white bread**

3 tbsp **milk**

¾ lb **chicken breast fillets**
or **ground chicken**

1 small **egg**, lightly beaten

4 tbsp **ketchup**

1 tsp **Worcestershire sauce**

2 tbsp chopped **fresh parsley**

½ tbsp **fresh thyme** (optional)

salt and freshly ground **black pepper**

1⅓ cups **canned sweet corn**,
drained

vegetable oil for frying

Diana's chicken & sweet corn fritters

🕐 Preparation: 15 minutes; cooking: 10 minutes   ✎ Makes 18 fritters

🖊 Provides iron, potassium, protein, B vitamins including folate, and vitamin C

❄ Suitable for freezing

My friend Diana, who comes from Russia, gave me this recipe. These mini fritters are popular and easy for little children to eat with their fingers. It's a good idea to make up the mixture and then cook one fritter to test; you can then add extra ketchup, herbs, or seasoning, according to taste, before you cook the rest.

▶ Heat the olive oil in a pan and sauté the onion with the garlic until softened but not golden brown. Soak the bread in the milk.

▶ Place the chicken in a food processor. If using chicken breasts, cut into chunks first, then chop for a few seconds. Tear the soaked bread into pieces and add to the chicken along with the beaten egg, ketchup, Worcestershire sauce, parsley, thyme (if using), and salt and pepper. Blend for a few seconds.

▶ Transfer the chicken to a bowl and stir in the sweet corn. At this stage, you can put the mixture in the refrigerator until you are ready to cook it—leave it there overnight if you wish.

▶ Form the mixture into 18 small rounds—it will be quite sticky, so it is helpful to use a wet spoon to shape the rounds. Sauté in vegetable oil until golden and cooked through.

▶ Serve with homemade ketchup (see below).

1 small **chicken breast fillet**
(about ¼ lb)

a little **vegetable oil**

Marinade

¾ tbsp **honey**

1 tbsp **lemon juice**

1 tbsp **soy sauce**

1 tsp light **olive oil**

ground **black pepper**

slice of **garlic** (optional)

Ketchup

1½ cups **tomato purée**

1 tbsp **balsamic vinegar**

1 tbsp **tomato paste**

1 tbsp **brown sugar**

Tender strips of griddled chicken & homemade ketchup

🕐 Preparation: 32 minutes, including 30 minutes to marinate; cooking: 15 minutes

✎ Makes 2 portions   🖊 Provides potassium, protein, B vitamins including folate, and vitamins C and E   ❄ Suitable for freezing

This is a delicious way to eat chicken and much healthier for your child than chicken nuggets.

▶ In a bowl, mix together all the ingredients for the marinade, add the chicken breast, and leave to marinate for about 30 minutes.

▶ Drain the marinade and reserve.

▶ Heat the griddle, brush it with a little oil, and cook the chicken for 4–5 minutes on each side or until cooked. (If you don't have a griddle, you can heat a little vegetable oil in a saucepan and sauté the chicken breast).

▶ Meanwhile, strain the marinade, pour it into a small saucepan, bring to a boil, and simmer for about 1 minute.

▶ Cut the chicken into strips and serve with the reduced marinade.

▶ To make the ketchup, put all the ingredients into a saucepan. Bring to a boil, then reduce the heat and cook, uncovered, for about 15 minutes.

Chicken chow mein

⟳ Preparation: 10 minutes; cooking: 18 minutes   ✎ Makes 6 portions   ✐ Provides beta-carotene, potassium, protein, B vitamins including folate, and vitamins C and E

"Chow mein" means stir-fried noodles. Shiitake mushrooms have a wonderful flavor but can sometimes be difficult to obtain. If you cannot find them, use button or cremini mushrooms instead.

▶ Mix together the ingredients for the marinade and marinate the chicken for 10 minutes. Strain and reserve the marinade. Cook the noodles in boiling, lightly salted water according to the instructions on the package, then set aside.

▶ Heat the vegetable oil in a wok or large frying pan and stir-fry the chicken for 5–6 minutes. Remove the chicken and set aside.

▶ Heat the sesame oil in the wok. Add the garlic and stir-fry for a few seconds. Add the shiitake mushrooms, sugar-snap peas, red pepper, and baby corn and cook for 4 minutes, stirring occasionally. Add the green onions, zucchini, and bean sprouts and continue to cook for 4 minutes, stirring occasionally.

▶ Add the chicken and noodles together with the reserved marinade. Stir-fry for 1–2 minutes or until the noodles are completely heated through.

1 large **chicken breast fillet** (about $1/2$ lb)

$1/4$ lb **fine Chinese egg noodles**

1 tbsp **vegetable oil**

$1 1/2$ tbsp **sesame oil**

1 **garlic clove,** peeled and crushed

$1 1/3$ cups **shiitake mushrooms**

$1 1/4$ cups **sugar-snap peas**

$1/2$ small **red pepper,** cut into thin strips

$1/2$ cup **baby sweet corn,** cut into quarters

4 **green onions,** finely sliced

1 cup **zucchini**

1 cup **bean sprouts**

Marinade

2 tbsp **soy sauce**

2 tbsp **sake (rice wine)**

1 tbsp **soft brown sugar**

½ cup **unsalted butter**

½ cup **granulated sugar**

½ cup **light brown sugar**

1 **egg**

1 tsp **vanilla extract**

1 cup **flour**

¼ tsp each of **cinnamon, ground cloves, ground nutmeg, allspice**

½ tsp **baking powder**

¼ tsp **baking soda**

¼ tsp **salt**

1 cup **quick oats**

1 cup **raisins**

Raisin & oatmeal cookies

Preparation: 20 minutes; cooking: 10 minutes   375°F
Makes 22 cookies   Provides fiber, iron, and potassium   Suitable for freezing

▶ Cream together the butter and sugars in an electric mixer or by hand. Beat in the egg and vanilla extract.
▶ Sift together the flour, spices, baking powder, baking soda, and salt. Add to the mixture and beat until combined. Stir in the oats and raisins.
▶ Lightly grease two baking sheets. Using your hands, form the dough into about 22 walnut-size balls. Put them on the baking sheets, widely spaced, and flatten them down a little.
▶ Put the cookies in the preheated oven and bake for about 12 minutes, or until lightly golden all over. Transfer to a wire rack and leave to cool.

---

2 cups **bran flakes**

1¼ cups **milk**

1 cup **whole-wheat flour**

½ tsp **salt**

1 tbsp **baking powder**

4 tbsp **butter**

⅓ cup **superfine sugar**

1 **egg**

2 **bananas,** peeled and mashed

½ cup **raisins**

Banana muffins

Preparation: 15 minutes; cooking: 30 minutes   350°F
Makes 12 muffins   Provides fiber, iron, and B vitamins including folate
Suitable for freezing

These muffins are full of good natural ingredients. They make superb portable food and can be eaten on the run if there's no time for a sit-down breakfast.

▶ Soak the bran flakes in the milk for 10 minutes. Sift together the flour, salt, and baking powder.
▶ Cream together the butter and sugar, then beat in the egg. Stir in alternate spoonfuls of soaked bran flakes and flour mixture. Gently fold in the mashed bananas and the raisins.
▶ Line a muffin pan with paper liners and half-fill each one with mixture. Bake in the preheated oven for 30 minutes.

½ cup **coconut milk**

½ cup **pineapple juice**

1 small **banana,** peeled and chopped

1 tsp **honey**

Pineapple, coconut & banana smoothie

Preparation: 3 minutes   Makes 2 glasses   Provides potassium and vitamins C and B6

Fruit smoothies and milkshakes make tasty and nutritious drinks.

▶ Place the coconut milk, pineapple juice, and chopped banana in a hand-held blender with the honey. Blend together until smooth.

Variations
▶ Add peeled ripe flesh of half a mango or one juicy ripe peach.
▶ Blend together 1½ cups pineapple juice, ⅓ cup coconut milk, 3 scoops vanilla ice cream, and 1 cup fresh pineapple.

Summer berry milkshake

⟳ Preparation: 5 minutes   ✂ Makes 2 glasses   ⚡ Provides calcium, potassium, protein, and vitamins B2, B12, and C (plus other nutrients depending on fruits used)

1½ cups frozen or fresh **summer fruits** or **berries**

2 tbsp **confectioner's sugar**

⅓ cup **raspberry drinking yogurt** or ⅔ cup **mixed berry yogurt**

¾ cup **milk**

▶ Blend together the berries and confectioner's sugar and then press through a sieve. Mix together with the yogurt and milk.

Frozen yogurt with fresh berries

⟳ Preparation: 20 minutes   ✂ Makes 4 portions   ⚡ Provides calcium, folate, potassium, protein, and vitamins A, B2, B12, C, and E

2 cups full-fat **natural yogurt**

⅔ cup **heavy cream**

½ cup **superfine sugar**

⅔ cup **strawberries**, hulled and quartered

¾ cup **blackberries**

⅔ cup **blueberries**

¾ cup **raspberries**

Raspberry coulis

2 cups **fresh** or **frozen raspberries**

2 tbsp sifted **confectioner's sugar**

▶ Mix together the yogurt, cream, and sugar and freeze and churn the mixture in an ice-cream maker. Alternatively, put into a plastic container and freeze for about 1½ hours. Remove from the freezer, transfer to a food processor, and blend until smooth, or simply stir thoroughly to remove ice particles. Freeze for another hour, blend again in the food processor, or stir once again, and then return to the freezer.

▶ To make the raspberry coulis, purée fresh raspberries, then press through a sieve to remove the seeds, and stir in the confectioner's sugar. If using frozen raspberries, heat them in a saucepan until mushy before puréeing them.
▶ Mix the fresh berries with the raspberry coulis and divide between four bowls. Serve scoops of the frozen yogurt on top of the berries and coulis.

2 to 3 years

Mock fried egg: vanilla yogurt with half an apricot on top becomes a simple visual joke.

Savory dip: a colorful array of vegetable and bread sticks has instant appeal.

Shepherd's pie: make a mini portion in a ramekin and let your child decorate it as she wishes.

Remember

• Don't make your child wait too long for a meal once she has announced she is hungry: she cannot yet wait patiently and may become irritable.

• Encourage a taste for foods that are not high in sugar. If sugar is kept to a minimum now, she is much less likely to develop a sweet tooth later.

• Leave snacks of sliced fruit or vegetable sticks on a low shelf in the refrigerator so your child can help herself when hungry.

Early childhood

Children in this age group are often highly appreciative of their food, especially when it has the lively presentation of a party spread. It's surprising how quiet a group of two- to three-year-olds can be around a table of edible goodies. Others are more erratic and selective. Whatever your child's eating habits, she will enjoy spending time in the kitchen with you, joining in with your cooking activities.

Eating for an active day

Two- and three-year-olds are highly active and often appear, if not thin, at least leggy. Your child will still need frequent small meals to meet her high energy requirements, and there may be times when she seems to need a rapid energy "fix" to keep her from becoming overtired (see page 89). Sugar and carbohydrates from refined sources (such as soda or cookies) are quickly broken down into glucose and provide an instant pick-me-up, but fruit or fruit juice are healthier sources of an energy boost. Unrefined carbohydrate foods, such as whole-wheat bread and pasta, take longer to break down into glucose, but provide a more sustained energy supply.

Making mealtimes work

By the age of two, your child will be able to sit on a secured booster seat at the table with you, and she will be eating very much what the rest of the family eats, though perhaps at different times. It is important, however, to keep her company at mealtimes if she is having her dinner before the rest of the family. Leaving her sitting alone at the table, even if you are in the same room, is bound to lead to trouble as she fights for your attention. Aim to

TIPS ON HOW TO HELP CHILDREN WHO ARE OVERWEIGHT

• Adopt a healthier eating pattern as a family instead of cutting down on the food offered to your child. Don't buy foods that you don't want her to eat.

• Serve less processed fatty food and more complex carbohydrates (brown rice, potatoes, whole-wheat bread), fruit and vegetables, low-fat dairy foods, and fish, chicken, or lean meat.

• Try to avoid fried food—broil or bake instead. Put only a scrape of butter or margarine on bread.

• Encourage your child to eat more vegetables—make stir-fries, vegetable soups, hidden vegetable tomato sauce, and raw vegetables with dip.

• Give your child plenty of fresh fruit— add fruit to breakfast cereals, make fruit smoothies and fresh fruit kebabs, and give fresh fruit for dessert.

• Encourage the drinking of water instead of juice or carbonated drinks. Low-fat milk can be introduced from two years if the child is eating a varied diet.

• Cut out between-meal snacks of chips or cookies and give healthy foods such as mini sandwiches or cottage cheese and fruit instead.

encourage her enjoyment of food: try to include her in the family's lunch or evening meal as often as possible. Don't feel obligated to make novelty foods all the time, but do think about giving everyday meals some "child appeal." Without spending more than a few moments, a simple plate of food can be made to appeal to a child's sense of form and color; fresh fruit arranged in a pattern will bring a smile to her face and stimulate her interest.

Cooking: a new activity

You can encourage your child's interest in food by involving her in its preparation. Children often take great pride in helping to set the table and knead dough or mix ingredients, and can be fascinated by the ordinary tasks that adults take for granted: just think how many ways there are to prepare an egg, or how ingredients change shape, texture, and color if heated or frozen. All of this is a new experience for your child. As long as you keep her away from sharp knives or electrical equipment, there are plenty of supervised activities she can take part in, from breaking eggs into a bowl to cutting out cookies or biscuits with shaped cutters. There are simple recipes in this book that would be ideal for your child to help you make. Try Mini pizzas (page 97), Cheesy bread animals (page 120), Character mini cakes (page 128), Shortbread cookies (page 131), and Chewy apricot & chocolate cereal bars (page 179).

"Let your child feel free to experiment with rolling dough and cutting out interesting cookie shapes."

Fun foods

By the time your child reaches her second birthday, she should regularly be joining in family meals and continuing to broaden her tastes. This is an excellent time to encourage an active interest in food, perhaps by allowing her to participate in fun, simple cooking activities, or to help choose favorite dishes for a birthday party with friends. Plan a party around a theme, perhaps serving foods with different distinctive shapes, or using foods of certain colors. Always bring out the healthier savory dishes before you serve the sweet things.

1 Open sandwiches
Daintily cut open sandwiches make easy finger foods for small children. These sandwiches are spread with butter or cream cheese, then topped with cucumber or tomato slices, squares of mild cheese or ham, or rosettes of smoked turkey. (See page 95 for recipe.)

2 Heart-shaped chicken nuggets
These chicken and apple patties, with their moist interior and crunchy coating, will be an instant hit with children. (See page 125 for recipe.)

3 Annabel's pasta salad
A dish of multicolored pasta with plenty of vegetable chunks and a lively dressing should appeal to both small children and any accompanying parents. (See page 122 for recipe.)

4 Present cake
Bold and bright birthday sponge cakes shaped to look like wrapped gifts make superb centerpieces. (See page 129 for recipe.)

1 tbsp **olive oil**

1 **garlic clove**, peeled and crushed

1 **onion**, peeled and chopped

1/2 cup **carrots**, peeled and diced

1 2/3 cups **canned chopped tomatoes** or 8 **fresh tomatoes**

1 tbsp **tomato purée**

2 1/2 cups **vegetable stock** (see page 47)

2 slices **white bread**, shredded

salt and freshly ground **black pepper**

pinch of **sugar**

2 tbsp torn **fresh basil leaves**

Tomato soup

Preparation: 10 minutes; cooking: 26 minutes   Makes 8 portions

Provides beta-carotene, folate, and potassium   Suitable for freezing

This quick tomato soup recipe differs from the one on page 106 because it is dairy-free and soothing for children when they're sick. I prefer to use canned tomatoes, since so many store-bought fresh tomatoes lack flavor, but if you have ripe, full-flavored, medium-size tomatoes, you can use them instead.

▶ Warm the olive oil in a large pan over a low heat, add the garlic, onion, and carrots, and sauté for 10 minutes.

▶ Add the remaining ingredients except for the basil. Simmer for 10 minutes, stirring occasionally, until all the vegetables are soft.

▶ Stir in the basil and simmer for a further 5 minutes. Purée the mixture using a blender.

---

2 cups **flour**, plus more to dust

pinch of **salt**

1/2 tbsp **fast-acting dried yeast**

1/2 tsp **honey**

pinch of **cayenne pepper**

1 tsp **ground dry mustard**

about 2/3 cup **warm water**

1/2 cup grated **cheddar cheese**

2 tbsp freshly grated **Parmesan cheese**

To decorate

1 **egg**, beaten

raisins

sesame seeds

poppy seeds

grated **cheddar cheese**

Cheesy bread animals

Preparation: 1 hour 30 minutes, including 1 hour rising; cooking: 20 minutes

400°F   Makes 6 bread rolls   Provides calcium, protein, and vitamin B12

Suitable for freezing

Children adore making bread, and they will have great fun forming this delicious, cheesy bread into animal shapes.

▶ Sift the flour and salt into a mixing bowl. Stir in the yeast, honey, cayenne pepper, and mustard and just enough of the water to form a soft dough.

▶ Transfer to a floured surface and knead lightly for about 5 minutes to make a smooth, pliable dough. Gradually knead the grated cheeses into the dough (this will produce a slightly streaky effect).

▶ Shape the dough into six animal figures and transfer to a floured baking sheet. Cover them loosely with a clean towel and leave to rise in a warm place for about 1 hour, or until doubled in size.

▶ Brush with beaten egg and add raisins for eyes. Sprinkle the tops with sesame seeds, poppy seeds, or grated cheese. Transfer to the preheated oven and bake for 20 minutes, or until golden brown. The underside should sound hollow when tapped. Leave on a wire rack to cool.

Variation

▶ To make cheese and onion bread rolls, add 1 tbsp of finely chopped green onion to the dough after adding the grated cheeses.

Mini baked potatoes with filling

⟳ Preparation: 10 minutes; cooking: 45 minutes   🔥 400°F

✂ Makes 6 portions   ⚡ Provides folate, protein, and vitamin B12 (cranberry & turkey filling); folate, protein, and vitamin B12 (tuna & sweet corn filling); fiber, folate, potassium, and protein (barbecue bean filling)   ❄ Suitable for freezing: undecorated only

Small baked potatoes look especially attractive when made into little sailing ships decorated with a cheese sail and a red-pepper flag. Each of the fillings suggested here is sufficient for three potatoes.

▶ Wash the potatoes, pat dry, prick with a fork, brush with oil, and sprinkle with sea salt. Place in the preheated oven and bake for about 40 minutes, or until crispy on the outside and tender inside (test with a skewer). Preheat the broiler to high.
▶ Cut the potatoes in half, scoop out the flesh into a bowl, and mash thoroughly. Mix the ingredients from your chosen topping with the mashed potato, then spoon the mixture back into the skins.

For a simple grated cheese topping, just sprinkle a little over each of the potatoes.
▶ Place the potatoes under the broiler (they can be arranged in a muffin tray to keep them upright). Heat for a few minutes, or just until lightly golden on top. If desired, decorate the potatoes as boats, securing the cheese sails and red pepper flags with cocktail sticks.

3 small **baking potatoes**

oil for brushing

sea salt

grated **cheddar cheese** (optional)

Cranberry & turkey filling

1 tsp **cranberry sauce**

1 tbsp **creamy peanut butter**

1 tsp **milk**

$^1\!/_2$ cup shredded **turkey**

Tuna & sweet corn filling

$^1\!/_3$ cup cooked **frozen** or **canned sweet corn**

2 tbsp **mayonnaise**

2 oz **canned tuna**, flaked and drained

1 **green onion**, finely sliced

freshly ground **black pepper**

1 tbsp grated **cheddar cheese**

Bean filling

1 cup **baked beans** seasoned with **Worcestershire sauce**

1 tbsp grated **cheddar cheese**

To decorate

cheddar cheese slices, cut into 6 triangles

red pepper slice, cut to make 6 flag shapes

6 **cocktail sticks**

NOTE If decorating, remove the cocktail sticks when serving.

Thousand Island salad dressing

⟳ Preparation: 2 minutes   ✂ Makes 4 portions

⚡ Provides calcium and vitamins B12 and E

This versatile dressing goes well with a green salad, or sliced tomatoes and avocado. You could add 1 tbsp of finely chopped parsley to garnish.

▶ Simply blend all the ingredients together, transfer to a clean container, and refrigerate, or whisk thoroughly and use immediately.

6 tbsp mild, full-fat **natural yogurt**

3 tbsp **mayonnaise**

3 tbsp **ketchup**

$^1\!/_2$ tsp **Worcestershire sauce**

salt and freshly ground **black pepper**

½ lb **pasta bows (farfalle)**

¾ cup **green beans**

⅔ cup **canned** or **frozen sweet corn**

½ cup **carrots**, peeled and grated

4 **cherry tomatoes**, quartered

Dressing

3 tbsp **onion**, peeled and grated

4 tbsp **vegetable oil**

1 tbsp **white wine vinegar**

2 tbsp **water**

½ tsp chopped **fresh ginger root**

1 tbsp **celery**, chopped

1 tbsp **soy sauce**

1½ tsp **tomato purée**

1 tsp **superfine sugar**

salt and freshly ground **black pepper**

Annabel's pasta salad

Preparation: 10 minutes; cooking: 12 minutes   Makes 4 portions   Provides beta-carotene, fiber, folate, protein (especially when tuna or chicken is added), and vitamin E

This salad's delicious dressing is popular with my children as a dip for raw vegetables (I make up a big bottle of it to keep in the refrigerator). The salad is great for lunchboxes, picnics, or as a side dish served warm or cold. Use three-color pasta if possible.

▶ Cook the pasta in boiling, lightly salted water according to the instructions on the package.

▶ Meanwhile, put the beans in a steamer and cook for 4 minutes. Add the sweet corn to the steamer and cook for 3–4 minutes, or until tender.

▶ Combine all the ingredients for the dressing in a blender or food processor, adding only a little salt and pepper, and process until smooth.

▶ Combine the cooked pasta with the steamed vegetables, grated carrots, and cherry tomatoes, and toss with some of the dressing.

Variation

Add ¼ cup diced cucumber and ½ cup diced cold chicken or tuna, and vary the vegetables according to taste.

½ lb **penne**

2 tbsp **olive oil**

1 **red onion**, peeled and chopped

4 **plum tomatoes**, quartered, deseeded, and roughly chopped

7 oz **canned tuna in oil**, drained

⅓ cup **sun-dried tomatoes**, chopped

1 tsp **balsamic vinegar**

⅔ cup **canned** or **frozen sweet corn**

small handful **basil leaves**, torn

salt and freshly ground **black pepper**

Penne with tuna, tomato & sweet corn

Preparation: 5 minutes; cooking: 10 minutes   Makes 4 portions   Provides fiber, iron, protein, B vitamins, and vitamin D

A simple, tasty pasta dish, this can be rustled up using mainly ingredients that you keep in your pantry.

▶ Cook the pasta in boiling, lightly salted water according to the instructions on the package.

▶ Heat the olive oil in a frying pan and sauté the onion for about 6 minutes, stirring occasionally until softened.

▶ Stir in the fresh tomatoes and cook for 2–3 minutes until heated through and beginning to soften.

▶ Add the tuna, sun-dried tomatoes, balsamic vinegar, sweet corn, and basil. Season and heat for 1 minute before stirring into the pasta.

Pasta with zucchini, peppers & sausage

⟳ Preparation: 10 minutes; cooking: 18 minutes ⌀ Makes 4 portions
🥄 Provides beta-carotene, fiber, folate, protein, and vitamin B12

1 tbsp **vegetable oil**

1 small **onion**, peeled and sliced

1/2 cup **red peppers**, cut into diamond shapes

1 cup **zucchini**, sliced

1 1/4 cups **tomato purée**

1/2 **chicken stock cube**, finely crumbled

1/4 lb **pasta bows (farfalle)**

1/4 lb **sausage**, cooked and sliced

▶ Warm the oil in a frying pan, add the onion, and sauté until softened. Add the peppers and cook for 3–4 minutes. Add the zucchini and cook for 3 minutes more.
▶ Pour the tomato purée into the pan, then stir in the crumbled stock cube. Bring the mixture to a boil, cover, and simmer for 10 minutes.

▶ Meanwhile, cook the pasta bows in boiling, lightly salted water, according to the instructions on the package.
▶ Add the sliced sausage to the sauce and cook until just heated through. Drain the pasta, toss it with the sauce, and serve at once.

Salmon teriyaki with noodles & bean sprouts

⟳ Preparation: 5 minutes; cooking: 40 minutes, including 30 minutes marinating ⌀ Makes 4 portions 🥄 Provides omega-3 fats, protein, B vitamins, and vitamins D and E

2 1/4 lb **salmon fillets**, skinned

1/4 lb **fine egg noodles**

1 tsp **cornstarch**

1 tbsp **vegetable oil**

3/4 cup **bean sprouts**

2 **green onions**, thinly sliced

3 1/2 tbsp **chicken stock** (see page 52)

Marinade

3 tbsp **soy sauce**

2 tbsp **sake**

2 tbsp **superfine sugar**

Simple to prepare, this dish is a great favorite with my three children. Oily fish, such as salmon, trout, tuna, sardines, and mackerel, contain omega-3 fatty acids, which protect against heart disease and strokes. Eating oily fish also helps brain development, and research shows that including oily fish in the diet can help children who are dyspraxic or dyslexic.

▶ Put the marinade ingredients in a small saucepan and boil rapidly for 2 minutes until slightly thickened. Allow to cool, then add the salmon and leave to marinate for at least 30 minutes.
▶ Cook the noodles in boiling, lightly salted water according to the instructions on the package and then rinse in cold water. Set aside.
▶ Drain the marinade from the salmon and reserve. Stir 1 tsp of cornstarch into the marinade.
▶ Heat 1/2 tbsp of oil in a small frying pan and sauté the salmon for about 2 minutes on each side, until just cooked. Pour some of the excess oil out of the pan, add half the reserved marinade, and cook for about 1 minute. Set aside.

▶ Heat the remaining oil in a wok or small frying pan and stir-fry the bean sprouts and green onions for 2 minutes, then stir in the noodles.
▶ Add the chicken stock to the remaining marinade. Pour this over the noodles and bean sprouts and cook for 1 minute.
▶ Serve the salmon on top of a bed of noodles and bean sprouts.

Chinese noodles with chicken & bean sprouts

⟳ Preparation: 10 minutes; cooking: 15 minutes   ✎ Makes 4 portions

✐ Provides potassium, protein, B vitamins including folate, vitamins C and E, and zinc

Don't be afraid to try out new tastes on your child—these noodles flavored with a mild curry and coconut sauce were very popular with my tasting panel. In fact, young children often like unusual flavors, such as olives or sweet-and-sour cucumbers, and tend to like mild curries.

▶ Heat the vegetable oil in a wok or frying pan and stir-fry the green onions, garlic, and chopped red chili for about 2 minutes. Add the chicken and continue to stir-fry for 2 minutes.

▶ Add the curry paste, chicken stock, and coconut milk and cook for 5 minutes over a low heat. Add the sweet corn and bean sprouts and cook for 3–4 minutes. Finally, add the peas, noodles, and shrimp and cook for about 3 minutes more.

½ tbsp **vegetable oil**

3 **green onions**, chopped

1 **garlic clove**, peeled and crushed

½ tsp **red chili**, chopped

1½ **chicken breast fillets** (about ½ lb) cut into strips

1 tsp **mild curry paste** (or 2 tsp, for more adventurous children)

⅔ cup **chicken stock** (see page 52)

⅔ cup **coconut milk**

½ cup **baby sweet corn**, cut into quarters

1 cup **bean sprouts**

½ cup defrosted **frozen peas**

¼ lb **Chinese noodles**

¼ lb small **shrimp**

Golden turkey fingers

↻ Preparation: 40 minutes, including 30 minutes marinating; cooking: 10 minutes
✂ Makes 4 portions 🔪 Provides protein, B vitamins including folate, and zinc
❄ Suitable for freezing: uncooked

½ lb **turkey breast fillets**
juice of 1 **lime** or ½ **lemon**
1 **shallot**, peeled and sliced
flour
salt and freshly ground **black pepper**
¾ cup **dry bread crumbs**
1½ tbsp snipped **chives**
1 **egg**, lightly beaten
vegetable oil for shallow frying

▶ Cut the turkey into 1-inch strips, removing any skin. Place in a bowl with the lime or lemon juice and shallot. Cover and refrigerate for 30 minutes.
▶ Spread some flour on a plate and season with salt and pepper. On another plate, mix together the bread crumbs and chives. Dip the turkey strips first in the seasoned flour, then in the beaten egg, and finally in the bread-crumb and chive mixture.
▶ Heat the oil in a frying pan, add the turkey strips, and sauté until golden and cooked through, about 10 minutes.

Heart-shaped chicken nuggets

↻ Preparation: 25 minutes; cooking: 6 minutes ✂ Makes 8 portions
🔪 Provides protein and B vitamins ❄ Suitable for freezing

¾ lb **chicken breast fillets**, cut into chunks
1 large **onion**, peeled and diced
2 tbsp chopped **fresh parsley**
1 small **apple**, peeled and grated
½ cup **fresh white bread crumbs**
1 **chicken stock cube**, crumbled
½ cup **dry bread crumbs**
1 cup **cheese and onion potato chips**, finely crushed
vegetable oil for frying

The addition of apple gives these nuggets a delicious, moist flavor. If you don't have a heart-shaped cutter, try another simple shape.

▶ Put the first six ingredients in a food processor and chop for a few seconds until well combined. Shape the mixture into a flat disk.
▶ Use a 2½-inch cookie cutter to press out heart shapes. Mix together the dry bread crumbs and chips on a plate and press the pieces into the coating.
▶ Heat enough oil for shallow frying in a large frying pan. Add the nuggets and cook for about 6 minutes, turning occasionally, until light golden and cooked through.

Caramelized chicken breasts

↻ Preparation: 5 minutes; cooking: 20 minutes ✂ Makes 4 portions
🔪 Provides protein, B vitamins including folate and zinc

1½ tbsp **olive oil**
1 **onion**, peeled and thinly sliced
1 small **garlic clove**, peeled and crushed
salt and freshly ground **black pepper**
2 **chicken breast fillets** (about ¾ lb)
1 tbsp **malt vinegar**
1½ tbsp **ketchup**
1 tbsp **soy sauce**
½ tbsp **soft brown sugar**

▶ Warm 1 tbsp of the oil in a heavy-bottomed saucepan. Add the onion and garlic and sauté for 10 minutes until soft and light golden.
▶ Remove the onion with a slotted spoon and add the remaining oil. Season the chicken and pan-fry for about 7 minutes on each side.
▶ When the chicken is nearly cooked, add the vinegar, ketchup, soy sauce, and brown sugar and cook over a high heat for 1 minute.
▶ Return the onion to the pan, cover, and cook for about 2 minutes. Serve with rice.

3/4 lb **chicken breast fillets**

1 1/2 tbsp **vegetable oil**

1 small **onion**, peeled and sliced

1 **garlic clove**, peeled and crushed

1/2 cup **baby sweet corn**, quartered

1/2 cup **carrots**, peeled and cut into strips

2/3 cup **cauliflower**, cut into florets

2/3 cup **zucchini**, cut into strips

black pepper, to taste

Marinade

2 tbsp **soy sauce**

2 tbsp **sake (Japanese rice wine)**

1/2 tsp **soft brown sugar**

1 tsp **sesame oil**

1 **green onion**, finely chopped

TIP For additional flavor, add 1/2 tsp finely chopped fresh ginger root to the marinade.

Teriyaki chicken stir-fry

○ Preparation: 40 minutes, including 30 minutes marinating; cooking: 15 minutes
◇ Makes 4 portions   ☡ Provides beta-carotene, folate and other B vitamins, iron, potassium, protein, vitamins C and E, and zinc

▶ Cut the chicken breasts into thin strips. Combine the marinade ingredients in a dish. Add the chicken and leave to marinate for at least 30 minutes.
▶ Heat the vegetable oil in a lidded wok or large frying pan, add the onion and garlic, and stir-fry, uncovered, for 2 minutes.
▶ Strain the marinade from the chicken and set aside. Add the chicken to the wok and stir-fry until it changes color. Add the baby sweet corn to the wok with the carrots and cauliflower, stir-fry for 3 minutes, add the zucchini, and continue to stir-fry for 2 minutes.

▶ Pour in the marinade. Cover the wok and cook for 2 minutes, or until the vegetables are tender and the chicken is cooked through. Season with a little freshly ground black pepper.

Variation
▶ Replace the chicken with 3/4 lb fillet or rump steak, pounded until tender and cut into strips.

---

4 **chicken breast fillets** (about 1 1/4 lb) cubed

1 cup **canned lychees**

1 **red pepper**, deseeded and cut into triangles

Marinade

3 tbsp **soy sauce**

3 tbsp **honey**

1/2 tbsp **lemon juice**

To decorate

8 **cherry tomatoes** or **radishes**

16 **whole cloves**

8 **green onion fans** (see below)

TIP To make green onion fans, cut green onions into 3-inch lengths. Make four slashes at one end of each. Place in ice water until the ends curl.

Chicken caterpillar kebabs

○ Preparation: 40 minutes, including 30 minutes marinating; cooking: 15 minutes
♨ 350°F   ◇ Makes 8 portions   ☡ Provides beta-carotene, iron, protein, B vitamins, vitamin C, and zinc

▶ Mix together the marinade ingredients in a shallow dish. Add the chicken and leave to marinate for at least 30 minutes. While the chicken marinates, soak eight bamboo skewers in water to keep them from burning.
▶ Thread the chicken onto the skewers, putting half a lychee and a red pepper triangle between each piece of chicken. Arrange on a baking sheet and transfer

to the preheated oven. Cook for about 15 minutes, basting with the marinade and turning occasionally, until cooked through.
▶ To decorate, make a face for each caterpillar using a cherry tomato or radish, studded with clove eyes. Attach it to the tip of the skewer, and thread on a green onion tail.

Annabel's tasty meatballs

⟳ Preparation: 10 minutes; cooking: 15 minutes   ⌖ Makes 8 portions
⚡ Provides iron, protein, B vitamins, and zinc   ❄ Suitable for freezing

These meatballs are easy to prepare and delicious (the apple keeps them wonderfully moist). They are good on their own or served with spaghetti and Special tomato sauce (see page 153).

▶ In a mixing bowl, combine all the ingredients except the flour and vegetable oil. Use your hands to form the mixture into about 24 walnut-size balls. Spread the flour on a plate and use it to coat the meatballs.

▶ Warm the oil in a frying pan, add the meatballs, and fry over a high heat for about 3 minutes, until browned on all sides. Lower the heat a little and fry for 12 minutes, or until cooked through.

1 lb **lean ground beef**

1 **onion**, peeled and finely chopped

1 tbsp chopped **fresh parsley**

1 **chicken stock cube** dissolved in 2 tbsp **hot water**

1 small **apple**, peeled and grated

1/2 tsp **Worcestershire sauce**

pinch of **brown sugar**

salt and freshly ground **black pepper**

flour for coating

vegetable oil for frying

Hungarian goulash

⟳ Preparation: 15 minutes; cooking: 2 hours 20 minutes   🔥 300°F
⌖ Makes 8 portions   ⚡ Provides beta-carotene, iron, potassium, protein, B vitamins including folate, vitamin C, and zinc   ❄ Suitable for freezing

For young children, chop the meat and vegetables into small pieces or process in a blender for just a few seconds. Serve with noodles.

▶ Spread the flour on a plate, season lightly, and use to coat the beef. Warm the vegetable oil in an ovenproof Dutch oven, add the beef, and sauté until browned all over. Remove with a slotted spoon and set aside.
▶ Add the onions to the casserole and sauté for 5 minutes. Add the red pepper and sauté for 3–4 minutes, then add the mushrooms and cook for 3 minutes. Sprinkle with paprika and cook for about 2 minutes.

▶ Return the sautéed meat to the pan, pour in the stock, and stir in the tomato purée, ketchup, Worcestershire sauce, and chopped parsley. Cover, transfer to the preheated oven, and cook for about 2 hours. Check that the meat is tender. Season to taste and stir in the sour cream. Set aside and keep warm.
▶ Cook the noodles in boiling, lightly salted water according to the instructions on the package. Drain, arrange a bed of noodles on each plate, and top with a serving of goulash.

flour for coating

salt and freshly ground **black pepper**

1 lb **lean chuck steak**, cut into cubes

2 tbsp **vegetable oil**

2 **onions**, peeled and chopped

1 **red pepper**, deseeded and chopped

3 cups **mushrooms**, sliced

1 tbsp **paprika**

1 1/2 cups **chicken stock** (see page 52) or **beef stock**

3 tbsp **tomato paste**

1 tbsp **ketchup**

1 tsp **Worcestershire sauce**

2 tbsp chopped **fresh parsley**

6 tbsp **sour cream**

1/2 lb **egg noodles**

Sponge cake mixture

½ cup **soft margarine**

½ cup **superfine sugar**

2 **eggs**

1 tsp **vanilla extract**

¼ tsp grated **lemon zest** (optional)

1 cup **self-raising flour**

½ cup **raisins** (optional)

To decorate as pigs

pink **food coloring**

6 oz **ready-to-roll white fondant**, plus **confectioner's sugar** to dust

3 tbsp **apricot jam**, sieved and warmed gently

pink **marshmallows**

colored **writing icing**

red **licorice laces**

To decorate as hedgehogs

Make a spiky hedgehog with chocolate buttercream icing and spikes made from flaked chocolate.

To decorate as clowns

Decorate a white-iced cake with yellow grated icing hair, a red icing nose and mouth, and black writing icing eyes.

TIP Fondant icing is easy to tint by kneading in some food coloring, as described in this recipe.

Character mini cakes

↻ Preparation: 20 minutes; cooking: 20 minutes, plus decorating time

🌡 350°F ⊘ Makes 15 cakes ✎ Provides vitamins A and B12

❄ Suitable for freezing: before decorating

Decorated mini cakes are great for parties. Here, I describe how to make a piggy face, but you could try clowns, spiky chocolate hedgehogs, or ladybugs made with red and black icing. Older children will enjoy helping to decorate these.

▶ Cream together the margarine and sugar until pale and fluffy. Beat in the eggs one at a time, then add the vanilla extract and lemon zest if using.

▶ Fold in the flour and raisins, if using, and mix until soft and creamy.

▶ Line a muffin pan with paper liners and half-fill each one. Transfer to the preheated oven and bake for about 20 minutes. Leave to cool on a wire rack.

▶ Add a few drops of the pink food coloring to the icing and knead until an even color tone is achieved. Lightly dust a work surface with confectioner's sugar and roll out the icing until it is about ⅛ inch thick.

▶ Use a round pastry cutter or glass to cut out disks of fondant slightly larger than the cakes. Brush the cake tops with a little warmed apricot jam and set the fondant on top.

▶ Make a pig's snout by attaching a marshmallow, halved across the diameter, to the center of the cake using jam; draw on nostrils with writing icing and use edible silver balls for the eyes. Add halved marshmallow ears and a short strip of licorice for the mouth.

Present birthday cake

Preparation: 20 minutes; cooking 1 hour, plus decorating time

350°F Makes 20 portions Provides vitamins A and B12

Suitable for freezing: undecorated only

► Pour the sponge cake mixture into a greased and lined 8-inch square cake pan and a 9-x-5-x-3-inch loaf pan. Transfer to the preheated oven and bake the loaf pan for 45 minutes and the square pan for 1 hour. Turn out and leave to cool on a wire rack.

► Divide the loaf cake into the desired number of blocks to form the presents. Slice all the cakes crosswise and sandwich the halves together with a layer each of raspberry jam and buttercream.

► Choose your colors, then tint the white fondant as described in the previous recipe.

► Brush the top and sides of the cake blocks with apricot jam. Lay the fondant over the top, either in a single sheet or in strips for a striped effect. Make icing bows in contrasting colors, sticking them down with jam. Decorate further with icing spots or flowers, or leave plain; or you can add a few marzipan animals.

4 batches **sponge cake mixture** (see Character mini cakes, opposite)

Filling

3/4 cup **raspberry jam**

1 quantity **buttercream** made with 3/4 cup **soft butter** beaten with 3 cups **confectioner's sugar**, 1 tbsp **milk**, and 1 tsp **vanilla extract**

To decorate

red, blue, green, and yellow **food coloring**

2 1/2 lb **ready-to-roll fondant** (see Tip, opposite), plus **confectioner's sugar** to dust

8 tbsp **apricot jam**, warmed gently and sieved

3 tbsp **butter**

²⁄₃ cup **soft brown sugar**

2 **eggs**

1¹⁄₃ cups **flour**, sifted

¾ tsp **baking powder**

1 cup **boiling water**

½ cup **pitted dates**, chopped

¾ tsp **baking soda**

¾ tsp **vanilla extract**

Butterscotch sauce

½ cup **soft brown sugar**

¼ cup **butter**

½ cup **heavy cream**

TIP *This dessert can be made in advance, kept in the refrigerator, and reheated before serving.*

Sticky toffee pudding

Preparation: 10 minutes; cooking: 40 minutes   375°F

Makes 8 portions   Provides vitamins A and B12   Suitable for freezing

This is a traditional English baked dessert that never fails to please children and adults alike.

► Cream together the butter and sugar. Beat the eggs into the mixture, then fold in the flour and baking powder.

► Pour the boiling water over the dates and add the baking soda and vanilla extract. Add this mixture to the batter and blend well.

► Butter an 11-x-7-inch ovenproof dish. Pour the batter into the dish (don't worry that the consistency is very runny) and bake in the preheated oven for 40 minutes.

► To make the sauce, put the brown sugar, butter, and cream in a pan and heat gently for about 5 minutes. Remove the pudding from the oven, pour on half the sauce, and place under a hot broiler until it bubbles. Serve the remaining sauce separately.

---

1 cup **self-raising flour**

2 tbsp **cocoa powder**

½ cup **soft margarine**

1 cup **superfine sugar**

2 **eggs**, lightly beaten

grated zest of 1 small **orange**

½ cup **semi-sweet chocolate chips**

Chocolate orange mini muffins

Preparation: 20 minutes; cooking: 12 minutes   350°F

Makes 30 mini muffins or 15 medium muffins   Provides vitamin A

Suitable for freezing

Mini muffins are just the right size for small children. However, if you prefer to make adult-size portions, bake this quantity of muffin mixture in medium muffin trays to make about 15 cakes.

► Sift together the flour and cocoa.

► Cream the margarine and superfine sugar. Add the eggs to the creamed mixture, a little at a time, together with 1 tbsp of the flour mixture.

► Mix in the remaining flour and cocoa until blended. Then stir in the orange zest and chocolate chips.

► Line some muffin pans with paper liners and fill each two-thirds full.

► Transfer to the preheated oven and cook for 10–12 minutes.

½ cup **butter** (cold)

⅓ cup **superfine sugar**

⅓ cup **ground almonds**

pinch of **salt**

¾ cup **flour,** plus more to dust

½ cup **cornstarch**

gel icing or **confectioner's sugar,** to decorate (optional)

edible silver balls to decorate (optional)

Shortbread cookies

🕐 Preparation: 15 minutes; cooking: 15 minutes   🌡 350°F
🍪 Makes 12–15 cookies   ✒ Provides vitamin A   ❄ Suitable for freezing

▶ Beat together the butter and sugar until fluffy. Add the remaining ingredients and beat until the mixture sticks together and begins to form a ball.
▶ Dust a pastry board with flour, turn out the mixture, and knead gently for 1–2 minutes to form a smooth dough. Roll the dough out until

¼ inch thick. Cut into shapes using cookie cutters.
▶ Using a spatula, transfer the shapes to a greased baking sheet. Bake in the preheated oven for 15 minutes, or until lightly golden. Leave to cool on the sheet, then lift off. Ice or decorate, as desired.

White chocolate chip cookies

🕐 Preparation: 25 minutes; cooking: 14 minutes   🌡 350°F
🍪 Makes 24 cookies   ❄ Suitable for freezing

The perfect recipe for chocolate chip cookies! I like them best with white chocolate, but you could use semi-sweet chocolate chips instead.

▶ Combine the butter, shortening, and sugars and beat in an electric mixer until the mixture is smooth. Add the egg and vanilla and continue to beat until all ingredients are well blended.
▶ In a mixing bowl, stir together the flour, baking powder, and salt. Stir the flour mixture into the first mixture, then add the chocolate chips.

▶ Using your hands, shape into walnut-size balls (about 1 inch in diameter). Place on greased baking sheets, spaced well apart, since the cookies will spread, and bake in the preheated oven for about 14 minutes. Let the cookies cool on the sheets, then transfer them to a wire rack. You can store the cookies in an airtight container for up to a week.

3 tbsp **unsalted butter**

3 tbsp **vegetable shortening**

½ cup **soft brown sugar**

½ cup **granulated sugar**

1 **egg**

1 tsp **vanilla extract**

1¼ cup **flour**

1 tsp **baking powder**

½ tsp **salt**

1 cup **white chocolate,** cut into small chunks

3 to 7 years

Preschool & beyond

"As your child reaches preschool age, this is a good time to educate him on the basics of good nutrition."

The greatest change in your child's life at this stage of development will probably be starting daycare and then school, and that means eating has to fit into more of a routine. Younger children will need a good breakfast to keep them alert until lunchtime. Later, packed lunches will become an essential part of your child's diet, too, and they will need to be nutritious and sustaining.

A healthy & varied diet

Between the ages of three and five, your child's manual dexterity should greatly improve and he should be able to master all the basic eating skills. He should also have his first full set of teeth. Around this age, many children will start noticing commercials that push unhealthy foods. This is a good time to explain the basic principles of nutrition to your child.

If parents offer fresh fruit and vegetables in a defensive or apologetic way, children will begin to reject them. So if you can make these fresh foods seem to be the appealing, tasty foods they really are, then your child will not equate "healthy" with "yucky." Vitamin pills are no substitute for fresh fruit and vegetables in your child's diet.

Breakfasts for brain power

The first meal of the day is the most important, since your child will not have eaten for at least 12 hours and his blood sugar levels will be very low. Your child's brain will also need a kick-start first thing in the morning. Although it makes up only 4 percent of your child's total body weight, the brain uses approximately 20 percent of the body's energy at rest. The brain's energy stores are also very small, so in order to keep it functioning at its best, it needs constant glucose replacement.

Improving blood sugar levels by eating a good breakfast after the night's fast raises blood glucose—"fuel for the brain"—and will help to improve your child's performance. Research has shown that children who eat a nutritionally balanced breakfast work faster, make significantly fewer mistakes on tasks requiring sustained attention, show greater physical endurance, and seem less tired to teachers than children who skip breakfast.

Breakfast sets the pattern for healthy eating throughout the rest of the day. When children miss breakfast, they often binge on cookies or chips later in the morning. For maximum energy and brain power to last throughout the morning, a good breakfast should ideally include food from each of these groups:
• **complex carbohydrate:** whole-grain cereal, bread
• **protein:** dairy products, eggs, nuts and seeds
• **vitamins and minerals:** fruit or fruit juice.

A healthy breakfast can take just 10 minutes to eat from start to finish. By giving your child cereal and milk or peanut butter on toast, some yogurt or cheese, and a glass of fruit juice, you are providing him with a food from each group and an excellent start to the day.

The key role of carbohydrates

Carbohydrates provide the body's main source of energy. Children need plenty of them not only because they are active and use up lots of energy, but also because they are growing. Make sure your child's breakfast includes some unrefined carbohydrates, such as whole-wheat bread, whole-grain cereals, and fruit. The fiber contained in these foods helps slow down the rate at which sugar is released, giving longer-lasting concentration and sustained energy.

If your child eats predominantly refined carbohydrates at breakfast, such as a bowl of sugary cereal or white bread with jam, he will have a burst of energy to fuel his activity for a while, but this be will be short-lived. When it is gone, his blood-sugar level starts to fall, which can result in poor concentration, erratic learning, disruptive behavior, and fatigue. He would be better off eating a breakfast of complex carbohydrates such as a bowl of muesli with fruit, or cheese on whole-wheat toast.

Nutritious, quick-to-prepare breakfast ideas

• Cheese on toast or sealed toasted sandwiches made in an electric sandwich-maker are delicious. Try cheese and tomato or ham and cheese.

• Make a fruit salad using seasonal fruits mixed with some fresh orange juice and a little lemon juice mixed with a little sugar—or mix fresh fruit with fruit yogurt. Different fruits contain different vitamins, so try to include plenty of variety.

• Make french toast: dip bread into beaten egg mixed with 2 tbsp of milk and fry in butter until golden.

• Fruity milkshakes or fruit smoothies are a good way to encourage your child to consume more fruit. Try sieved berries sweetened with confectioner's sugar, mixed with milk and some raspberry or strawberry yogurt drink (you can also use frozen berries).

• Make scrambled eggs extra-special by adding ingredients such as chopped fresh tomatoes, grated cheese, or ham. Allow an extra minute for the eggs to cook.

• Boiled eggs and toast fingers spread with butter are popular with most children.

• Dried fruit compote or stewed fruit, such as apples or rhubarb, is delicious with brown sugar.

• Make toast with peanut butter, honey, and banana. Spread slices of toasted multigrain bread with peanut butter and a little honey, and top with sliced bananas.

• Children are great mimics and will be affected by adults' attitudes to eating. If parents do not eat healthily themselves, or refuse to try new dishes, children are likely to copy their conservative eating habits. If a member of the family is dieting, don't discuss it in front of the children. You need to avoid creating eating anxieties.

• When setting up a healthy eating plan, enlist the help of visitors, grandparents, and other caregivers. If everyone is aware of your food policies, your child will be treated consistently.

• Ensure that your child eats a substantial breakfast, particularly on weekdays if he will be at daycare or preschool. If he is a very slow eater and you are running late, give him a sandwich or healthy muffin to eat on the way.

• Iron absorption can be inhibited by the tannin in tea, so it's best to avoid giving tea to children for breakfast.

Good iron-boosting breakfast combinations
• boiled eggs with whole-wheat toast, yogurt, and a glass of orange juice
• bowl of fortified cereal with milk and dried fruit, kiwi fruit

Refined carbohydrates have fewer nutrients than complex carbohydrates because many are lost in processing. For example, white flour contains less zinc than whole-wheat flour. Zinc is vital for growth and aids resistance to infection.

Increasing iron in the diet
Iron deficiency is the most common nutritional deficiency, affecting about 25 percent of young children. Two symptoms are tiredness and lack of concentration, so increasing iron intake could improve your child's schoolwork. Iron is important for transporting oxygen in the blood to all the body's organs, including the brain, so iron is important for good brain function.

Fortified cereals and whole-wheat bread are good sources of iron. However, it is difficult for our bodies to absorb iron from vegetable sources—red meat provides the form of iron that is most easily absorbed by the body. To improve the absorption of iron from a plant source, you will need to consume a vitamin C–rich fruit (such as kiwi fruit or berries) or vitamin C–rich juice (such as orange or cranberry juice) along with the plant source.

Breakfast cereals
Many of the cereals designed to appeal to children contain up to 50 percent sugar, are high in salt, and are so highly processed that, unless they are fortified, they contain very little fiber, vitamins, or minerals. Healthy cereals include shredded wheat, unsweetened granola, muesli, and oatmeal. Even if your child adds sugar, it will be a lot less than the 4–5 teaspoons per bowl you might find in other cereals.

Outside the home

Some time after his third birthday, if not before, your child may go to daycare or start attending nursery school. If lunch is provided, make sure it is well-balanced and nutritious. Where a packed lunch is required, try to make it interesting and healthy.

Briefing caregivers
If you find that your child is always hungry when he comes out of preschool, ask a staff member to monitor what he eats and report back to you. Children are usually quite hungry after a preschool day, and it can be a good time to encourage them to snack healthily. If you bring a nutritious snack, such as a banana or a cheese and tomato sandwich, when you pick up your child, you will usually find that he will eat it eagerly.

If you have a policy of no candy or chocolate between meals, then let caregivers and relatives know so that you can be consistent with your rules. You might suggest other treats, such as exotic fruits or homemade cookies.

It may not be a good idea to ban sweets altogether, because there is a danger of making them into an even more desirable "forbidden fruit." It is probably easier to limit sweets to certain specific times, such as after meals or at weekends. If you keep to your rule, your child will soon stop asking for them at any other time.

Fast food
Many fast foods are high in saturated fat, salt, or sugar relative to their nutrient content. To encourage your children to eat a nutritious diet, make healthy versions of their fast-food favorites, such as Mini pizzas (page 97), Crunchy chicken fingers (page 101), Oven-baked chips (page 163), and Seriously strawberry freezer pops (page 177).

Tasty & nutritious packed lunches

When your child brings his lunch to school, he carries a little piece of home with him. Whenever I make packed lunches for my three children, it is a challenge to come up with something new to entice them to eat healthy food and bring smiles to their faces after a long morning at school. Simple touches can make all the difference: try drawing a face on your child's banana with a felt-tip and decorating it with stickers, or cutting sandwiches into interesting shapes using cookie cutters.

If you want to boost your child's brainpower and concentration at school, you need to make sure that his lunch box contains a variety of foods from the following groups:
• a source of protein for growth and alertness throughout the day
• complex carbohydrates for slow-release energy
• calcium for growing bones

Remember
• Keep food in your child's packed lunch cool and well-wrapped so that it remains free from bacteria.

"You don't have to give your child a sandwich for lunch; try tortilla wraps or pita pockets, chicken drumsticks, or tubs of pasta or rice salad."

- vitamins and minerals from fruit and vegetables
- a little fat for staying power
- water, pure fruit juice, or a fruit smoothie.

So a typical healthy lunch box might include a whole-wheat sandwich or pita bread pocket with tuna, chicken, egg salad, cheese, or peanut butter; a carton of yogurt or a yogurt drink; a piece of fruit or some dried fruit, and a treat like a small chocolate bar or some cookies, mini muffins, or chips.

"Young children like miniature portions, such as individual wrapped cheeses, tiny boxes of raisins, and mini muffins."

Lunch box combinations

There are a huge number of options for creating a nourishing packed lunch for your child. Here are some healthy yet tasty suggestions for each nutrient. Choose from each category to create a well-balanced lunch for your child.

- **Protein** Choose lean meats, such as turkey slices, chicken skewers, and roast beef, for his sandwich. Fish, such as tuna, is also a good source of protein: try tuna and pasta salad. Boiled eggs wrapped in plastic wrap and individually wrapped mini cheeses are also popular sources of protein.
- **Carbohydrates** Choose complex carbohydrates such as whole-grain bread, pasta, potatoes, or basmati rice. These release calories slowly and help to keep up energy levels and concentration. Refined carbohydrates provide more short-lived energy. Sandwiches don't have to be made using sliced bread. Try tortilla wraps, pita bread, or bagels; for example, toast a bagel or an English muffin, spread with a little spaghetti sauce, top with some grated Swiss, cheddar, or mozzarella cheese, and place under the broiler until the cheese is melted. Wrap in foil. Alternatively, try making little tubs of pasta or rice salad.
- **Calcium** After your child has reached the age of one and has been weaned, switch to full-fat cows' milk. He should be drinking 13 fl oz (375ml) of milk a day or eating the equivalent in dairy products. One carton of yogurt and 1 oz (30g) of hard cheese provide the same amount of calcium as 7 fl oz (200ml) of milk. Until the age of two, your child needs full-fat milk because it provides necessary calories and vitamin A. Children under five shouldn't eat a low-fat diet, so choose whole-milk products, such as full-fat yogurt, rather than low-fat versions.

Many supermarkets stock "live" yogurt and yogurt drinks containing friendly bacteria known as probiotics, packaged in small containers that are an ideal size for lunch boxes. Probiotics can help prevent food poisoning and other digestive system infections.

Dried figs, seeds, and nuts also provide moderate amounts of calcium. Canned sardines are a rich source.

• **Vitamins and minerals** Always include some fresh fruit in your child's lunch box; dried fruits, such as dried apricots or raisins, are good, too. Raw vegetables with an accompanying dip are usually popular with children, or you can prepare salad kebabs with cherry tomatoes, cucumber chunks, bell pepper strips, and cheese.

Include a vitamin C–rich drink, such as orange juice, or a vitamin C–rich fruit such as kiwi fruit, to help boost iron absorption. Choose unsweetened pure fruit juice or make a fruit smoothie. Don't give vitamin-enriched fruit juice drinks: many contain a lot of water and sugar or artificial sweeteners.

Preserving lunch box contents

• In hot weather, keep the contents of your child's lunch box cool by including a small ice pack. Alternatively, put a carton or plastic container of juice in the freezer overnight and add it to the lunch box in the morning. By lunchtime the juice will have defrosted.
• Wrap sandwiches in plastic wrap or aluminum foil to keep them fresh.
• To keep sandwiches from getting squashed by bottles of juice, pack them in a rigid plastic container.
• To avoid soggy sandwiches, make sure you dry the ingredients before you put them in the sandwich. For example, if you wash lettuce, dry it before putting it in the sandwich. A layer of dry lettuce between filling and bread can also help stop sandwiches from turning soggy. If you are going on a picnic, some of the wet ingredients can be packed separately and added to the sandwich just before eating.

Hot food at lunchtime

When the weather gets colder, it's a good idea to include something hot in your child's lunch box. A wide-mouthed mini Thermos bottle is ideal for serving up a delicious cup of homemade soup.

Remember
If your child suffers from a nut allergy or any other serious food allergy, it is important that you inform his school. Sometimes children trade items of food with their friends, and many schools have a policy of asking parents not to include any foods containing peanuts in school lunch boxes.

Handy tricks
• It's sometimes good to get children to make their own sandwiches for their lunch box. They are more likely to eat them if they have chosen the bread and the filling.

• Start a cookie-cutter collection. Sandwiches cut into funny shapes will appeal to your child.

MORE IDEAS FOR LUNCH BOXES & PICNICS

Sandwich fillings

• Bacon, lettuce, and tomato
• Sliced turkey with lettuce, mayonnaise, and cranberry sauce
• Sliced turkey with Swiss cheese, tomatoes, cucumber slices, and alfalfa sprouts mixed with mayonnaise
• Chopped pineapple, slivers of ham or turkey, and honey mustard
• Roast beef, lettuce, pickled cucumbers, tomatoes, and mild horseradish or mustard
• Shredded chicken, chopped tomatoes, chopped hard-boiled egg, snipped chives, lettuce, and mayonnaise

• Tuna, lettuce, finely chopped green onion, and mayonnaise
• Shrimp with lettuce and mayonnaise mixed with a little ketchup
• Cream cheese and smoked salmon
• Chopped hard-boiled egg mashed with a little mayonnaise, snipped chives or parsley, salt, and freshly ground pepper
• Sliced Swiss cheese, cherry tomatoes, and shredded lettuce
• Cream cheese and cucumber
• Grated cheese and carrots with a little mayonnaise

• Tomatoes, mozzarella, avocado, and French dressing
• Hummus, grated carrots, and cucumber slices
• Peanut butter and sliced banana with a little honey
• Peanut butter and jelly
• Peanut butter and bacon
• Peanut butter and raisins

Snack ideas

• A bag of bite-size carrots, cucumber sticks, and cherry tomatoes with a small container of hummus or sour cream and chive dip
• Dried fruit such as apricots, figs, apples, or raisins

• Thin slices of ham or turkey wrapped around cheese sticks
• Very small vegetables and fruits, such as baby carrots, cherry tomatoes, tangerines, or small bananas
• Popcorn, as long as it is not covered in salt or caramel
• Rice cakes
• Mini cheeses
• Nuts—for example, honey-roasted cashew nuts for children over five, as long as there is no history of nut allergy in the family
• Probiotic yogurt drinks

Healthy snacks

Young children expend a lot of energy running around, their stomachs are small, and it is often difficult for them to eat enough at mealtimes to keep them going all day. Also, many young children just don't have the patience to sit down and eat a decent meal. Snacks are therefore a very important part of their diet, and if you encourage your child to eat healthy snacks in preference to cookies and chips, it is likely that these habits will continue later in life and your child will enjoy a much healthier diet.

1 Fruit skewers

Children should eat five portions of fruit and vegetables each day, and this is a fun way of encouraging your child to eat more fruit. (See page 147 for recipe.) You can also make skewers using a mixture of fresh and dried fruit.

2 Turkey & pasta salad

This dish is a delicious combination of moist turkey, sweet corn, cherry tomatoes, and pasta, tossed in a dressing flavored with soy sauce, honey, and lemon. (See page 145 for recipe.) Keep salads like this in the refrigerator for your child to snack on when he is hungry.

3 Cherry tomato & mozzarella salad

Quick and easy to put together, this is an attractive salad of sweet cherry tomatoes with mini balls of mozzarella cheese and fresh basil. (See page 144 for recipe.)

1

2

3

1 tbsp **sunflower oil**

¹⁄₂ cup **pumpkin seeds**

¹⁄₂ cup **sunflower seeds**

1 tbsp **honey**

1 tbsp **soy sauce**

TIP Toasted pumpkin seeds make a nutritious snack and are full of valuable vitamins and minerals.

Toasted seeds with honey & soy sauce

Preparation: 2 minutes; cooking: 3 minutes   Makes 4 portions   Provides iron, magnesium, omega-3 fatty acids, potassium, protein, B vitamins, vitamin E, and zinc

These make a delicious nibble any time of the day and can also be sprinkled over salads. You can mix the toasted seeds with raisins if you like.

▶ Heat the oil in a nonstick frying pan and cook the seeds, stirring constantly, for 2 minutes or until lightly browned.

▶ Remove from the heat, add the honey and soy sauce, return to the heat for 1 minute, then leave to cool.

---

1 **English muffin**

generous pat of **butter**

2 **eggs**

2 tbsp **heavy cream**

salt and freshly ground **black pepper**

butter for spreading

Muffins with creamy scrambled eggs

Preparation: 5 minutes; cooking: 5 minutes   Makes 1 portion
Provides calcium, protein, B vitamins including folate, and vitamins A and D

If you wish, you could top these muffins with grilled tomato halves or perhaps add some snipped chives to the scrambled eggs.

▶ Preheat the broiler to high. Split the muffin in half and toast until golden. Meanwhile, melt the butter in a pan over a gentle heat. Whisk the eggs with the cream and season with salt and pepper.
▶ Swirl the melted butter in the pan and pour in the eggs. Leave for a few seconds, then stir with a wooden spoon until the eggs are just beginning to set.
▶ Spread the split muffin with butter and pile the scrambled eggs on top.

Variation

▶ To make a delicious tuna topping instead of scrambled eggs, flake a small can of tuna into a bowl and stir in 2 tbsp of ketchup, 3 tbsp of sour cream, and two chopped green onions. Top the toasted muffin with the tuna mixture, sprinkle with cheddar cheese, and return to the broiler for 2–3 minutes until golden and bubbling.

---

7 oz **canned tuna in oil**

3 tbsp **mayonnaise**

2 tsp **white wine vinegar**

4 **green onions**, chopped

salt and freshly ground **black pepper**

a few drops of **Tabasco sauce**

2 **eggs**, hard-boiled

1 large or 2 small **tomatoes**, deseeded and chopped

a handful of **salad greens**

2 **pita breads**

Pita pockets with tuna, eggs & tomatoes

Preparation: 8 minutes; cooking: 10 minutes   Makes 2 portions
Provides beta-carotene, magnesium, potassium, protein, B vitamins including folate, and vitamins A, D and E

Stuffed pita pockets with a nutritious filling make a good snack or light lunch. This tuna mix is delicious.

▶ Drain the oil from the can of tuna and, in a bowl, mix flaked tuna together with the mayonnaise, white wine vinegar, green onions, salt and pepper, and Tabasco sauce.

▶ Peel and roughly chop the hard-boiled eggs and add to the tuna mix with the tomato and salad greens, stirring well.
▶ Cut the pita breads in half to make four pita pockets. Toast the bread and divide the mixture between them.

Chicken wraps

⟳ Preparation: 8 minutes; cooking: 10 minutes   ✄ Makes 4 rolls   ⚡ Provides beta-carotene, potassium, protein, B vitamins including folate, and vitamins A, C, and E

1 tbsp **vegetable oil**

1 small **onion**, sliced

1/2 small **red pepper,** sliced

1 large **chicken** or **turkey breast fillet** (about 1/2 lb)

1/2 tsp **dried oregano**

1/2 tsp **mild chili powder**

salt and freshly ground **black pepper**

1/2 **iceberg lettuce**

2 tbsp **mayonnaise**

4 **mini flour tortillas**

2 tbsp grated **cheddar cheese**

▶ Heat the vegetable oil in a frying pan. Fry the onion and red pepper for 4–5 minutes until softened.
▶ Cut the chicken into thin strips and add to the pan with the oregano and chili powder. Fry for 3–4 minutes until cooked. Season with salt and pepper.

▶ Finely shred the lettuce and mix with the mayonnaise.
▶ Heat the tortilla according to the instructions on the package. Divide the lettuce between the four tortillas, sprinkle with the cheddar cheese, and add the chicken mixture on top. Roll up.

Ham & cheese sandwich

⟳ Preparation: 4 minutes   ✄ Makes 1 portion   ⚡ Provides calcium, iron, potassium, protein, B vitamins including folate, and vitamin A

2 oz wafer-thin slices of **ham**

2 tbsp grated **cheddar cheese**

a handful of shredded **lettuce**

1 1/2 tsp **mayonnaise**

2 slices **bread**

a little **butter** or **margarine**

▶ Cut the ham into strips and mix together with the grated cheese, lettuce, and mayonnaise. Spread each slice of bread thinly with butter.
▶ Arrange the filling on top of one of the slices and top with the remaining slice.
▶ Remove the crusts and cut the sandwich into four squares, or cut horizontally into three fingers.

Variation

▶ To make a toasted version, preheat the broiler, then mix 1 oz wafer-thin slices of ham, cut into pieces, with 3 tbsp grated cheddar cheese and 1 tsp of mayonnaise. Toast and butter a slice of multigrain bread and arrange the cheese and ham on top. Place under the broiler until the cheese has melted.

1 cup small **cherry tomatoes**, cut in half

1 cup **mozzarella**, diced

4 fresh **basil leaves**, torn into pieces (optional)

Dressing

1½ tbsp **light olive oil**

1 tsp **soy sauce**

1 tsp **balsamic vinegar**

pinch of **sugar**

salt and freshly ground **black pepper**

Cherry tomato & mozzarella salad

Preparation: 5 minutes Makes 2–3 portions Provides calcium, potassium, protein, B vitamins including folate, and vitamins A and E

Mini balls of mozzarella, called mozzarelline, can be substituted for regular mozzarella. These create a very attractive dish. If you are taking this salad on a picnic, pack the dressing in a small plastic container and mix with the tomatoes and cheese when you're ready to eat.

▶ Mix together the cherry tomatoes and diced mozzarella.
▶ To make the dressing, simply whisk together all the ingredients.

▶ Toss the tomatoes and mozzarella in the dressing and then add the fresh basil, if using.

⅕ lb **pasta bows (farfalle)**

1 cup **canned sweet corn**

16 **cherry tomatoes**, cut in half

4 **green onions**, finely sliced

5-oz ball **mozzarella**, cut into small cubes

½ **cucumber**, peeled, quartered, deseeded, and cut into small chunks

Dressing

3 tbsp **light olive oil**

1 tbsp **honey**

1 tbsp **soy sauce**

1 tbsp **red wine vinegar**

freshly ground **black pepper**

Summer pasta salad

Preparation: 8 minutes; cooking: 12 minutes Makes 4 portions Provides beta-carotene, calcium, folate, potassium, protein, and vitamins A, B12, C, and E

Light and energizing, this delicious, healthy pasta salad is a favorite with adults as well as children of all ages.

▶ Cook the pasta in boiling, lightly salted water according to the instructions on the package. Drain and refresh under cold water.
▶ To make the dressing simply whisk together all the ingredients.

▶ Place the pasta in a large serving bowl. Add all the remaining ingredients and pour on the dressing. Toss the salad in the dressing and serve immediately.

1½ oz **pasta shapes**

1 tbsp **vegetable oil**

1 **chicken breast fillet** (about ¼ lb), cut into bite-size pieces

2 tbsp freshly grated **Parmesan cheese**, divided

1 **baby Boston lettuce** or ½ **Romaine lettuce**, cut into pieces

Dressing

2 tbsp **mayonnaise**

1 tsp **lemon juice**

½ **garlic clove**, peeled and crushed

⅛ tsp **Dijon mustard**

few drops **Worcestershire sauce**

few drops **Tabasco sauce**

Chicken caesar salad

Preparation: 6 minutes; cooking: 4 minutes Makes 1 portion Provides beta-carotene, potassium, protein, B vitamins including folate and vitamins C and E

This is a classic recipe—and deservedly so. To save time, use store-bought cooked chicken breast.

▶ Cook the pasta in boiling, lightly salted water according to the instructions on the package.
▶ Meanwhile, heat the oil in a pan, add the chicken, and fry for 3–4 minutes until cooked through. Leave to cool.
▶ Mix the dressing ingredients with 1 tbsp of the Parmesan cheese.

▶ Combine the lettuce, drained pasta, and chicken and toss with most of the dressing (there will probably be a little too much).
▶ Sprinkle on the remaining 1 tbsp of Parmesan cheese.

Pasta salad with shrimp

🕑 Preparation: 5 minutes; cooking: 12 minutes 🗡 Makes 1–2 portions ⚡ Provides beta-carotene, potassium, protein, B vitamins including folate, vitamins C and E, and zinc

---

Shrimp is the perfect ingredient for a pasta salad. Avocados really add to the flavor, but if your child doesn't like them, simply leave them out.

▶ Cook the pasta in boiling, lightly salted water according to the instructions on the package. Put the shrimp, avocado, cherry tomatoes, and shredded lettuce into a bowl with the drained, cooked pasta.

▶ Mix together the mayonnaise, ketchup, Worcestershire sauce, and lemon juice, if using, and toss the salad with this dressing.

1/4 lb **pasta shapes**

1/4 lb **cooked shrimp**

1/2 small **avocado**, peeled and chopped

4 **cherry tomatoes**, quartered

1/2 **gem lettuce**, shredded

Dressing

3 tbsp **mayonnaise**

1 tbsp **ketchup**

dash of **Worcestershire sauce**

squeeze of **lemon juice** (optional)

Turkey & pasta salad

🕑 Preparation: 10 minutes; cooking: 10 minutes 🗡 Makes 2 portions ⚡ Provides beta-carotene, potassium, protein, B vitamins including folate, and vitamins C and E

Turkey & pasta salad is a definite hit with my children and an ideal candidate for including in your child's lunch box. Select moist slices of turkey at the deli counter of the supermarket.

▶ Cook the pasta in boiling, lightly salted water according to the instructions on the package. Meanwhile, whisk together all the ingredients for the dressing.

▶ Put the chopped turkey, avocado (if using), sweet corn, tomatoes, and green onions into a bowl together with the drained pasta and toss with the dressing.

2 oz **pasta shapes**

1/4 lb **turkey** or **chicken breast fillet,** cooked and chopped

1/2 small **avocado**, peeled, pitted, and chopped (optional)

2/3 cup **canned** or **frozen sweet corn**

2 **tomatoes,** skinned, deseeded, and chopped, or 6 **cherry tomatoes**

2 **green onions**, thinly sliced

Dressing

3 tbsp **light olive oil**

1 tbsp **honey**

1 tbsp **soy sauce**

1 1/2 tbsp freshly squeezed **lemon juice**

Shakes

Many of the fruit juices marketed for children are full of sugar and water and often contain less than 10 percent juice. If you are ready to compromise on nutrition because of their convenience, you should consider that in just a few short minutes, you can make your own delicious and nutritious shakes using fresh or frozen fruit, yogurt, milk or ice cream.

Fruity cranberry shake

Defrost ²⁄₃ cup frozen summer fruits, such as strawberries, raspberries, blueberries, blackberries, or cherries, purée, and push through a sieve.

Blend together the puréed fruit with ¹⁄₂ cup of strawberry yogurt, ¹⁄₂ cup cranberry juice, and one chopped banana. Serves two.

Cookies & cream shake

Place six chocolate Oreo cookies, broken into pieces, 1¹⁄₄ cup milk, and two scoops of vanilla ice cream in a

blender and process until smooth. Serves two.

---

juice of 1 large **orange** (about ²⁄₃ cup)

²⁄₃ cup **apple juice**

1 small **banana**, peeled

2 large or 4 small **strawberries**, hulled

Energy-boosting smoothie

↻ Preparation: 3 minutes   ✎ Makes 2 glasses   ⚗ Provides folate, potassium, and vitamins B6 and C

Fruit smoothies provide instant energy and are quick and easy to prepare. Experiment with various combinations of fruits to suit your child's taste.

▶ Simply blend all the ingredients together and serve. You could also add

a ripe peach or half a small, ripe mango to this smoothie.

---

1 tbsp **butter**

2 ripe **peaches**, pitted and chopped but not peeled

2 **plums**, pitted and chopped

3 **strawberries**, hulled and quartered

1¹⁄₂ tbsp **soft brown sugar**

¹⁄₂ cup **raspberries**

¹⁄₂ cup **blueberries**

1 tbsp **rose water** or **water**

Peach & berry compote

↻ Preparation: 5 minutes; cooking: 5 minutes   ✎ Makes 2 portions
⚗ Provides beta-carotene, fiber, folate, potassium, and vitamin C

You can use peaches, nectarines, and any berries, or even pitted and halved cherries, to make this delicious fruit compote.

▶ Melt the butter and sauté the peaches and plums for 2 minutes. Add the strawberries, sprinkle with sugar,

and cook for 2 minutes more. Stir in the raspberries, blueberries, and water and heat through for one minute.

Fruit salad

🕐 Preparation: 5 minutes ⏲ Makes 2 portions ⚡ Provides beta-carotene, fiber, potassium, and vitamins C and E

The citrus juice and choice of fruit make this a refreshing fruit salad. If you wish, you could add a little fresh chopped mint for even greater zing.

▶ Mix together the orange, lemon, or lime juice and honey and pour over the prepared fruits. If using, sprinkle the mint over the top to decorate.

juice of 1 **orange** (about ⅓ cup)

1 tbsp **lime** or **lemon juice**

1 tbsp **honey**

2 **kiwi fruit**, peeled and chopped

2 ripe **peaches**, peeled, pitted, and chopped

6 **strawberries,** hulled

½ small **mango**, peeled, pitted, and chopped

8 **grapes**

chopped **fresh mint** (optional)

Fruit skewers

🕐 Preparation: 5 minutes ⏲ Makes 2 portions
⚡ Provides beta-carotene, fiber, potassium, and vitamins C and E

A good way of encouraging your child to eat more fruit is to thread chunks of different fruits onto skewers—use either bamboo skewers or thin straws. Your child will have fun pulling off the fruit pieces one by one.

▶ Take a chunk of each of your chosen fruits and thread them, one at a time, onto each skewer, to provide a colorful and tasty mix. Stick the skewers in half an upturned melon and serve.

Use any combination of the following fruits

seedless grapes

chunks of **pineapple**

slices of **kiwi fruit**

strawberries

chunks of **mango**

chunks of **plum**

dried fruits, such as **apricots** or **figs**

½ **melon** made into melon balls (optional)

TIP *With these brownies, always err on the side of underdone rather than overdone. They will firm up as they cool down.*

$^3/_4$ cup **unsalted butter**

1 cup **semi-sweet chocolate,** broken into squares

3 large **eggs**

1$^1/_3$ cups **superfine sugar**

$^1/_2$ cup **cocoa powder**

$^3/_4$ cup **flour**

$^1/_4$ cup **white chocolate,** chopped

$^1/_4$ cup **milk chocolate,** chopped

My favorite brownies

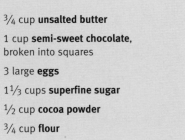 Preparation: 15 minutes; cooking: 35–40 minutes   350°F
Makes 16 squares   Provides vitamins A, B12, and D

My son Nicholas likes to make these himself. They are irresistible to all the family and disappear in no time.

▶ Grease and line an 8-inch square baking pan. Cut the butter into pieces and place in a heatproof bowl with the semi-sweet chocolate.
▶ Set the bowl on top of a pan of simmering water (the base of the bowl should not touch the water) and stir until the butter and chocolate are melted. Alternatively, melt the chocolate and butter in a microwave on a high setting for about 2 minutes, stirring halfway through. Set aside to cool.
▶ Break the eggs into a large bowl, add the sugar, and whisk for about 3–5 minutes until pale and creamy and roughly double the original volume.

▶ Gently fold in the cooled chocolate mixture, then sift the cocoa and flour into the chocolate/egg mixture and fold in. When folding in, take care not to overmix or the brownie will become heavy. Stir in the white and milk chocolate chunks.
▶ Pour the mixture into the prepared pan and bake in the preheated oven for about 35 minutes. If the mixture is very liquid in the center when you remove it from the oven, cook for a few minutes longer until fudgy in the middle. Take care not to overcook. The mixture will firm up as it cools.
▶ Leave until completely cool before cutting into squares.

Summer berry muffins

Preparation: 15 minutes; cooking: 25 minutes 400°F

Makes 8 large muffins Provides vitamins A and E

White chocolate and a mixture of tempting berries complement each other beautifully in these delicious, easy-to-prepare muffins.

► Line a muffin pan with 8 paper muffin liners. In a large bowl, combine the flour, brown sugar, salt, and baking powder and set aside.

► In a separate bowl, whisk together the vegetable oil, egg, vanilla extract, and milk. Add the mixed dry ingredients and stir until blended. Gently fold in the berries and white chocolate.

► Spoon the mixture into the muffin liners and sprinkle with demerara sugar.

► Bake for about 25 minutes until risen and just firm. Allow to cool a little, then transfer to a wire cooling rack.

$1\frac{1}{2}$ cups **flour**

$1\frac{1}{2}$ cups **soft brown sugar**

$\frac{1}{2}$ tsp **salt**

2 tsp **baking powder**

$\frac{1}{4}$ cup **vegetable oil**

1 **egg**

1 tsp **vanilla extract**

$\frac{1}{4}$ cup **full-fat milk**

$\frac{3}{4}$ cup **fresh raspberries**

$\frac{1}{2}$ cup **blueberries**

$\frac{1}{3}$ cup **white chocolate chips**

1 tbsp **demerara sugar**

White chocolate & cranberry cookies

Preparation: 30 minutes; cooking: 10 minutes 375°F

Makes 35 cookies Provides vitamins A and D Suitable for freezing

Delicious, chewy white chocolate and cranberry cookies are very easy to make. They should be quite soft when you take them out of the oven, so that when they cool down, they are crisp on the outside but moist inside.

► Beat the butter together with the sugars. With a fork, beat the egg together with the vanilla extract and add this to the butter mixture.

► In a bowl, mix together the flour, baking powder, and salt. Add this to the butter and egg mixture and blend. Mix in the white chocolate and cranberries.

► To make the cookies, line four baking sheets with nonstick baking paper. Using your hands, form the dough into walnut-size balls and arrange on the baking sheets, spaced well apart.

► Bake in the preheated oven for 10 minutes. Allow to cool for a few minutes and then transfer to a wire rack.

$\frac{1}{2}$ cup softened **unsalted butter**

$\frac{1}{2}$ cup **superfine sugar**

$\frac{1}{2}$ cup **light muscovado sugar**

1 **egg**

1 tsp **vanilla extract**

$1\frac{1}{3}$ cups **flour**

$\frac{1}{2}$ tsp **baking powder**

$\frac{1}{2}$ tsp **salt**

1 cup **white chocolate,** cut into small chunks

$\frac{1}{2}$ cup **dried sweetened cranberries**

Chocolate chip, raisin & sunflower-seed cookies

Preparation: 15 minutes; cooking: 12–14 minutes 350°F Makes 14 cookies

Provides fiber, iron, potassium, protein, and vitamin E Suitable for freezing

Packed full of nutrients, these cookies provide sustained energy.

► Cream together the butter and sugar until light and fluffy. Beat in the egg and vanilla extract. Stir in the remaining ingredients until combined.

► Using a tablespoon, spoon the mixture onto two nonstick or lined baking sheets, leaving enough space between the cookies for the dough to spread.

► Bake for 12–14 minutes until golden in the preheated oven. Cool on a wire rack.

$\frac{1}{3}$ cup **unsalted butter**

$\frac{1}{3}$ cup **superfine sugar**

1 small **egg,** beaten

1 tsp **vanilla extract**

$\frac{1}{2}$ cup **raisins**

$\frac{1}{4}$ cup **semi-sweet** or **milk chocolate chips**

$\frac{1}{3}$ cup **sunflower seeds**

$\frac{1}{3}$ cup **flour**

$\frac{1}{2}$ tsp **baking soda**

$\frac{1}{2}$ tsp **salt**

$\frac{1}{2}$ cup **quick oats**

Family meals

They say the family that eats together, stays together, and this section is all about finding recipes with that magical ingredient, "child appeal," so you can make one meal to suit everyone in the family. It's a shame that so many children live on a very limited junk-food diet when there are so many other wonderful foods they would enjoy eating if only they were given the chance. Encourage your child to eat a varied diet and try some of these recipes, many of which are my family's favorites. I've done the hard work already—every one of my recipes is tested on a panel of children, and without their seal of approval, the dishes would not be featured in this book.

1 Sleeping cannelloni
Make humorous, decorative additions to this Italian classic for instant appeal. The stuffed cannelloni tubes have the usual "blanket" of cheese sauce, but with mushroom faces, grated-cheese hair with green-pepper bows, and black-olive boots. (See page 156 for recipe.)

2 Beef tacos
Crispy corn tacos stuffed with ground beef or chicken strips, beans, and salad are always popular with children. The filling in these tacos has a hint of chili and cilantro to give it a little kick. (See page 173 for recipe.)

3 Paella
Give dinner a Spanish flavor with this festive one-pot meal of chicken, sausages, shrimp, and vibrant yellow rice. A colorful dish packed with goodness. (See page 166 for recipe.)

1

2

3

2 tbsp **butter**

1 medium **onion,** peeled and chopped

1 **garlic clove,** peeled and crushed

1 **leek,** rinsed well between the layers and thinly sliced

¾ lb **potatoes,** peeled and cut into chunks

1 **bay leaf**

1 sprig of **thyme** (optional)

1½ quarts unsalted **chicken stock** (see page 52) or **vegetable stock** (see page 47)

salt and freshly ground **black pepper**

2 oz **orzo**

2 cups **watercress**

Leek, potato & watercress soup with orzo

↻ Preparation: 10 minutes; cooking: 27 minutes   ✂ Makes 6 portions

⚡ Provides beta-carotene, folate, potassium, and vitamins A, B6, C, and E

❄ Suitable for freezing

The combination of leek and potato makes a classic soup that has always been very popular. The addition of watercress gives it a particularly special flavor and a wonderful freshness to balance the earthy flavor of the vegetables. Orzo is a tiny pasta shape that looks like grains of rice. Like other small and unusual pasta shapes, it goes down very well with children.

▶ Melt the butter in a large pan and sauté the onion and garlic for 5 minutes. Add the leek and continue to cook for 2 minutes. Add the potatoes, bay leaf, and thyme, if using. Add the stock and season to taste. Bring to a boil and then simmer, covered, for 15 minutes.

▶ Meanwhile, cook the orzo in boiling, lightly salted water according to the instructions on the package. Add the watercress to the soup. Cook for 5 minutes longer. Remove the bay leaf and thyme and purée in a blender. Stir in the orzo, heat through, and adjust the seasoning.

1 large **chicken** plus **giblets**

12 **carrots,** peeled and cut in half

1 large **red onion,** peeled and cut into pieces

1 **leek,** white part only, washed and cut into pieces

2 **celery stalks with leaves,** cut into pieces

sea salt

white pepper

3 or 4 sachets **bouquet garni**

4 **bay leaves**

4 **chicken stock cubes**

1 tsp **sugar**

7 quarts **water**

vermicelli noodles

Old-fashioned chicken soup

↻ Preparation: 20 minutes; cooking: 3 hours 20 minutes   ✂ Makes 15–20 portions

⚡ Provides beta-carotene, potassium, protein, B vitamins, and vitamin C

❄ Suitable for freezing

I make large quantities of this nutritious soup, which I divide into smaller batches and freeze. Then, when I want to give my children chicken soup, I simply reheat a batch and add some cooked vermicelli for extra substance.

▶ Cut the chicken into about eight pieces, clean well, and put into a very large pan with the giblets. Cover with water and boil for 20 minutes. Skim off the scum from the surface with a slotted spoon.

▶ Add the rest of the ingredients (except the vermicelli), cover, and simmer over a low heat for about 3 hours.

▶ Remove the bay leaves and bouquet garni. Allow to cool, and then leave in the refrigerator overnight.

▶ The next day, skim off the layer of fat on the surface of the mixture and strain the soup through a sieve into another bowl. Take the chicken meat off the bones and tear it into pieces.

▶ Place some of the shredded chicken and a few of the carrots into the bowl of soup. Freeze in batches.

▶ When you want to use the soup, cook some vermicelli (thin pasta), if using, in lightly salted water according to the instructions on the package, and reheat a batch of the soup. Add the cooked pasta to the soup and serve.

TIP When all else fails, pasta is a great standby for children. It's a good idea to keep tasty homemade pasta sauces in the freezer.

Sloppy Joe sauce

⏱ Preparation: 5 minutes; cooking: 40 minutes   🍴 Makes 4 portions   🥄 Provides beta-carotene, iron, potassium, B vitamins, vitamins C and E, and zinc   ❄ Suitable for freezing

A good source of iron for your child, this tasty meat sauce is very versatile: it can be served on a toasted hamburger bun or as a sauce for pasta or rice.

▶ Heat the oil in a frying pan and sauté the onion and garlic for about 5 minutes or until softened.
▶ Add the ground beef and sauté until browned, stirring occasionally. After it has browned, I like to chop the meat in a food processor for a few seconds to make it less lumpy and easier to chew.
▶ Return the beef to the pan and stir in the remaining ingredients. Simmer over a low heat for about 30 minutes or until the sauce is thick.

1 tbsp **olive oil**

1 small **onion,** peeled and finely chopped

1 **garlic clove,** peeled and crushed

1/2 lb lean **ground beef**

1 2/3 cups **canned chopped tomatoes**

1 tsp **red wine vinegar**

1 tsp **brown sugar**

1/2 tsp **salt**

1/2 tsp **Worcestershire sauce**

1/2 tbsp **ketchup**

Special tomato sauce

⏱ Preparation: 5 minutes; cooking: 12 minutes   🍴 Makes 4 portions   🥄 Provides beta-carotene, calcium, protein, and vitamins B12 and E   ❄ Suitable for freezing

Try this full-flavored tomato sauce as a base for pizza topping, or add a few mini meatballs or a small can of tuna to make a simple pasta sauce.

▶ Heat the oil in a frying pan over a low heat, add the garlic, and sauté for 30 seconds. Stir in the tomatoes and break them up with a spoon. Add the remaining ingredients except the basil and Parmesan cheese. Season, then simmer gently for 10 minutes.
▶ Stir in the basil and Parmesan, and cook just until the cheese has melted.

1 tsp **olive oil**

1 **garlic clove,** peeled and crushed

1 2/3 cups **canned tomatoes**

2 tbsp **pesto**

1/4 tsp **mild chili powder**

1 tsp **balsamic vinegar**

1 tsp **superfine sugar**

salt and freshly ground **black pepper**

1 tbsp shredded **fresh basil**

2 tbsp freshly grated **Parmesan cheese**

Pasta twists with zucchini

1 tbsp **olive oil**

1 small **onion**, peeled and sliced

1 **garlic clove**, peeled and chopped

1 cup **zucchini**, sliced

1 cup small **button mushrooms**, sliced

1¼ cups **tomato purée**

1 **vegetable stock cube** dissolved in 3½ tbsp **boiling water**

½ tsp **balsamic vinegar**

½ tsp **sugar**

salt and freshly ground **black pepper**

½ lb **pasta twists (rotini)**

¼ cup freshly grated **Parmesan cheese**

⟳ Preparation: 10 minutes; cooking: 25 minutes   ⚙ Makes 4 portions

⚡ Provides calcium, fiber, folate, potassium, and protein   ❄ Suitable for freezing

Another quick recipe that will encourage children to enjoy eating vegetables. Vary the vegetables according to seasonal availability.

► Heat the oil in a pan, add the onion and garlic, and sauté for 2 minutes. Add the zucchini and button mushrooms, and sauté for 5 minutes. Stir in the tomato purée, vegetable stock, vinegar, and sugar, and season to taste. Simmer, uncovered, for 15 minutes.

► Meanwhile, cook the pasta in lightly salted, boiling water according to the instructions on the package.

► Remove the sauce from the heat and toss with the drained pasta. Serve with some freshly grated Parmesan.

Creamy chicken with penne

¼ lb **penne**

1 tbsp **olive oil**

1 **shallot**, peeled and chopped, or 3 tbsp **onion**, peeled and chopped

1 **garlic clove**, peeled and crushed

1 **chicken breast fillet** (about ¼ lb), cut into thin strips

2 ripe **plum tomatoes**, skinned, deseeded, and chopped

½ cup **sun-dried tomatoes**, chopped

⅓ cup **chicken stock** (see page 52)

½ tsp **lemon juice**

⅓ cup h**eavy cream**

2½ tbsp freshly grated **Parmesan cheese**

1 tbsp **fresh basil** (optional)

salt and freshly ground **black pepper**

⟳ Preparation: 5 minutes; cooking: 12 minutes   ⚙ Makes 2 portions

⚡ Provides calcium, potassium, protein, and B vitamins

► Cook the penne in lightly salted, boiling water according to the instructions on the package.

► Meanwhile, heat the oil in a frying pan and sauté the shallot and garlic for about 2 minutes.

► Add the chicken and continue to cook until browned, turning occasionally. Add the fresh and sun-dried tomatoes, and cook for 2 minutes.

► Add the stock and lemon juice and cook for 6–7 minutes on a low heat. Stir in the cream and Parmesan and heat through. Stir in the fresh basil and season with salt and black pepper.

► Drain the penne and mix thoroughly with the sauce.

Picky eater's pasta

¼ lb **pasta twists (rotini)**

a little **salt**

2 tbsp **butter**

4 tbsp freshly grated **Parmesan cheese**

⟳ Preparation: 3 minutes; cooking: 11–12 minutes   ⚙ Makes 1 portion

⚡ Provides calcium, protein, vitamins A, B2, and B12, and zinc

When all else fails, most children will eat this simple pasta dish. Serve with a side portion of carrots, sweet peppers, cucumber sticks, and cherry tomatoes.

► Cook the pasta in lightly salted, boiling water according to the instructions on the package.

► Melt the butter. Drain the pasta shapes and toss in the melted butter and freshly grated Parmesan cheese.

Tagliolini with cheese & Parma ham

⟳ Preparation: 5 minutes; cooking: 5 minutes ⊘ Makes 4 portions
✐ Provides calcium, potassium, protein, and B vitamins

2 tbsp **butter**

3 tbsp **flour**

1³/₄ cup **milk**

¹/₃ cup freshly grated **Parmesan cheese**

salt and freshly ground **black pepper**

¹/₄ lb **Parma ham,** thinly sliced and cut into strips

1 lb **tagliolini**

This is a version of a very famous pasta dish that is served in Harry's Bar in Venice. There, they make it with very thin, fresh green tagliolini, and it tastes absolutely wonderful.

▶ Melt the butter in a saucepan, add the flour, and cook for 1 minute, stirring occasionally.
▶ Gradually whisk in the milk. Bring to a boil, stirring continuously until thickened and smooth. Remove from the heat and stir in half the cheese. Season to taste, then stir in the Parma ham.
▶ Cook the tagliolini in boiling, lightly salted water according to the instructions on the package. Drain and mix with the cheese sauce.

▶ Transfer to an ovenproof dish and sprinkle with the remaining Parmesan cheese. Place under a preheated broiler for a few minutes until the top is golden and bubbling.

Marina's bow-tie stir-fry

⟳ Preparation: 35 minutes, including 30 minutes marinating; cooking: 15 minutes
⊘ Makes 4 portions ✐ Provides potassium, protein, and B vitamins including folate

1 **chicken breast fillet** (about ¹/₄ lb), cut into strips

¹/₄ lb **pasta bows (farfalle)**

1 tbsp **vegetable oil**

1 tbsp **sesame oil**

1 **onion,** peeled and thinly sliced

1 cup **zucchini,** cut into matchsticks

¹/₂ cup **frozen peas**

1 cup **bean sprouts**

salt and freshly ground **black pepper**

Marinade

1 tbsp **soy sauce**

¹/₂ tbsp **brown sugar**

Sauce

1 tbsp **soy sauce**

1 tbsp **oyster sauce**

1 tbsp **apricot** or **plum jam**

²/₃ cup **chicken stock** (see page 52)

¹/₂ tbsp **cornstarch** mixed with 1 tbsp **cold water**

Stir-fries are great because everything is cooked in the same pan, so they're quick and easy to make. This is an appealing combination of chicken, vegetables, and pasta with a tasty sauce.

▶ Marinate the chicken in the soy sauce and sugar for about 30 minutes.
▶ Cook the pasta in lightly salted, boiling water according to the instructions on the package.
▶ Heat the vegetable and sesame oils in a wok, add the onion, and stir-fry for 3 minutes. Add the marinated chicken and stir-fry for 3 minutes. Add the zucchini, peas, and bean sprouts and stir-fry for 4 minutes. Add the pasta, stirring for 1 minute.

▶ Put the soy sauce, oyster sauce, apricot jam, and chicken stock in a small saucepan and stir over a gentle heat for about 1 minute. Stir the cornstarch paste into the sauce. Bring to a boil and then heat, stirring for 1 minute.
▶ Pour the sauce over the chicken, and stir-fry until heated through. Season to taste.

1²/₃ cups **frozen spinach**

2 tbsp **butter**

1 **onion,** peeled and finely chopped

1 small **garlic clove,** peeled and crushed

1 cup **mushrooms,** sliced

1 tbsp **flour**

¹/₃ cup **milk**

2 tbsp **heavy cream**

salt and freshly ground **black pepper**

8 **parboiled cannelloni tubes**

Cheese sauce

2 tbsp **butter**

¹/₄ cup **flour**

1³/₄ cups **milk**

1 cup each grated **Gruyère** and **cheddar cheese**

¹/₂ tsp **ground dry mustard**

salt and freshly ground **black pepper**

To decorate

tomato purée or **Special tomato sauce** (see page 153)

8 sautéed **button mushrooms**

8 **black olives**

tiny **green pepper** bows and squares

red pepper strips

handful of grated **cheddar cheese**

Sleeping cannelloni

Preparation: 35 minutes; cooking: 45 minutes   350°F   Makes 8 portions
Provides beta-carotene, calcium, iron, potassium, protein, B vitamins including folate, and zinc   Suitable for freezing: undecorated

▶ Place the spinach in a pan without water, cover, set over a low heat, and cook gently for 5 minutes, or according to the instructions on the package. Squeeze out any excess water.

▶ Warm the butter in a pan, add the onion and garlic, and sauté until softened. Add the mushrooms and cook for 5 minutes. Stir in the flour and cook for 1 minute. Add the cooked spinach, stir in the milk, and cook for 2 minutes. Remove the pan from the heat, stir in the cream, and season to taste.

▶ Lightly grease a 10-x-8-inch ovenproof dish. Use a teaspoon to push the stuffing into the cannelloni tubes, then arrange them in the dish next to one another in a single layer.

▶ To make the cheese sauce, melt the butter in a pan over a low heat, add the flour, and stir to make a paste. Cook gently for 2 minutes, then whisk in the milk and cook, stirring, until thickened. Remove from the heat, stir in the cheeses until melted, add the mustard, and season to taste.

▶ Pour the sauce over the cannelloni, transfer to the preheated oven, and bake for 30 minutes.

▶ Decorate to make the dish look like four matchstick bodies sleeping under a sheet and blanket with their heads appearing at one end and their feet at the other. Spread a narrow band of tomato sauce from one side of the dish to the other near the top of the cannelloni tubes to create a turned-down red sheet. Arrange the eight olives in pairs at the bottom of each tube to indicate the feet. Use the mushrooms to make the heads; make three slits in each for two eyes and a mouth, then position at the top of each cannelloni tube. Push the squares of green pepper in each eye slit and the strips of red pepper in each mouth slit. Arrange the grated cheese around each head for the hair and place green pepper bows in it.

6 sheets **parboiled** or **fresh lasagna**

4 tbsp freshly grated **Parmesan cheese**

Tomato sauce

2 tbsp **olive oil**

1 large **onion**, peeled and chopped

1 **garlic clove**, peeled and crushed

1 tbsp **balsamic vinegar**

3$\frac{1}{2}$ cups **canned chopped tomatoes**

4 tbsp **sun-dried tomatoes**, chopped

2 tbsp **tomato purée**

1 **bay leaf**

Spinach and ricotta filling

1 lb fresh **spinach**, carefully washed and tough stalks removed

2 tbsp **olive oil**

1 cup **ricotta cheese**

2 tbsp freshly grated **Parmesan cheese**

salt and freshly ground **black pepper**

Cheese sauce

2 tbsp **butter**

$\frac{1}{4}$ cup **flour**

1$\frac{3}{4}$ cups **milk**

$\frac{2}{3}$ cup grated **cheddar cheese**

salt and freshly ground **black pepper**

Cheese, tomato & spinach lasagna

Preparation: 15 minutes; cooking: 45 minutes   350°F

Makes 6 portions   Provides beta-carotene, calcium, potassium, protein, B vitamins including folate, and vitamins A, C, and E   Suitable for freezing

▶ For the tomato sauce, heat the olive oil and sauté the onion and garlic for 3–4 minutes. Add the balsamic vinegar and cook for about 30 seconds. Stir in the canned chopped tomatoes, sun-dried tomatoes, tomato purée, and bay leaf. Bring to a boil and simmer for 10 minutes. Remove and discard the bay leaf. Set aside.

▶ Meanwhile, sauté the spinach in the olive oil until wilted, then drain and roughly chop. Mix with the ricotta cheese, stir in 2 tbsp of freshly grated Parmesan cheese and season with a little salt and pepper. Set aside.

▶ For the cheese sauce, melt the butter and stir in the flour and cook for about 1 minute. Gradually stir in the milk and

cook for about 2 minutes until thickened. Stir in the cheddar cheese until melted and season to taste.

▶ If using fresh lasagna, you will need to cook it in boiling water first, according to the instructions on the package.

▶ To assemble the lasagna, spoon a third of the tomato sauce onto the base of a fairly deep ovenproof lasagna dish (about 7 inches square) and cover with a layer of the spinach and ricotta. Cover with 2 sheets of lasagna, followed by a layer of the cheese sauce, then a layer of tomato sauce. Repeat each layer twice, finishing with a layer of cheese sauce.

▶ Sprinkle with the Parmesan cheese and bake in the preheated oven for 30 minutes.

9 sheets **parboiled lasagna**

1/3 cup freshly grated **Parmesan cheese**

Meat sauce

1 tbsp **olive oil**

1 **onion**, peeled and finely chopped

1 **carrot**, peeled and finely chopped

1 **celery stalk**, finely chopped

1 **garlic clove**, peeled and crushed

1 lb **lean ground beef**

1 1/4 cups **beef stock**

3/4 cup **canned chopped tomatoes**

1 tbsp **tomato purée**

2 sprigs **thyme**

2 **bay leaves**

1 tbsp chopped **fresh parsley**

salt and freshly ground **black pepper**

White sauce

3 tbsp **butter**

1/3 cup **flour**

1 3/4 cups **milk**

pinch of freshly ground **nutmeg**

1/2 cup grated **Gruyère cheese**

salt and freshly ground **black pepper**

Beef lasagna

🕐 Preparation: 15 minutes; cooking: 1 hour 5 minutes　🔥 350°F

🍴 Makes 6 portions　🥄 Provides beta-carotene, calcium, iron, potassium, B vitamins, vitamins C and E, and zinc　❄ Suitable for freezing

Lasagna is often a favorite dish with children, and the sauce for this recipe can also be used as a tasty meat sauce with pasta.

▶ To make the meat sauce, heat the olive oil in a saucepan, add the onion, carrot, and celery, and sauté over a low heat for 3–4 minutes. Add the garlic and ground beef and cook until the meat is browned all over.

▶ Transfer the mixture to a food processor and chop for a few seconds to give it a smoother texture.

▶ Return the mixture to the pan, add the stock, bring to a boil, then simmer for 3–4 minutes. Stir in the canned chopped tomatoes, tomato purée, thyme, bay leaves, parsley, salt, and pepper. Bring to a boil, then reduce the heat and simmer, covered, for 20 minutes.

▶ Remove the lid and cook for a further 5 minutes, stirring occasionally until most of the liquid has evaporated.

▶ Adjust the seasoning if necessary, remove and discard the thyme and bay leaves, take off the heat, and set aside to cool slightly.

▶ To make the white sauce, melt the butter in a saucepan and stir in the flour. Cook over a medium heat for 1 minute, stirring all the time, then gradually whisk in the milk. Bring to a boil, add the nutmeg, and simmer for 2 minutes. Remove from the heat, stir in the Gruyère cheese until melted, and season to taste.

▶ Cover the bottom of a large lasagna dish with a couple of tablespoons of each sauce. Cover with three sheets of lasagna. Spoon over half the meat sauce and cover with a third of the white sauce. Cover with three more sheets of lasagna. Now cover with the remaining meat sauce and another third of the white sauce. Cover with the last three sheets of lasagna and finish off by spooning on the remaining white sauce and then sprinkling on the Parmesan cheese.

▶ Bake in the preheated oven for about 30 minutes, until golden and bubbling.

1 tbsp **olive oil**

1 **onion**, peeled and finely chopped

1 **garlic clove**, peeled and crushed

1 small **red pepper,** deseeded and diced

1 lb **lean ground beef** or **lamb**

1 tbsp **pesto**

1 tbsp **tomato purée**

1/2 cup **chicken stock** (see page 52)

1 tbsp **fresh oregano** or 1/2 tbsp **dried oregano**

1 tbsp chopped **fresh parsley**

salt and freshly ground **black pepper**

1/2 lb **pasta twists (rotini)**

2 tbsp freshly grated **Parmesan cheese**

Pasta twirls with a meat sauce

🕐 Preparation: 8 minutes; cooking: 28 minutes　🍴 Makes 4 portions　🥄 Provides iron, potassium, B vitamins, vitamins C and E, and zinc　❄ Suitable for freezing

▶ Heat the olive oil in a large pan and sauté the onion, garlic, and red pepper for about 5 minutes, until softened. Add the meat and cook until browned. At this stage, chop the meat in a food processor to give it a softer texture if preferred.

▶ Return the meat to the pan and stir in the tomatoes, pesto, tomato purée, chicken stock, and herbs, and season to taste. Cover and cook over a medium heat for 20 minutes.

▶ Meanwhile, cook the pasta in boiling, lightly salted water according to the instructions on the package. Mix the pasta with the sauce and serve.

Variation

▶ Put the pasta and sauce in an 8-inch-square ovenproof dish, cover with half the white sauce used for Beef lasagna (see above), sprinkle with 2 tbsp grated Parmesan, and broil for a few minutes.

2/3 cup **butternut squash**, peeled and cut into small cubes

1 tbsp **olive oil**

generous pat of **butter**

1 **onion**, peeled and finely chopped

1 **garlic clove**, peeled and crushed

1 cup **risotto rice**

2¹/₂ cups hot **vegetable stock** (see page 47) or **chicken stock** (see page 52)

8 **sage leaves**, torn into small pieces

3 tbsp freshly grated **Parmesan cheese**

salt and freshly ground **black pepper**

Butternut squash risotto

Preparation: 10 minutes; cooking: 30 minutes   Makes 4 portions
Provides beta-carotene, calcium, potassium, and vitamins B2, B12, and E

Risottos are easy to make, and this one has a great blend of flavors. To make a good risotto, you need a heavy-bottomed pan that will allow even, slow cooking: a large, fairly deep frying pan is ideal. Add the stock gradually for perfect results and stir continuously! If reheating, stir in a little extra stock first.

▶ Steam the squash for 5 minutes.
▶ Heat the olive oil and butter in a heavy-bottomed pan and sauté the onion and garlic over a low heat until soft but not colored.
▶ Add the rice and stir until well coated. Cook over a medium heat for about 25 minutes, adding the stock one ladleful at a time and stirring occasionally, allowing the rice to absorb each ladleful of liquid before adding the next.

▶ About 10 minutes before the end of the cooking time, add the squash and sage. Continue to add the stock until it is all used up.
▶ Stir in the Parmesan cheese and season to taste. The risotto should be thick and creamy, and the texture of the rice should be soft on the outside but firm in the center.

1 cup **basmati rice**

2 tbsp **vegetable oil**

1 **onion,** peeled and chopped

1 **carrot,** peeled and sliced

1 cup **broccoli,** cut into small florets

1 cup **cauliflower,** cut into small florets

1 small **garlic clove,** peeled and crushed

1 tbsp **tomato purée**

1 tbsp **medium curry paste**

1½ cups **canned coconut milk**

½ cup **baby sweet corn,** cut into bite-size pieces

⅓ cup **frozen peas**

Curried vegetables with rice

⟳ Preparation: 15 minutes; cooking: 25 minutes   ⌒ Makes 4 portions   ⚡ Provides beta-carotene, fiber, folate, potassium, and vitamins C and E   ❄ Suitable for freezing

It's important to encourage young children to be a little adventurous. The flavor of mild curry and coconut makes these vegetables really tasty.

► Cook the rice in boiling, lightly salted water according to the instructions on the package.
► Meanwhile, heat the oil in a large saucepan and sauté the onion and carrot for 3 minutes to soften. Add the broccoli and cauliflower and cook for 5 minutes.
► Stir in the garlic, tomato purée, and curry paste and stir for 1 minute.

► Stir in the coconut milk and simmer for 10 minutes.
► Add the baby sweet corn and cook for a further 3 minutes. Finally, add the peas and cook for 2 to 3 minutes.
► Serve on a bed of the cooked rice.

½ tbsp **vegetable oil**

½ **onion,** peeled and very finely chopped

½ **garlic clove,** peeled and crushed

¼ tsp each **curry powder, ground ginger,** and **ground cumin**

1 cup **button mushrooms,** finely chopped

1 cup **cauliflower,** cut into very small florets

1 **carrot,** peeled and very finely chopped

2 tsp **superfine sugar**

3 tsp mild **natural yogurt**

salt and freshly ground **black pepper**

1 package **filo pastry sheets**

4 tbsp **butter,** melted

TIP When handling filo pastry, keep the piece you are not working with covered with a clean, damp towel to prevent it from drying out and becoming brittle.

Mildly spiced vegetable samosas

⟳ Preparation: 35 minutes; cooking: 35 minutes   🌡 350°F   ⌒ Makes 8 portions   ⚡ Provides beta-carotene and potassium   ❄ Suitable for freezing: uncooked

► Heat the oil in a frying pan, add the onion and garlic, and sauté for 2–3 minutes. Stir in the spices and sauté for 1 minute. Add the vegetables and cook for 5 minutes, stirring occasionally. Stir in the sugar and yogurt. Season and cook for 3–4 minutes.
► Lay the filo pastry out flat and cover with a clean, damp dish towel. Place one sheet of pastry on the work surface and brush with melted butter. Fold the pastry in half lengthwise and brush again with butter.
► Place 1 tbsp of filling on one end of the strip, leaving a 1-inch border around it. Fold over the corner to make a triangle, then keep folding the parcel over on itself, along the length of the pastry. Seal the flap left at the end with melted butter. Repeat with the remaining pastry and filling.

► Place the samosas on a lightly greased baking sheet and brush with more butter. Bake in the preheated oven for 20–25 minutes, or until crisp.

Mini bean & veggie enchiladas

⟳ Preparation: 10 minutes; cooking: 15 minutes ⚲ Microwave on high or conventional oven at 350°F ⚲ Makes 4 portions ⚲ Provides calcium, fiber, folate, iron, and protein

Small flour tortillas can be filled with a variety of ingredients. Kidney beans are a good source of protein.

▶ Heat the oil in a frying pan, add the onion, garlic, and chili if using, and cook gently for 3 minutes.
▶ Roughly chop the kidney beans. Add the beans to the frying pan with the sweet corn and chopped tomatoes. Season to taste and cook over a medium heat for 5 minutes. Sprinkle with parsley. Preheat the broiler to high.
▶ Divide the filling among the tortillas, roll them up, and top with cheese. Heat through in a microwave for 1–2 minutes, or in a conventional oven for 6 minutes, then broil until golden and bubbly.

Variation

▶ Replace the beans with two chicken breasts, cut into strips, seasoned, and fried. Replace the sweet corn and tomatoes with half a small red pepper, chopped and sautéed. Heat the enchiladas through and dress with a spoonful each of salsa and sour cream.

1 tbsp **vegetable oil**

½ **onion**, peeled and chopped

1 small **garlic clove**, peeled and crushed

¼ **red chili**, finely chopped (optional)

⅔ cup **canned red kidney beans** or **refried beans**

¾ cup **canned** or **frozen sweet corn**, cooked

1 cup **canned chopped tomatoes**, drained

salt and freshly ground **black pepper**

1 tbsp chopped **fresh parsley**

4 **mini flour tortillas**

½ cup grated **cheddar cheese**

Vegetable stir-fry with jumbo shrimp in sweet & sour sauce

⟳ Preparation: 15 minutes; cooking: 20 minutes ⚲ Makes 2 portions ⚲ Provides beta-carotene, potassium, protein, B vitamins including folate, vitamins C and E, and zinc

▶ Cook the rice in boiling, lightly salted water according to the instructions on the package.
▶ Heat the vegetable oil in a wok and stir-fry the mushrooms, sweet corn, and red pepper for 2 to 3 minutes. Add the sake or water, shrimp, and green onions, and cook for 2–3 minutes.
▶ Mix together all the sauce ingredients and add to the pan along with the spinach leaves. Cook for 2 to 3 minutes until thickened slightly.
▶ Serve on a bed of the cooked rice.

⅔ cup **basmati** or **long-grain rice**

1 tbsp **vegetable oil**

1 cup **button** or **cremini mushrooms**, quartered

½ cup **baby sweet corn**, halved lengthwise

½ **red pepper**, thinly sliced

1 tbsp **sake** or **water**

¼ lb **cooked jumbo shrimp**

2 **green onions**, sliced

½ cup **baby spinach leaves**

Sauce

⅓ cup **chicken stock** (see page 52) or **vegetable stock** (see page 47)

2 tsp **soy sauce**

1 tsp **sesame oil**

1 tbsp **rice wine vinegar**

1 tbsp **tomato purée**

1 tbsp **brown sugar**

$^1\!/_4$ lb skinned **salmon fillets**, cut into about 2-inch cubes

Marinade

1$^1\!/_2$ tbsp **soy sauce**

2 tbsp **ketchup**

1 tbsp **white wine vinegar**

1 tsp **sweet chili sauce**

2 tbsp **dark brown sugar**

Sticky salmon

Preparation: 1 hour 5 minutes, including 1 hour marinating; cooking: 20 minutes
400°F   Makes 2 portions   Provides magnesium, omega-3 fatty acids, potassium, protein, B vitamins, vitamins D and E, and zinc

Salmon is an excellent food for children because it's quick to cook and a good source of essential fatty acids, which are important for brain function. The flavor of the marinade is addictive. It's funny how the simplest and easiest recipes can very often be the best.

▶ Place all the ingredients for the marinade in a small saucepan and stir over a gentle heat until the sugar has dissolved completely.

▶ Remove from the heat, pour into an ovenproof dish, and leave to cool. Add the salmon fillets and turn to coat them in the marinade. Leave to marinate for at least 1 hour.

▶ Cook the salmon fillets in the preheated oven for 20 minutes, basting occasionally until cooked through. Serve with boiled white rice with a dash of soy sauce, or with the noodle and bean sprout mixture used in the recipe for salmon teriyaki on page 123.

$^1\!/_4$ cup **sliced almonds**

$^1\!/_2$ tbsp **flour**

salt and freshly ground **black pepper**

1 tbsp **butter**

a little **vegetable oil**

2 small **trout fillets**, skin on

squeeze of **lemon juice**

1 tbsp chopped **fresh parsley**

Trout with almonds

Preparation: 5 minutes; cooking: 15 minutes   Makes 2 portions
Provides calcium, magnesium, omega-3 fatty acids, potassium, protein, B vitamins, and vitamins D and E

You can use rainbow trout for this recipe, but if you want to make it for a special meal, such as a birthday dinner, use pink salmon trout, which is a very tasty fish. This dish is quick to prepare, so is perfect for fast evening meals if your child has friends over after school. The toasted almond slices are highly nutritious and add a wonderful flavor.

▶ Toast the almond slices on a baking tray in the oven for 5–6 minutes, or in a dry frying pan for a few minutes until golden. Keep moving them around in the pan or they will burn very quickly. Set aside.

▶ Dust the skin side of the trout fillets with flour, and season both sides with salt and pepper.

▶ Heat half the butter together with a drizzle of vegetable oil. Place the trout, skin side down, in the pan and cook for about 5 minutes until the skin is golden and the fish is cooked through. Remove the trout and place on a serving dish.

▶ Add the remaining butter to the frying pan along with the lemon juice, parsley, and toasted almonds. Cook for about 1 minute and spoon over the fish. Serve with mashed potatoes with carrots (see page 165) and peas or broccoli.

¾ lb small to medium **potatoes**, scrubbed

1½ tbsp **olive oil**

freshly ground **sea salt** and **black pepper**

seasoned salt (optional)

½ cup **flour**, to coat

4 cups **corn flakes**

½ lb **flounder fillets** or **cod fillets**, cut into about 16 strips

1 **egg**, lightly beaten

vegetable oil for frying

TIP The fish can be fried in advance and then reheated in the oven. It can also be baked on a greased baking sheet for 10–12 minutes rather than fried.

Fish & oven-baked chips

⏱ Preparation: 5 minutes; cooking: 35 minutes   🔥 400°F   ✂ Makes 4 portions
📈 Provides potassium, protein, B vitamins including folate, and vitamins C and E

If you make these for a children's party, wrap portions in greaseproof paper and serve British-style in a newspaper cone—use the comics section!

▶ Halve the potatoes lengthwise, then cut into wedges. Toss in a bowl together with the oil, a little seasoned salt (if using), and salt and pepper until well coated.

▶ Transfer the potatoes to a roasting pan and bake in the preheated oven for approximately 30 minutes, turning occasionally, until crisp on the outside but tender inside.

▶ Meanwhile, spread the flour on a plate and season with salt and pepper. Crush the corn flakes by putting them in a plastic bag and smashing them with a rolling pin, then pour on another plate.

▶ Dip each strip of fish first in the seasoned flour, then in the egg, then roll in the crushed cornflakes.

▶ Heat the vegetable oil in a frying pan, add the strips in batches, and fry for 2 to 3 minutes, turning halfway through.

2 tbsp **vegetable oil**

1 medium **onion,** peeled and finely chopped

1 cup **leeks,** washed and sliced

3/4 lb **potatoes,** peeled and cut into chunks

1 1/2 tbsp **milk**

2 tbsp **butter**

salt and freshly ground **black pepper**

1/2 lb **ground chicken** or **turkey**

1/2 stalk **celery,** chopped

1 small **carrot,** grated

2 tbsp **ketchup**

1/3 cup boiling **chicken stock** (see page 52)

1/2 tsp **fresh thyme** or pinch of **dried thyme**

an extra pat of **butter**

To decorate

1 **leek,** washed and sliced

2 **baby sweet corn,** halved

1 **tomato,** sliced

1 **carrot**

6 **frozen peas**

basil leaves

Mini chicken & potato pie

⟳ Preparation: 15 minutes; cooking: 25 minutes   ⚀ Makes 3 mini pies
✎ Provides beta-carotene, potassium, protein, B vitamins including folate, and vitamins A, C, and E   ✳ Suitable for freezing

Children like individual portions, so I make this recipe in three small ramekins, and decorate each pie with vegetables to make humorous faces. These "funny face" pies were very popular with a tasting panel of young consumers!

▶ Heat the oil in a pan and sauté the onion and leeks for 5 minutes to soften.
▶ Meanwhile, cook the potatoes in a pan of lightly salted water until tender, then mash with the milk and butter. Season to taste.
▶ Add the ground chicken, celery, and grated carrot to the onion and leeks and cook for about 7 minutes. Transfer to a food processor and chop for a few seconds to give the mixture a smooth texture, if desired. Return to the pan, add the ketchup, boiling stock, and herbs. Cover and cook for about 5 minutes.

▶ Preheat the broiler. Divide the chicken mixture between three 4-inch ramekin dishes and top with mashed potatoes. Dot the tops with a little butter and place under the broiler until golden.
▶ Decorate each with vegetables to create a funny face of your design. You could use sliced leeks and peas for the eyes, halved baby sweet corn for the nose, two thin slices of tomato to make the mouth, carrot strips for the hair, and green beans for a distinctive mustache. You could also add a bow tie made out of basil leaves.

Chicken with gravy & mashed potatoes with carrots

⟳ Preparation: 10 minutes; cooking: 30 minutes   🔪 Makes 4 portions   🗡 Provides beta-carotene, potassium, protein, B vitamins including folate, and vitamins C and E

Creamy mashed potatoes and carrots are the perfect partner for succulent griddled chicken, and both are made all the more delicious by the gravy.

▶ For the gravy, heat 1 tbsp of the vegetable oil in a saucepan and cook the onion for 7–8 minutes until it begins to turn golden. Stir in the sugar and water, increase the heat, and cook for about 1 minute, until the water has evaporated.
▶ Stir in the beef stock, cornstarch mixed with water, Worcestershire sauce, and tomato purée. Season with salt and pepper. Stir for 2–3 minutes until thickened, then set aside.
▶ For the mashed potatoes and carrots, put the vegetables into a pan of lightly salted water. Bring to a boil, then cook for 20 minutes or until tender. Drain and mash with the butter, salt, pepper, and enough milk to give the mash a creamy consistency.

▶ Cover the chicken breasts with plastic wrap and pound with a mallet so they are not too thick. Season with salt and pepper.
▶ Heat the griddle, brush with the remainder of the vegetable oil, and cook the chicken for about 3 minutes on each side, or until cooked through. Alternatively, heat the oil in a frying pan and fry on each side for approximately 4 minutes, or until lightly golden and cooked all the way through.
▶ Serve with domes of mashed veggies made with an ice-cream scoop.

4 **chicken breast fillets**

Gravy

2 tbsp **vegetable oil**

1 **onion,** peeled and thinly sliced

1 tsp **superfine sugar**

1 tbsp **water**

³⁄₄ cup **beef stock**

1 tsp **cornstarch** mixed with 1 tbsp **water**

few drops of **Worcestershire sauce**

1 tsp **tomato paste**

salt and freshly ground **black pepper**

Mashed potatoes and carrots

1 lb **potatoes,** peeled and cut into chunks

1 large **carrot,** peeled and thinly sliced

2 tbsp **butter**

salt and **white pepper**

a little **milk**

TIP The gravy, potatoes, and carrots can be prepared in advance—at mealtime, just cook the chicken.

Sticky barbecue drumsticks

⟳ Preparation: 45 minutes, including 30 minutes marinating; cooking: 20 minutes
🔪 Makes 4 portions   🗡 Provides protein and B vitamins   ❄ Suitable for freezing

Barbecued drumsticks are excellent whether eaten hot off the broiler or cold from the lunch box. Wrap the ends of the drumsticks in foil so that they can be eaten with the fingers without getting messy.

▶ To make the marinade, heat the oil in a frying pan, add the onion, and sauté until soft. Stir in the sugar and cook gently for 1–2 minutes. Add the remaining ingredients and simmer for 5 minutes.
▶ Pour the mixture into a glass or ceramic bowl and allow to cool. Add the drumsticks and marinate for at least 30 minutes and up to 12 hours in the refrigerator.

▶ Preheat the broiler to a high heat. Transfer the drumsticks to a baking dish, baste well with the marinade, and place under the broiler. Cook for 20 minutes, turning halfway through and basting again with the marinade.
▶ Make sure the drumsticks are cooked through, wrap the ends in foil, and serve hot or cold.

4 large **chicken drumsticks,** scored with a knife (remove the skin first if preferred)

Marinade

¹⁄₂ tbsp **vegetable oil**

1 small **onion,** peeled and chopped

¹⁄₃ cup **dark muscovado** or **dark brown sugar**

juice of ¹⁄₂ **lemon**

¹⁄₂ tbsp **Worcestershire sauce**

4 tbsp **ketchup**

1 tbsp **white wine vinegar**

2 **part-boned chicken breasts** (about ¾ lb)

⅓ cup **flour**

1 tsp **salt** and a little freshly ground **black pepper**

1 **egg**, lightly beaten

½ cup **fresh bread crumbs**

vegetable oil for frying

Marinade

pinch of **cayenne pepper**

⅔ cup **buttermilk**

Gravy

1 small **onion**, peeled and chopped

1 tsp **flour**

1 tsp **tomato purée**

½ tsp **Worcestershire sauce**

1¼ cups **chicken stock** (see page 52)

Southern fried chicken

Preparation: 10 minutes, plus several hours marinating; cooking: 15 minutes
Makes 2 portions   Provides potassium, protein, B vitamins, and vitamins A and D

Marinating the chicken in buttermilk gives it a terrific flavor and makes it wonderfully tender.

▶ To make the marinade, mix the cayenne pepper into the buttermilk.
▶ Place the chicken breasts in the marinade and refrigerate for several hours. Either marinate the chicken overnight and cook it for lunch the next day, or set it in the marinade in the morning and cook that evening.
▶ In a shallow bowl, mix together the flour and the salt and pepper. Shake off the excess buttermilk from the chicken breasts and coat with the seasoned flour. Dip into the beaten egg, then coat with the bread crumbs.
▶ Either deep fry or shallow fry in at least ½ inch of oil in a frying pan for about 10 minutes or until golden brown and cooked through.

▶ To make a gravy, pour off the oil and sauté the chopped onion until softened. Add the flour, cook for 30 seconds, and stir in the chicken stock with the tomato purée and Worcestershire sauce. Bring to a boil and simmer for a few minutes. Serve with oven-baked potatoes or sweet-potato wedges (see page 108).

1 tbsp **sunflower oil**

1 **garlic clove,** peeled and crushed

1 **onion**, peeled and chopped

2 small **chicken breast fillets** (about ½ lb), cut into chunks

1 **red pepper**, deseeded and diced

1⅔ cups **long-grain rice**

1 tsp **turmeric**

1 tsp **mild chili powder**

3 cups **chicken stock** (see page 52)

1 **bay leaf**

⅔ cup **frozen peas**

2 **pork sausages**, grilled and sliced diagonally

¼ lb small **cooked, peeled shrimp**

salt and freshly ground **black pepper**

Paella

Preparation: 10 minutes; cooking: 25 minutes   Makes 8 portions
Provides beta-carotene, magnesium, potassium, protein, B vitamins, vitamin E, and zinc   Suitable for freezing

Paella is a great all-in-one dish that's easy to cook and full of flavor. While the traditional Spanish paella contains a mixture of seafood, including mussels, my child-friendly version is made with chicken, sausage, and shrimp. The turmeric gives the rice a rich yellow tint.

▶ Heat the oil in a deep, heavy-bottomed frying pan, add the garlic and onion, and sauté for 3 minutes. Add the chicken and sauté until browned on all sides.
▶ Add the red pepper and cook, stirring, for 1 minute. Rinse the rice, then stir it in with the turmeric and chili powder. Sauté for 1 minute, stirring the mixture constantly.

▶ Pour in the stock, add the bay leaf, stir well, and leave to simmer for 15 minutes, covered, until all the liquid is absorbed by the rice.
▶ Add the peas, sausages, and shrimp to the pan and simmer, covered, for a further 4–5 minutes. Season, remove the bay leaf, and serve.

Enchiladas with turkey & tomato sauce

⟳ Preparation: 10 minutes; cooking: 45 minutes 🔥 350°F

🔪 Makes 8 enchiladas 💉 Provides beta-carotene, calcium, potassium, protein, B vitamins including folate, and vitamins A, C, and E ❄ Suitable for freezing

This is a fabulous recipe that has become a family favorite. It's great for dinner parties, too, and can be made in advance. These enchiladas are tortilla wraps filled with a delicious ground turkey mixture and then covered with tomato sauce and grated cheese and baked in the oven. Highly recommended!

▶ To make the sauce, heat the olive oil in a medium saucepan and sauté the onion and garlic for 5 minutes until softened. Stir in the tomato purée and oregano, then season with salt and pepper. Cover and leave to simmer for 10 minutes.

▶ For the turkey filling, heat the olive oil in a large frying pan or wok and stir in the garlic, onion, pepper, and zucchini. Cook for 5 minutes, then add the turkey, stirring occasionally.

Season with salt and pepper. After 7–8 minutes, the turkey should be completely cooked through. Stir in half of the cheese until melted.

▶ Divide the mixture between the mini tortillas and roll up each one to form a cigar shape. Place the rolled tortillas in an ovenproof dish and cover with tomato sauce. Sprinkle with the remaining cheese. Bake in the preheated oven for 15–20 minutes until golden.

8 **flour tortillas,** about 8 inches in diameter

Sauce

2 tbsp **olive oil**

1 **onion,** peeled and chopped

1 **garlic clove,** peeled and crushed

1²/₃ cups **tomato purée**

1 tsp **fresh oregano**

salt and freshly ground **black pepper**

Turkey filling

1 tbsp **olive oil**

1 **garlic clove,** peeled and crushed

1 **red onion,** peeled and chopped

1 **red pepper,** deseeded and diced

1 small **zucchini,** diced

³/₄ pound **ground turkey**

salt and freshly ground **black pepper**

1¹/₂ cups grated **cheddar cheese**

1 tbsp **vegetable oil**

1 small **onion**, peeled and chopped

1 **garlic clove**, peeled and crushed

2 **chicken breasts** (about ¾ lb), skinned and cut into chunks

1 cup **button mushrooms**, cut into quarters

1 tbsp **mild curry paste**

1 tsp **tomato purée**

¾ cup **evaporated milk**

1 **eating apple**, peeled, cored, and diced

2 tbsp **raisins**

salt and freshly ground **black pepper**

1 tsp **lemon juice**

Mild chicken curry with apple

↻ Preparation: 10 minutes; cooking: 25 minutes   ✂ Makes 4 portions

⚗ Provides beta-carotene, iron, potassium, protein, and B vitamins including folate

❄ Suitable for freezing

If your child prefers, you could leave out the mushrooms and add some frozen peas about 5 minutes before the end of the cooking time.

► Heat the vegetable oil in a medium saucepan. Add the onion and garlic and cook for 5 minutes until softened. Stir in the chicken and the mushrooms and cook for 3–4 minutes, until the chicken has turned opaque.

► Stir in the curry paste and tomato purée and continue to cook, stirring for about 6 minutes. Stir in the evaporated milk, apple, and raisins and cook for 10 minutes, stirring occasionally.

► Season with salt and pepper and stir in the lemon juice.

---

2 **chicken breast fillets** (about ¾ lb), cut into chunks

Marinade

2 tbsp **black bean sauce**

2 tbsp **soy sauce**

2 tbsp **peanut butter**

1 tbsp **rice wine vinegar**

2 tbsp **honey**

Note Remove the skewers before serving to young children.

TIP Try threading vegetables, such as pieces of onion or pepper, onto the skewers, alternating with the chicken, to get some extra vegetables into your child's diet.

Chicken satay

↻ Preparation: 35 minutes, including 30 minutes marinating; cooking: 10 minutes

✂ Makes 3 portions   ⚗ Provides iron, potassium, protein, B vitamins, and zinc

Here are two delicious ways to make chicken satay. They should be a great hit with any child who likes peanut butter.

► Preheat the broiler to high.

► Mix all the marinade ingredients with the chicken in a glass or ceramic bowl. Leave to marinate for at least 30 minutes. While the chicken marinates, soak four bamboo skewers in water to prevent them from getting scorched when under the broiler.

► Thread the chicken onto the skewers and cook under the preheated broiler for 8–10 minutes until cooked through, turning and basting occasionally with the marinade.

Variation

► Sandwich two chicken breasts between two pieces of plastic wrap and pound them out with a rolling pin or mallet until they are quite thin. Remove the plastic wrap and cut each breast into six strips. Make a marinade by mixing 4 tbsp peanut butter, 5 tbsp coconut milk, 2 tbsp lime juice, ½ tsp sweet chili sauce, 2 tsp soy sauce, 2 tsp honey, and 1 tsp vegetable oil. Marinate the chicken in the refrigerator for at least 30 minutes. Meanwhile, soak six bamboo skewers to prevent them from getting scorched when under the broiler. Remove the chicken from the marinade and thread it onto the skewers in a snake pattern. Reserve the marinade. Cook under a medium-hot broiler for 8 to 10 minutes, turning halfway through. Alternatively, cook them first on a griddle, then finish off under the broiler. You can make a tasty dipping sauce for the chicken satay using the reserved marinade. Put in a saucepan, bring to a boil, and stir in 3½ tbsp boiling water. Cook, stirring, for 1 minute over a medium heat.

2 **chicken breast fillets** (about
$3/4$ lb), cut in half

Marinade

2 tbsp **mango chutney**

1 tbsp **dark brown sugar**

juice of $1/2$ **lime**

1 tsp **soy sauce**

freshly ground **black pepper**

Spinach and mango salad

$1^{1}/_2$ cups **baby spinach**, carefully
washed

$1/2$ large **mango**, peeled, pitted,
and chopped

$1/3$ cup **dried cranberries**

$1^{1}/_2$ tbsp **toasted pine nuts**
(optional)

Dressing

3 tbsp **vegetable oil**

1 tbsp **balsamic vinegar**

1 tsp **sugar**

salt and freshly ground **black pepper**

Sticky mango chicken

Preparation: 1 hour, including 1 hour marinating; cooking: 9 minutes

Makes 2–4 portions   Provides beta-carotene, fiber, iron, magnesium, potassium,
protein, B vitamins including folate, and vitamins C and E

*The spinach and mango salad that accompanies this dish is one of my
favorite salads. I love the combination of baby spinach, fresh mangoes, and
dried cranberries. If I'm making it for older children, I add toasted pine nuts.*

▶ Mix together the mango chutney,
sugar, lime juice, soy sauce, and pepper.
Pour this over the chicken and leave to
marinate for at least 1 hour, turning
occasionally. Preheat the broiler to
medium-high.

▶ Drain the marinade from the chicken
and reserve. Place the chicken on a
baking sheet. Broil for about 6 minutes
and then drizzle with a little of the
marinade and continue to cook for

about 3 minutes or until the chicken
is turning golden and cooked through.

▶ Meanwhile, mix together all the
ingredients for the salad dressing.

▶ In a bowl, combine the spinach,
mango, cranberries, and pine nuts, if
using, reserving some for sprinkling.
Toss with the dressing. Serve the chicken
on a bed of the salad. Sprinkle with
toasted pine nuts, if using.

1 cup **basmati rice**, rinsed in cold water then drained

4 tbsp **vegetable oil**

1 small **onion**, peeled and finely chopped

1/2 cup **red pepper**, deseeded and finely chopped

salt and freshly ground **black pepper**

1 beaten **egg**

1/3 cup **frozen peas**

1/3 cup **frozen sweet corn**

1 large **green onion**, sliced

1 **chicken breast fillet** (about 1/4 lb), cut into thin strips

1/4 lb **cooked shrimp** (optional)

1 tbsp light **soy sauce**

Egg fried rice with chicken & shrimp

🔄 Preparation: 10 minutes; cooking: 30 minutes ✎ Makes 4 portions

✎ Provides beta-carotene, protein, B vitamins including folate, vitamin C, and zinc

❄ Suitable for freezing

Egg fried rice with vegetables and chicken is an appealing, simple meal. Your child may be eager to practice eating with chopsticks; this will be slow going at first, so provide a fork, too.

▶ Cook the rice in boiling, lightly salted water according to the instructions on the package.

▶ Heat half the oil in a large frying pan or wok, add the onion, and sauté for 2 minutes. Add the red pepper and cook for 7–8 minutes.

▶ Season the beaten egg with a little pepper. Pour it into the pan, tipping the pan to spread it evenly, and cook until set. Remove from the heat and break the egg up into small pieces with a wooden spatula.

▶ Return the pan to the heat, add the peas and sweet corn, and cook until tender. Remove the egg/vegetable mixture from the pan and set aside.

Add the remaining oil and sauté the green onion for 1 minute. Add the chicken and sauté for 3–4 minutes or until cooked, then season.

▶ Add the cooked rice and shrimp, if using, and toss the rice over a high heat for 2 minutes. Return the egg/vegetable mixture to the pan, add the soy sauce, and toss together until heated through.

1/4 lb **dried rice noodles**

3 tbsp **oil**

2 **chicken breast fillets** (about 3/4 lb), cut into very thin strips

1 or 2 **garlic cloves**, peeled and crushed

1 1/2 cups **bean sprouts**

5 **green onions**, cut diagonally into 3/4-inch pieces

2 **eggs**, beaten

3 tbsp **brown sugar**

1 1/2 tbsp **lemon** or **lime juice**

2 tbsp **soy sauce**

3 tsp **sweet chili sauce**

2 tbsp **oyster sauce**

Pad Thai noodles with chicken

🔄 Preparation: 15 minutes; cooking: 15 minutes ✎ Makes 4 portions

✎ Provides potassium, protein, and B vitamins

▶ Cook the noodles in boiling, lightly salted water according to the instructions on the package.

▶ Heat the oil in a wok and stir-fry the chicken for about 4 minutes. Add the garlic, bean sprouts, and green onions, and cook for about 3 minutes.

▶ Add the beaten eggs, stirring continuously until set, and then the sugar, lemon or lime, soy sauce, sweet chili sauce, and oyster sauce.

▶ Finally, add the noodles and stir until heated through.

Singapore noodles

🕑 Preparation: 45 minutes, including 30 minutes marinating; cooking: 20 minutes

⚔ Makes 4 portions   🍴 Provides beta-carotene, fiber, iron, protein, B vitamins including folate, vitamin C, and zinc

These noodles can be made spicier with added chili and curry powder. If preferred, replace the shrimp with pork or more chicken. For extra flavor, fry the beaten egg in 1/2 tbsp of sesame oil.

► Mix together the marinade ingredients in a bowl, cut the chicken into thin strips, add to the bowl, and marinate for at least 30 minutes.

► Heat 1/2 tbsp of oil in a frying pan, add the egg, and fry to make a thin omelet. Remove from the pan and cut into ribbons. Heat 1 tbsp of oil in the pan or a wok and sauté the garlic and chili, if using, for 30 seconds. Drain the chicken, add to the pan, and cook for 3–4 minutes, then set aside.

► Heat the remaining oil in the wok. Add the baby corn and carrots and stir-fry for 2 minutes. Add the zucchini and bean sprouts and cook for 2 minutes. Stir the curry powder into the stock and add to the wok. Return the chicken to the pan with the shrimp, green onions, and egg, and fry for 2 minutes.

► Cook the noodles in boiling, lightly salted water according to the instructions on the package. Drain, mix with the stir-fry, and heat through.

1/4 lb **chicken breast fillet**

2 1/2 tbsp **vegetable oil**

1 beaten **egg**

1 **garlic clove**, peeled and chopped

1/4 tsp finely chopped **red chili** (optional)

1/2 cup **baby sweet corn**

1/2 cup each **carrots** and **zucchini**, cut into thin strips

3/4 cup **bean sprouts**

1/4 tsp **mild curry powder**

4 tbsp **strong chicken stock**

1/4 lb small **peeled shrimp**

3 **green onions**, thinly sliced

1/4 lb **Chinese noodles**

Marinade

1 tbsp each **soy sauce** and **sake**

1/2 tsp **sugar**

1 tsp **cornstarch**

2 tbsp **vegetable oil**

1 **onion,** peeled and finely chopped

1/2 lb **lean ground beef**

1/2 tsp **dried thyme**

salt and freshly ground **black pepper**

1 lb **potatoes,** peeled and boiled for 12 minutes, then mashed with 2 tbsp **butter**

1 tbsp chopped **fresh parsley**

1 tbsp **ketchup**

1/2 tsp **Worcestershire sauce**

flour for dusting

Gravy

1 tbsp **vegetable oil**

1 **onion,** peeled and thinly sliced

1 tsp **demerara** or **brown sugar**

2 tbsp **water**

1 **beef stock cube**

1 3/4 cups **boiling water**

1 tbsp **cornstarch**

1 tsp **tomato paste**

a few drops **Worcestershire sauce**

1/2 tsp **ground dry mustard**

Beef croquettes

Preparation: 15 minutes; cooking: 25 minutes Makes 12 croquettes Provides iron, potassium, protein, B vitamins, vitamins C and E, and zinc Suitable for freezing

I think this dish is probably my kids' favorite ground meat recipe, and their dad loves it, too! The mashed potatoes give these croquettes a nice, soft texture.

▶ Heat 1 tbsp of the vegetable oil in a saucepan and fry the onion for 3–4 minutes. Add the beef and fry for a further 3–4 minutes. Stir in the thyme and season with salt and pepper. Cook for 1 minute more.

▶ Stir the mixture into the mashed potatoes with the parsley, ketchup, and Worcestershire sauce. Season to taste. Cool, then refrigerate until cold.

▶ Using your hands, form the mixture into 12 croquettes, dust with flour, and refrigerate for at least 1 hour.

▶ Heat the remaining vegetable oil in a large frying pan and sauté the croquettes for about 5 minutes or until golden and cooked through.

▶ To make the gravy, heat the oil in a saucepan and, over a low heat, cook the onion for about 8 minutes until softened. Stir in the sugar and 1 tbsp of water. Dissolve the stock cube in the boiling water and add.

▶ Mix 1 tbsp of cold water with the cornstarch and stir into the beef stock. Pour into the saucepan. Stir in the tomato purée, Worcestershire sauce, and mustard. Bring to a boil and simmer for 3–4 minutes. Season to taste. Serve with the croquettes.

Beef tacos

⟳ Preparation: 10 minutes; cooking: 15 minutes   ⬇ 350°F   ✂ Makes 4 portions
🥕 Provides beta-carotene, fiber, iron, protein, B vitamins including folate,
vitamin C, and zinc

*Children seem to love tacos. Try stuffing them with a variety of delicious
ingredients. Beans make a great filling, and this is a good way of getting
them into your child's diet.*

▶ Heat the oil in a saucepan, add the onion and garlic, and sauté for about 2 minutes. Add the peppers and continue to cook, stirring occasionally, for 3 minutes. Add the ground beef and cook, stirring, until browned.
▶ Stir in the chopped tomatoes, mild chili sauce, and stock, then simmer uncovered for 15 minutes. Stir in the red kidney beans and cook for 3 minutes. Stir in half the cilantro (if using) and heat through. Season to taste.

▶ Meanwhile, warm the taco shells in the preheated oven for 2 to 3 minutes, or in a microwave on full power for 1 minute. Remove from the oven, line with lettuce, spoon in the beef mixture, and garnish with the remaining cilantro.

1 tsp **vegetable oil**

½ small **onion**, peeled and finely diced

1 **garlic clove**, peeled and crushed

¼ cup each **red pepper** and **green pepper**, cored, deseeded, and finely diced

¼ lb **lean ground beef**

¾ cup **canned chopped tomatoes**

1 tsp **sweet** or **mild chili sauce**

⅓ cup **chicken stock** (see page 52)

1¼ cups **canned red kidney beans**

salt and freshly ground **black pepper**

½ tbsp chopped **fresh cilantro**

4 **taco shells**

4 **lettuce leaves**

Minute steak with teriyaki sauce, mushrooms & bean sprouts

⟳ Preparation: 45 minutes, including 30 minutes marinating; cooking: 12 minutes
✂ Makes 3 portions   🥕 Provides iron, potassium, B vitamins including folate,
vitamin C, and zinc

*Minute steak is made from very thin slices of tender steak, preferably fillet
steaks. You need to cook the steak for only one minute on each side. These
steaks are also good served with the gravy from Chicken with gravy and
mashed potatoes with carrots on page 165.*

▶ To make the marinade, mix together the sugar, soy sauce, lime juice, beef stock, and cornstarch mixed with water. Add the steaks and leave to marinate for 30 minutes. Reserve the marinade.
▶ To make the sauce, heat the sesame oil in a wok and stir-fry the mushrooms and garlic for 5 minutes. Add the green onions and bean sprouts and cook for

about 1 minute. Stir in the marinade and cook for 3–4 minutes until thickened slightly.
▶ Heat a large frying pan with a few drops of vegetable oil. Pat the marinated steaks dry with some paper towels and fry each steak for 1 minute on each side. Serve with the stir-fried vegetables and sauce.

¾ lb **minute steaks** (very thin steaks)

Sauce

1 tbsp **sesame oil**

1½ cups **oyster mushrooms**, sliced

1½ cups **button** or **cremini mushrooms**, sliced

1 **garlic clove**, peeled and crushed

4 **green onions**, thinly sliced

1½ cups **bean sprouts**

a little **vegetable oil**

Marinade

1 tbsp **brown sugar**

2 tbsp **soy sauce**

1 tbsp **lime** or **lemon juice**

⅓ cup **beef stock**

1 tsp **cornstarch**, mixed with 1 tsp **water**

3 tbsp **soy sauce**

4 tbsp **mirin (sweet rice wine)**

1 tsp **sesame oil**

1 **garlic clove**, peeled and crushed

1-inch piece fresh **ginger root**, grated

3/4 lb **fillet steak**, cubed

1 tsp **cornstarch**

Beef teriyaki skewers

🕑 Preparation: 1 hour 5 minutes, including 1 hour marinating; cooking: 10 minutes
🔪 Makes 4 portions   ⚗ Provides iron, protein, B vitamins including B12, and zinc

Marinating the beef not only gives it a wonderful flavor, but also makes it more tender. You can serve the skewers with or without vegetables.

▶ Combine all the ingredients except the cornstarch in a bowl and marinate for at least 1 hour. While the steak marinates, soak four bamboo skewers in water to prevent scorching when under the broiler. Preheat the broiler to high.

▶ Thread the beef onto the skewers, reserving the marinade. Transfer the skewers to the broiler (or grill) and cook for 4–5 minutes on each side.

▶ Meanwhile, mix the cornstarch to a paste with 1 tbsp of the marinade, then pour into a pan with the remaining marinade. Heat for 2 minutes, or until thickened. Serve as a dipping sauce.

3/4 lb **lean beef frying steak**, cut into strips

1 tbsp **corn oil**

1 small **onion**, peeled and sliced

1 tbsp **sesame oil**

1 **garlic clove**, peeled and crushed

1 **carrot**, peeled and cut into strips or stars

1 cup **broccoli**, cut into florets

1 cup **baby sweet corn**

1 cup **sugar-snap peas** or **zucchini**, cut into strips

1 **red pepper**, cut into strips

Marinade

1 tbsp each **sake** and **oyster sauce**

2 tbsp **soy sauce**

1 tsp **light brown sugar**

Beef stir-fry with oyster sauce

🕑 Preparation: 45 minutes, including 30 minutes marinating; cooking: 25 minutes
🔪 Makes 4 portions   ⚗ Provides beta-carotene, fiber, iron, protein, B vitamins including folate, vitamins C and E, and zinc   ❄ Suitable for freezing

This quick Oriental dish uses oyster sauce, but there are other good, ready-made stir-fry sauces available—just make sure they are additive-free.

▶ Combine the marinade ingredients in a bowl. Add the beef strips and leave for 30 minutes.

▶ Remove the beef and set aside, reserving the marinade.

▶ Meanwhile, heat the corn oil in a wok or frying pan. Add half the onion and stir-fry until softened. Add the beef and stir-fry until cooked, then remove and set aside.

▶ Heat the sesame oil in the wok and stir-fry the remaining onion and the garlic for 2–3 minutes. Add the carrot, broccoli, and sweet corn and stir-fry for 3–4 minutes. Add the peas and red pepper, then stir-fry for a further 3–4 minutes.

▶ Return the beef strips to the pan, pour in the marinade, and stir-fry for 2–3 minutes more. Serve with rice.

Marinated lamb cutlets

⏱ Preparation: 1 hour 5 minutes, including 1 hour marinating; cooking: 14 minutes
🍴 Makes 2 portions 🥗 Provides iron, potassium, protein, B vitamins, and zinc

I've never had any problems getting children to eat these lamb cutlets.
Make sure you trim away any visible fat from the meat.

▶ Whisk the marinade ingredients together, then pour into a dish and marinate the lamb cutlets for at least 1 hour.

▶ Broil or grill for 5–6 minutes on each side. Trim the fat off the lamb cutlets and cut them into slices. Serve with boiled potatoes and vegetables.

4 **lamb cutlets**

Marinade

1 tbsp **lemon juice**

1 tbsp **soy sauce**

1 tbsp **soft brown sugar**

$1/2$ tsp *herbes de Provence*

1 tsp **vegetable oil**

salt and freshly ground **black pepper**

Small leg of lamb with rosemary

⏱ Preparation: 8 minutes; cooking: 1 hour 10 minutes 🌡 400°F & 350°F
🍴 Makes 6 portions 🥗 Provides iron, potassium, protein, B vitamins, and zinc

Children tend to like traditional roasts of lamb or chicken. This dish, served
with roast potatoes, would make a good centerpiece for a special meal.

▶ Make about 12–14 holes in the lamb with a small, sharp knife. Push a slice of garlic into each hole, with a little chopped rosemary. Brush the lamb with the oil and season with salt and pepper. Place on a rack in a roasting pan.
▶ Roast the lamb in the preheated oven for 20 minutes at 400°F, then at 350°F for a further 50 minutes. Baste the lamb a couple of times with juices and fat during cooking and turn it over a couple of times.
▶ Once cooked, remove from the oven and keep warm on a plate. Pour the excess fat out of the tray and keep the juices.

▶ To make the gravy, place the pan on the burner and bring the juices to a boil. Pour in the wine and add the sprigs of rosemary. Cook for about 1 minute. Pour in the stock and the red currant jelly or honey, then bring to a boil.
▶ Mix the cornstarch with a little water to make a paste and add enough to thicken the gravy. Season with salt and pepper and strain through a sieve. Carve the lamb and serve with the gravy.

$3^{1}/_{4}$ lb **boneless leg of lamb**

2 **garlic cloves,** peeled and sliced

2 sprigs **rosemary,** chopped

1 tbsp **vegetable oil**

salt and freshly ground **black pepper**

Gravy

$3/_{4}$ cup **red wine**

2 sprigs **rosemary**

$1^{1}/_{4}$ cups **beef stock**

1 tbsp **red currant jelly** or **honey**

1–2 tbsp **cornstarch**

1 tbsp **water**

salt and freshly ground **black pepper**

5 **Granny Smith** (or other) **apples**

1½ tbsp **ground cinnamon**

2 tbsp freshly squeezed **orange juice**

2¼ cups **granulated sugar**

3 cups **flour**

½ tsp **salt**

3 tsp **baking powder**

4 **eggs**

½ tsp **almond extract**

2 tsp **vanilla extract**

1 cup **sunflower oil**

confectioner's sugar for dusting

Annabel's apple cake

⟳ Preparation: 25 minutes; cooking: 1 hour 30 minutes   🔥 350°F

✂ Makes 8 portions   ⚡ Provides potassium and vitamins B12 and E

❄ Suitable for freezing

Apart from how simple it is to prepare, the beauty of this truly delicious apple cake is that it will stay moist for as long as a week, because it is made with sunflower oil instead of butter.

► Peel and thinly slice the apples and place in a bowl. Toss with the cinnamon, orange juice, and ½ cup of the granulated sugar.

► In a separate bowl, mix together all the dry ingredients (the flour, salt, and baking powder and the remaining sugar). Add the eggs one at a time (this can be done in an electric mixer on a low setting, if you wish), then add the almond and vanilla extract along with the oil.

► Grease a deep ring pan or other decorative molded cake pan, such as a bundt pan. Pour in a third of the batter, then half the sliced apple

mixture, then a third more of the batter, followed by the rest of the apple mixture. Finish with the remaining third of batter.

► Bake in the preheated oven for about 1½ hours or until a toothpick inserted comes out clean. When mostly cool, remove from the pan and cool further.

► To serve, dust the top of the cake with sieved confectioner's sugar.

---

1 tbsp **butter**

3 cups **apples**, peeled, cored, and thinly sliced

2 tsp **soft brown sugar**

1¾ cups **canned prunes**

Crumble topping

1¼ cups **flour**

a generous pinch of **salt**

⅓ cup **demerara** or **brown sugar**

½ cup cold **butter**, cut into pieces

½ cup **ground almonds**

Apple & prune crumble

⟳ Preparation: 10 minutes; cooking: 32 minutes   🔥 375°F

✂ Makes 6 portions   ⚡ Provides fiber, iron, potassium, and vitamins A, C, and E

❄ Suitable for freezing

If apple and prune is not to your child's taste, there are many other fillings that can be used with this wonderful crumble topping. Try rhubarb or apple and blackberry instead.

► To make the topping, mix the flour with the salt and sugar, then rub in the butter with your fingertips until the mixture resembles bread crumbs. Finally, rub in the ground almonds.

► Melt the butter in a pan, add the sliced apples and sugar, and cook for 2 minutes. Spoon the apples into an ovenproof dish about 8 inches square and 2½ inches deep.

► Pit the prunes, reserving the juice. Mix the prunes and 6 tbsp of the prune juice from the can with the apples. Cover the fruit with the crumble topping and sprinkle with a little water.

► Bake in the preheated oven for about 30 minutes or until the topping is golden.

Seriously strawberry freezer pops

↻ Preparation: 3–4 hours, including freezing time   ✓ Makes 6 freezer pops
✎ Provides calcium and vitamin C

*The one food that children are almost guaranteed to like is freezer pops.
These are made with ingredients that are actually good for your child: puréed
strawberries, yogurt, and fresh fruit juice. The three-tier version looks very
attractive, but you can make up a single fruit flavor if you prefer.*

► Put the sugar and water in a saucepan
and boil for about 3 minutes until
syrupy. Set aside to cool.
► Quarter the strawberries and purée
in a hand blender. Press through a sieve
to remove the seeds.
► Combine the strawberry purée with
the cooled syrup and orange juice and
pour into six freezer-pop molds until
about a third full. Freeze until solid.
When the first layer is set, pour in yogurt
to a depth of 1 inch and freeze. Once
this layer is frozen, pour in the purée,
syrup, and juice mixture almost to the
top, and insert a stick in each freezer
pop. Freeze again.

► When ready to eat, run the mold
under hot water for a few seconds to
loosen the freezer pops.

Variations

► Mix the orange juice with 1⅔ cups
pineapple juice or exotic fruit juice. Add
the strained juice of three passionfruits.
Pour into the molds and freeze.
► Cook a selection of fresh or frozen
berries with a little sugar. Purée and
sieve, then mix with superfine sugar
and grape or cranberry juice to sweeten.

1½ tbsp **superfine sugar**
3½ tbsp **water**
1⅓ cups **strawberries**, hulled
juice of 1 **orange** (about ⅓ cup)
1¼ cups **strawberry yogurt**

*TIP It's easy to make your own
healthy freezer pops by pouring
fruit juice or fruit smoothies
into freezer-pop molds.*

Base

2¹/₂ cups **graham crackers, crushed**

¹/₂ cup **butter**

Filling

1 cup **superfine sugar**

3 tbsp **cornstarch**

3 cups **cream cheese** such as Philadelphia

2 **eggs**

1 tsp **vanilla extract** or grated zest of ¹/₂ **lemon**

1 cup **whipping cream**

¹/₂ cup **raisins** (optional)

Baked cheesecake

⟳ Preparation: 15 minutes; cooking: 1 hour   ⬇ 350°F   ⊘ Makes 8–10 portions   🔪
Provides calcium and vitamins A and B12   ❄ Suitable for freezing

This is a foolproof recipe for delicious cheesecake.

► To make the base, break the graham crackers into pieces, put into a plastic bag, and crush with a rolling pin. Melt the butter in a pan over a low heat and stir in the crushed crackers.

► Line a 9-inch spring-form cake pan with parchment paper and grease the sides. Press the graham cracker mix over the base of the pan with a potato masher.

► To make the filling, mix together the sugar and cornstarch. Beat in the cream cheese until smooth, then add the eggs and vanilla extract. Beat until smooth.

► Slowly whisk in the cream until the mixture thickens slightly. Stir in the raisins if using. Pour the cheesecake mixture over the base. Bake in the preheated oven for 1 hour.

---

¹/₂ cup **butter** (at room temperature)

1²/₃ cups **confectioner's sugar**, sifted

1³/₄ cups **self-raising flour**, sifted

¹/₂ tsp **salt**

¹/₂ tsp grated **orange zest**

1 cup **semi-sweet chocolate chips**

Chocolate chip & orange cut-out cookies

⟳ Preparation: 1 hour 15 minutes, including 1 hour chilling; cooking: 10 minutes
⬇ 350°F   ⊘ Makes 25–30 cookies   🔪 Provides vitamin A
❄ Suitable for freezing

Children love interestingly shaped cookies and will enjoy helping you cut them out. The subtle orange flavor combines well with the chocolate chips to make these very addictive.

► Put all the ingredients except the chocolate chips in a food processor and mix until blended together. Alternatively, beat the ingredients together by hand.

► Stir in the chocolate chips. Knead the dough until pliable and form it into a ball. If you have time, wrap it in plastic wrap and set aside in the refrigerator for about 1 hour.

► Roll out the dough to a thickness of ¹/₄ inch and cut into shapes using a variety of cookie cutters. Arrange on a lightly greased baking sheet (or one sprayed with nonstick cooking spray) and bake in the preheated oven for about 10 minutes.

Chocolate cream puffs & choux pastry mice

⏱ Preparation: 10 minutes; cooking: 35 minutes plus decoration
🌡 400°F ⚗ Makes 20 cream puffs
💉 Provides vitamin A ❄ Suitable for freezing: undecorated

▶ To make the pastry, put the butter and water in a saucepan and slowly bring to a boil. Remove from the heat and sift in the flour, then stir to combine. Beat the mixture vigorously with a wooden spoon until it comes away from the sides of the saucepan, then allow it to cool a little.
▶ Add the eggs, a little at a time, until the mixture is soft and smooth and has a dropping consistency (you may not need to add all the egg).
▶ Fit a size 8 plain round tip into a piping bag and pipe small, round mounds of the mixture onto a greased baking sheet. Bake in the preheated oven for 20–25 minutes. Remove and leave to cool.
▶ Whisk the cream with the confectioner's sugar until thick and fluffy. Cut a slit in the cream puffs and fill with the sweetened cream.

▶ Melt the chocolate in a heatproof bowl set over a saucepan of simmering water, or in a microwave on full power for 1 minute. Stir in the butter, allow it to melt, and combine to make a smooth mixture. Leave it to cool slightly.
▶ Spread a little of the chocolate mixture over the top of each cream puff with a spatula. If you wish, the cream puffs can be decorated to look like mice: add a pair of sliced-almond ears, a chocolate-chip nose, glacé-cherry eyes and a red-licorice tail.

Choux pastry

$1/3$ cup **lightly salted butter**, cut into small pieces

$3/4$ cup **water**

$3/4$ cup **flour**

3 **eggs**, lightly beaten

Cream filling

$2^1/2$ cups **heavy cream**

2 tbsp **confectioner's sugar**

Chocolate icing

1 cup **semi-sweet chocolate**, broken into small pieces

$1/3$ cup **unsalted butter**, cut into small pieces

To decorate as mice (optional)

sliced almonds

chocolate chips

glacé cherries

red licorice laces

TIP The pastry will expand during cooking, so do not make the pastry mounds for the choux mice longer than $1^1/2$ inches.

Chewy apricot & chocolate cereal bars

⏱ Preparation: 15 minutes plus refrigeration time ⚗ Makes 10 portions
💉 Provides fiber, iron, magnesium, potassium, B vitamins including folate, and vitamin A

Great for special treats, these are popular with adults and children alike. They are fun for children to make themselves, since they require no oven cooking.

▶ Combine the oats, puffed rice, chopped apricots, and nuts (if using) in a mixing bowl.
▶ Put the butter, corn syrup, and white chocolate into a small saucepan and heat gently until melted. Stir the mixture into the dry ingredients until well coated.

▶ Press the mixture into a shallow 11-x-7-inch foiled-lined pan, using a potato masher to level the surface. Place in the refrigerator to set. Cut into bars and store in the refrigerator.

2 cups **rolled oats**

$3^1/2$ cups **puffed rice cereal** (such as Rice Krispies)

$2/3$ cup **dried apricots**, chopped

$1/2$ cup **pecans**, chopped (optional)

$1/2$ cup **unsalted butter**

$1/3$ cup **golden syrup** or **corn syrup**

$1/2$ cup **white** or **semi-sweet chocolate**, broken into pieces

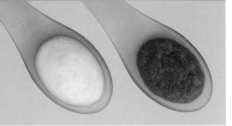

Menus: first tastes

Start with one meal of solids a day, building up to three meals a day by week five or six of weaning, when the third solid meal can be introduced at dinnertime. It may be a good idea to offer half the usual milk feeding before the solids, then finish the meal with more breast milk or formula (see page 29). Some babies may need an extra milk feeding or a little cooled boiled water during the day.

| | Weeks 1 and 2 | | | Weeks 3 and 4 | | | |
	Early morning and breakfast	Lunch	Evening and bedtime	Early morning	Breakfast	Lunch	Evening and bedtime
Day 1	Milk	Milk First fruit purée (apple) *see page 36*	Milk	Milk	Milk First fruit purée (apple) *see page 36*	Milk First vegetable purée (carrot) *see page 37*	Milk
Day 2	Milk	Milk First vegetable purée (carrot) *see page 37*	Milk	Milk	Milk First vegetable purée (carrot) *see page 37*	Milk First vegetable purée (potato) *see page 37*	Milk
Day 3	Milk	Milk Fruity baby rice cereal (pear) *see page 37*	Milk	Milk	Milk Fruity baby rice cereal (pear) *see page 37*	Milk First vegetable purée (sweet potato) *see page 37*	Milk
Day 4	Milk	Milk First vegetable purée (potato) *see page 37*	Milk	Milk	Milk First vegetable purée (potato) *see page 37*	Milk Butternut squash purée *see page 39*	Milk
Day 5	Milk	Milk First fruit purée (apple) *see page 36*	Milk	Milk	Milk First fruit purée (apple) *see page 36*	Milk Avocado purée *see page 38*	Milk
Day 6	Milk	Milk Sweet potato purée *see page 39*	Milk	Milk	Milk Sweet potato purée *see page 39*	Milk Creamy vegetable purée (carrot) *see page 37*	Milk
Day 7	Milk	Milk Mashed bananas *see page 36*	Milk	Milk	Milk Mashed bananas *see page 36*	Milk First vegetable purée (sweet potato) *see page 37*	Milk

Menus: exploring tastes

You can now offer a wider variety of flavors and textures. Let your baby's appetite guide you as to whether you give one or two courses of solids. I have suggested some simple desserts to give at lunchtime, and you can include something similar at dinner or give fresh fruit or whole-milk yogurt. Offer a drink of water or well-diluted juice from a cup with lunch and dinner.

	Breakfast	Snacks	Lunch	Snacks	Dinner	Bedtime
Day 1	Milk Cereal Mashed bananas *see page 36*	Milk	Potato, leek & pea purée *see page 48* Apples & pears with raisins & cinnamon *see page 45*	Milk	Fish with carrots & orange juice *see page 51*	Milk
Day 2	Milk Bananas, prunes, and yogurt plus toast fingers, lightly buttered	Milk	First chicken casserole *see page 53* First fruit purée (apple) *see page 36*	Milk	Tomato & cauliflower gratin with cooked carrot sticks *see page 49*	Milk
Day 3	Milk Cereal First fruit purée (apple & pear) *see page 36*	Milk	Braised beef with carrots, parsnips & potatoes *see page 53* Yogurt	Milk	Cheesy leeks, sweet potato & cauliflower purée *see page 47*	Milk
Day 4	Milk Well-cooked scrambled eggs with toast Yogurt	Milk	Lentil & vegetable purée *see page 49* Apricot & banana custard *see page 46*	Milk	Trio of root vegetables *see page 47*	Milk
Day 5	Milk First fruit purée (apple) *see page 36*	Milk	Fish with carrots & orange juice *see page 51* Peach, apple & strawberry purée *see page 45*	Milk	Sweet potato, carrot & broccoli purée *see page 49*	Milk
Day 6	Milk Apricot, pear, peach & apple compote *see page 45* Yogurt	Milk	Chicken with sweet potatoes & grapes *see page 52* Yogurt	Milk	Fillet of cod with a trio of vegetables *see page 50*	Milk
Day 7	Milk Cereal with milk Mashed papayas or bananas *see page 36*	Milk	Tomato & cauliflower gratin *see page 49* Chunks of soft, ripe fruit such as pears or peaches	Milk	Spinach, potato, parsnip & leek purée *see page 48*	Milk

Menus: 9 to 12 months

Most of these recipes are found in the 9-to-12-month section, but dishes from previous chapters are also suitable. You can substitute a selection of finger foods, such as strips of roast chicken, cheese, fruit, and rice cakes, for cooked meals. Serve the snacks with a drink of breast milk or formula between main meals, perhaps midmorning and midafternoon.

	Breakfast	**Lunch**	**Dinner**	**Snacks**
Day 1	Fruity baby muesli *see page 63* Yogurt	Quick chicken couscous *see page 66* Fruit	Cheesy pasta stars *see page 64* Exotic fruit salad *see page 63*	Milk Sandwiches *see page 95* Dried fruit
Day 2	Scrambled eggs with toast First fruit purée (apple) *see page 36*	Fillet of fish mornay with vegetables *see page 65* Fruit	Tomato & tuna pasta sauce *see page 64* Fruit	Milk Vegetable fingers and toast strips with dips Yogurt
Day 3	Cereal Fruit Yogurt	Baby's bolognese *see page 67* Fruit	Easy mashed vegetable duo *see page 62* Banana	Milk Sandwiches *see page 95* Grated apples
Day 4	Toast with yeast extract or jam Fruit	Flaked cod with tomatoes & zucchini *see page 66* Yogurt	Creamy chicken & broccoli *see page 67* Fruit	Milk Sandwiches *see page 95* Fruit
Day 5	Apple & date oatmeal *see page 63* Fruit	Fruity chicken with carrots *see page 67* Yogurt	Cheesy pasta stars *see page 64* Apple purée *see page 36*	Sweet potato, carrot & broccoli purée *see page 49*
Day 6	Raisin toast fingers Apple & pear purée *see page 36*	Braised beef with carrots, parsnips & potatoes *see page 53* Yogurt	Steamed vegetable fingers and cheese sticks Fruit	Milk Cheese on toast Fruit
Day 7	Cereal Juicy pear & prune purée *see page 44*	California chicken *see page 66* Fruit	Cauliflower gratin (variation) *see page 49* Fruit	Milk Sandwiches *see page 95* Yogurt

Menus: 12 to 18 months

Your child is now able to join in family meals, and many of these recipes are suitable for the whole family. Choose your preferred accompaniments to the main courses—perhaps pasta, potatoes, bread, or rice, and a selection of vegetables. Your child should also drink at least 14 fl oz (400ml) of milk daily, which can be given with his snacks. You can now give him full-fat cow's milk.

	Breakfast	Lunch	Dinner	Snacks
Day 1	Toast with jam Yogurt Fruit	Turkey balls & pepper sauce *see page 82* Fruit	Orzo with colorful diced vegetables *see page 79* Apricot & pear purée *see page 43*	Milk Raisin toast fingers *see page 85* Yogurt
Day 2	Cereal Yogurt Fruit	Shepherd's pie *see page 83* Raspberry frozen yogurt *see page 84*	Zucchini & tomato frittata *see page 76* Fruit	Milk Toasted ham and cheese sandwich Dried fruit
Day 3	Scrambled egg with toast Fruit	Chicken sausage snail *see page 81* Yogurt	Pasta cartwheels (variation) *see page 77* Banana	Milk Creamy avocado dip & vegetable sticks *see page 62* Fruit
Day 4	Pancakes or waffles with bananas & maple syrup *see page 76* Yogurt	Turkey balls & pepper sauce with rice *see page 82* Fruit salad	Pasta & sauce with hidden vegetables *see page 78* Fruit	Milk Baked beans with toast Yogurt and fruit
Day 5	Boiled egg with toast fingers Yogurt Fruit	Finger-licking chicken & potato balls *see page 83* Banana	Tomato & tuna pasta sauce *see page 64* Fruit	Milk Vegetable fingers and other finger foods Ice cream
Day 6	Cereal Yogurt and fruit	Bow-tie pasta with ham & peas *see page 79* Fruit	Mini veggie bites *see page 77* Fruit	Milk Baked beans with toast Banana
Day 7	Yogurt pancakes with maple syrup *see page 84* Fruit	Pasta cartwheels with cheese & broccoli *see page 77* Ice cream	Joy's fish pie *see page 80* Fruit	Milk Vegetable fingers or root vegetable chips *see page 76* Dried fruit

Menus: 18 months to 2 years

Shared family meals are not always possible, so I have included recipes in this weekly menu that can be prepared in advance or frozen, so that your toddler can eat the same food as you but at an earlier time. At this age, most children tend not to eat much at one sitting but are physically very active, so between-meals snacks with milk are especially important.

	Breakfast	Lunch	Dinner	Snacks
Day 1	Cereal Cheese Fruit	Annabel's vegetable fritters *see page 99* Frozen yogurt with fresh berries *see page 113*	Chicken bolognese *see page 102* Fruit	Milk Sandwiches *see page 95* Yogurt
Day 2	Scrambled eggs with cheese & tomatoes *see page 94* Apple purée *see page 36*	Bow-tie pasta with spring vegetables *see page 96* Fruit	Shepherd's pie *see page 83* Fruit	Milk Baked beans with toast Yogurt
Day 3	Pancakes or waffles with bananas & maple syrup *see page 76* Yogurt	Honey & soy salmon skewers with rice *see page 109* Fruit	Salmon starfish *see page 100* Fruit	Milk Cheese on toast Dried fruit and rice cakes
Day 4	Cereal Summer berry milkshake *see page 113*	Tender strips of griddled chicken with steamed vegetables *see page 110* Frozen yogurt with fresh berries *see page 113*	Tuna melt *see page 109* Fruit	Milk Raisin & oatmeal cookies *see page 112* Fruit
Day 5	Apple, mango & apricot muesli *see page 94* Yogurt	Mini pizzas *see page 97* Flavored gelatin and ice cream	Chicken kebabs with honey & citrus marinade *see page 102* Fruit	Milk Raw vegetables and other finger foods Banana muffins *see page 112*
Day 6	Banana muffin *see page 112* Yogurt Fruit	Honey chicken *see page 101* Fruit	Zucchini & tomato frittata *see page 76* Ice cream or mock fried egg *see page 116*	Milk Sandwiches *see page 95* Fruit
Day 7	Toast with jam Fruit Yogurt and honey	Macaroni and cheese *see page 107* Fruit	Diana's chicken & sweet corn fritters *see page 110* Fruit	Milk Raisin & oatmeal cookies *see page 112* Summer berry milkshake *see page 113*

Menus: 2 to 3 years

This menu plan shows a progressively wider choice of recipes that will accustom your child to new tastes. As with the other menu charts, you can substitute a few healthy convenience foods, such as pizzas, cooked chicken pieces, or fish sticks, and vary or omit desserts, but do aim to keep snacks nutritious and provide milk, fruit juice, or water with them.

	Breakfast	Lunch	Dinner	Snacks
Day 1	Apple, mango & apricot muesli *see page 94* Yogurt and honey	Pasta with zucchini, peppers & sausages *see page 123* Fruit and ice cream	Teriyaki chicken stir-fry *see page 126* Yogurt	Milk Sandwiches *see page 95* Fruit
Day 2	Boiled egg with toast fingers Fruit Yogurt	Tomato soup *see page 120* Fruit	Annabel's tasty meatballs *see page 127* Ice cream	Milk Banana muffins *see page 112* Natural yogurt and honey
Day 3	Cereal Energy-boosting smoothie *see page 146*	Chinese noodles with chicken & bean sprouts *see page 124* Flavored gelatin and ice cream	Mini baked potatoes with filling *see page 121* Yogurt	Milk Baked beans with toast Fruit
Day 4	Oatmeal Raisin toast Fruit	Annabel's vegetable fritters *see page 99* Sticky toffee pudding *see page 130*	Golden turkey fingers *see page 125* Yogurt	Milk Cheese and vegetable sticks Fruit
Day 5	Toast with jam Yogurt Fruit	Heart-shaped chicken nuggets *see page 125* Fruit	Annabel's pasta salad *see page 122* Raw vegetables & dip Ice cream	Milk Cheese on toast Summer berry milkshake *see page 113*
Day 6	Cereal Yogurt Fruit	Golden turkey fingers *see page 125* Peach & berry compote *see page 146*	Hungarian goulash *see page 127* Fruit	Milk Cheese on toast Dried fruit
Day 7	Muffins with creamy scrambled eggs *see page 142* Fruit	Caramelized chicken breasts *see page 125* Fruit salad *see page 147*	Mini baked potatoes with filling *see page 121* Salad Fruit	Milk Sandwiches *see page 95* Seriously strawberry freezer pop *see page 177*

Menus: 3 to 7 years

At this age, children love to help prepare their meals, and there are many simple things they can do, such as cut sandwich shapes or cookies. Although I have suggested fruit after most meals, it is fine to offer occasional treats such as cheesecake or pudding. If your child eats lunch at preschool or school, just balance her evening meal at home accordingly.

	Breakfast	Lunch	Dinner	Snacks
Day 1	Boiled or fried eggs with toast fingers Cereal Fruit	Special tomato sauce with spaghetti *see page 153* Salad Yogurt	Paella *see page 166* Fruit	Milk Vegetable sticks with hummus Chocolate chip, raisin & sunflower-seed cookies *see page 149*
Day 2	Apple, mango, & apricot muesli *see page 94* Yogurt Fruit	Beef teriyaki skewers *see page 174* Salad Fruit	Egg fried rice with chicken & shrimp *see page 170* Seriously strawberry freezer pops *see page 177*	Milk Cheese on toast Chewy apricot & chocolate cereal bar *see page 179*
Day 3	Oatmeal with honey or jam Thinly sliced cheese or miniature cheeses Fruit	Sticky salmon with rice and vegetables *see page 162* Seriously strawberry freezer pops *see page 177*	Singapore noodles *see page 171* Exotic fruit salad *see page 63*	Milk Baked beans with toast Chocolate chip & orange cut-out cookies *see page 178*
Day 4	Muffins with creamy scrambled eggs *see page 142* Toast Fruit	Chicken satay *see page 168* Fruit	Fish & oven-baked chips *see page 163* Flavored gelatin and ice cream	Milk Sandwiches *see page 95* Fruit skewers *see page 147*
Day 5	Yogurt pancakes with maple syrup *see page 84* Yogurt Fruit	Mini baked potatoes with filling *see page 121* Fruit	Beef stir-fry with oyster sauce *see page 174* Sticky toffee pudding *see page 130*	Milk Vegetable and cheese sticks Raisin & oatmeal cookies *see page 112*
Day 6	Cereal Cheese Energy-boosting smoothie *see page 146*	Sloppy Joe with rice *see page 153* Fruit	Turkey & pasta salad *see page 145* Flavored gelatin & ice cream	Milk Cherry tomato & mozzarella salad *see page 144* Dried fruit
Day 7	Waffles with maple syrup Fruit Yogurt	Sticky mango chicken *see page 169* Apple & prune crumble *see page 176*	Butternut squash risotto *see page 159* Fruit	Milk White chocolate & cranberry cookies *see page 149* Fruit

Menus: snacks and party food

Snacks form an important part of every young child's diet, so it's important to have a selection of healthy snacks ready for when your child is hungry. Encourage children to eat healthily now and you will lay the foundation for a lifetime of healthy eating. For special meals, such as a birthday party, you could make up an individual picnic box for each child instead of setting a table.

Healthy snacks		Party planner	
Recipes for snacks		**Prepare in advance**	**Make on the day**

<table>
<tr><td>

Recipes for snacks

Pineapple, coconut &
banana smoothie
see page 112

Chunky tomato & cream
cheese dip/Creamy avocado
dip & vegetable sticks
see pages 94 and 62

Mock fried egg (vanilla yogurt
& canned peach half)
see page 116

Raisin & oatmeal cookies
see page 112

Banana muffins
see page 112

Seriously strawberry freezer pops
see page 177

Raspberry frozen yogurt
see page 84

Root vegetable chips
see page 76

Sandwiches
see page 95

Scrambled eggs with
cheese & tomatoes
see page 94

Mixed salad with dressing
from Annabel's pasta salad
see page 122

Toasted tuna English muffins
see page 142

Tuna melt
see page 109

Mini pizzas
see page 97

Toasted seeds with
honey & soy sauce
see page 142

</td><td>

Turkey & pasta salad with
honey & soy dressing
see page 145

Pasta salad with shrimp
see page 145

Pita pockets with tuna,
eggs & tomatoes
see page 142

Chocolate chip, raisin &
sunflower-seed cookies
see page 149

Energy-boosting smoothie
see page 146

Fruity cranberry shake
see page 146

Other ideas

Boiled egg with toast fingers

French bread

Cheese on toast

Toasted raisin-bread fingers
with cream cheese

Toasted sandwiches

Miniature cheeses &
cheese slices

Dried fruit

Fresh fruit & fruit salad

Whole-grain breakfast cereal
with milk

Baked beans on toast

Glass of milk or
fresh orange juice

Popcorn

Yogurt

Rice cakes, crispbreads,
bread sticks

Vegetables, on their own
or with a dip

</td><td>

Prepare in advance

Present birthday cake
see page 129

Heart-shaped chicken
nuggets
see page 125

Chunky tomato & cream
cheese dip (cut up raw veggies
the day before the party)
see page 94

Character mini cakes
(decorate the day before
the party)
see page 128

Chocolate choux pastry mice
(decorate the day before
the party)
see page 179

Chewy apricot & chocolate
cereal bars
see page 179

Gelatin boats (cut in half and
decorate on party day)
see page 85

Shortbread cookies
see page 131

White chocolate &
cranberry cookies
see page 149

Chocolate orange
mini muffins
see page 130

My favorite brownies
see page 148

</td><td>

Make on the day

Sandwich selection
see page 95

Annabel's pasta salad
see page 122

Chicken kebabs with
honey & citrus marinade
see page 102

Chicken satay
see page 168

Pasta with zucchini,
peppers & sausages
see page 123

Golden turkey fingers
see page 125

Mini pizzas
see page 97

Fresh fruit platter with
chocolate-dipped fruit

Fruit skewers
see page 147

</td></tr>
</table>

Index

Acknowledgments

Author's acknowledgments

I am indebted to the following people for their help and advice during the writing of his book: Dr. Margaret Lawson, Senior Lecturer in Pediatric Nutrition, Institute of Child Health; Dr. Stephen Herman FRCP, consultant Pediatrician, Central Middlesex Hospital; Dr. Barry Lewis FRCP, FRCPH, Consultant Pdiatrician; Luci Deniels, State Registered Dietitian; Simon Karmel; David Karmel; Evelyn Etkind; Jane Hamilton; Marian Magpoc; Letty Catada; Jo Pratt; Joy Skipper; Jacqui Morley; Lara Tankel; and Mary Jones. I would especially like to thank Nicolas, Lara, and Scarlet Karmel, and all the other discerning young tasters who have eaten their way through the recipes in this book. Thanks also to Dave King for the beautiful photography, and Daniel Pangbourne for the lovely portrait of myself and Scarlett. And thanks to all the team at DK who have worked on this project.

Dorling Kindersley would like to thank: Lyndel Costain and Martin Edelstein, MD for advice on nutrition; Wesley Martin for recipe advice, Annaïck Guitteny for photographic assistance; Bethany Heald and Dagmar Vesely for food styling; Clare Louise Hunt for prop styling; Stokke for the Tripp Trapp high chair; Hilary Bird for the index.

Many thanks to all our models:

Louix Ball, Hanni Blaskey, Henry Boag, Clara Boucher, Jordan Chan, Susan Colyer, Connor Fitzjohn, Hebe Harvey, Thomas Leman, Scarlett McKelvie, Lavinia McKelvie, Luc McNally-Drew, Alexandra Mellor, Emilia Momen, Alexander Moore-Smith, Ella Moriarty, Jacob Moriarty, Sophie Moriarty, Patrick Moriarty, Ethan Myers, Sabina Netherclift, Sabina Regan, Finnegan Regan, Mike Rogers, Felix Rogers, Max Salzer, Georgia Sargent, Harvey Sidebottom, Erin Somes, Gabrielle Somes, Ben Somes, Kai Takahashi.

Picture credits

Picture research: Anna Bedewell.
Picture librarian: Romaine Werblow.
The publisher would like to thank the following for their kind permission to reproduce their photographs:
page 7: Daniel Pangbourne
page 12: Corbis/George Shelley
page 59: Bubbles/Chris Miles
page 73: Mother & Baby Picture Library/Ian Hooton.
All other images © Dorling Kindersley. For more information, see www.dkimages.com.

Useful addresses

Annabel Karmel's Cooking for Children
www.cookingforchildren.com

Food Allergy & Anaphylaxis Network
11781 Lee Jackson Hwy., Suite 160
Fairfax, VA 22033-3309
(800) 929-4040
www.foodallergy.org

Asthma and Allergy Foundation of America
233 20th St. NW, Suite 402
Washington, DC 20036
(202) 466-7643
www.aafa.org

American Diabetes Association
1701 North Beauregard Street
Alexandria, VA 22311
(800) DIABETES (342-2383)
www.diabetes.org

Celiac Disease Foundation
13251 Ventura Boulevard, Suite 1
Studio City, CA 91604-1838
(818) 990-2354
www.celiac.org

Celiac Sprue Association/United States of America, Inc.
P.O. Box 31700
Omaha, NE 68131
(402) 558-0600
www.csaceliacs.org

Gluten Intolerance Group
15110 10th Ave SW, Suite A
Seattle, WA 98166-1820
(206) 246-6652
www.gluten.net

American Celiac Society
59 Crystal Avenue
West Orange, NJ 07052
(973) 325-8837

U.S. Food and Drug Administration
5600 Fishers Lane, Rockville MD 20857
(888) INFO-FDA (463-6332)
www.fda.gov

Martha Stewart
www.marthastewart.com

Williams-Sonoma
www.williams-sonoma.com
(877) 812-6235

North American Vegetarian Society
P.O. Box 72
Dolgeville, NY 13329
(518) 568-7970
www.navs-online.org

Boelter Direct
11100 W. Silver Spring Road
Milwaukee, WI 53225
(800) 392-3278
www.boelter.com

Edward Don & Co. Foodservice Equipment
(800) 777-4366
www.don.com

Oneida, Ltd.
Oneida, NY 13421-2899
(315) 361-3000
www.oneida.com